OXF[ ]RD
TEACHING GUIDES

HOW TO

Teach
Even Better:
An Evidence-Based
Approach

GEOFF PETTY

OXFORD

T0346680

OXFORD
UNIVERSITY PRESS

Great Clarendon Street, Oxford, OX2 6DP, United Kingdom

Oxford University Press is a department of the University of Oxford.
It furthers the University's objective of excellence in research, scholarship, and
education by publishing worldwide. Oxford is a registered trade mark of Oxford
University Press in the UK and in certain other countries

© Oxford University Press 2018

The moral rights of the authors have been asserted

First published in 2018

All rights reserved. No part of this publication may be reproduced, stored in a
retrieval system, or transmitted, in any form or by any means, without the prior
permission in writing of Oxford University Press, or as expressly permitted by
law, by licence or under terms agreed with the appropriate reprographics rights
organization. Enquiries concerning reproduction outside the scope of the above
should be sent to the Rights Department, Oxford University Press, at the address
above.

You must not circulate this work in any other form and you must impose this
same condition on any acquirer

British Library Cataloguing in Publication Data
Data available

978-0-19-841410-0

Kindle edition

978-0-19-841702-6

10 9 8 7

Paper used in the production of this book is a natural, recyclable product made
from wood grown in sustainable forests. The manufacturing process conforms to
the environmental regulations of the country of origin.

Printed and bound by CPI Group (UK) Ltd, Croydon, CR0 4YY

Links to third party websites are provided by Oxford in good faith and for
information only. Oxford disclaims any responsibility for the materials
contained in any third party website referenced in this work.

The Publisher would like to thank Doug Forbes, of Out Of House Publishing
Solutions, and Anthony Haynes for their help in the production of this book.

Foreword

'Evidence' should surely be the most contested term in our profession. Some privilege evidence published in journals, others their experience as educators; but the skill is in combining these types of evidence, which this book does wonderfully.

In my work under the Visible Learning titles, I have provided evidence based on research published in journals and dissertations. My intention was to compare the story of those influences with above- and below-average effectiveness. The idea was to identify interventions that have a high probability of success, and then invite educators to evaluate the impact of their implementations. But there is a more important underlying message – less about what educators do, more about how they think – hence the Mindframes – and 'know thy impact'.

Geoff Petty has the talent to provide the methods and tools to help educators know their impact. He's excellent at highlighting the importance of previous knowledge – and then making meaning from this knowledge, which he does in a most engaging and convincing way.

Critically, he emphasises that learning is more than remembering – it is also meaning-making. But it is clear that before a student can relate and extend ideas, they need ideas themselves. At the start of the learning process, the emphasis could be on gaining knowledge, but then meaning-making becomes imperative.

Petty has a style of writing and a gift for language that makes these themes come alive, and he provides many core ideas that can be implemented in any classroom. It is this balance of critical ideas, based on a major corpus of research studies and on classroom experiences, which make this book so worthwhile.

Using evidence is somewhat like making a meal. My last meeting with Geoff was at his daughter's London restaurant. I had the mussels, and wow – I asked for the recipe.

I bought the mussels (green-lipped NZ ones, of course!), chopped the onion and garlic, put the wine, mussels, garlic and onions in the heavy bottom pan, waited until the mussels opened, added the cream, waited two minutes and added the parsley and served. But they were not the same – and it was only reading the last line "the magic might be in this reduction...." that made me realise just following the recipe was not sufficient. This book has helped put the magic into the reduction of so many research studies, so much experience, so much wisdom. Enjoy, and you will teach even better.

John Hattie, Laureate Professor of Education at the University of Melbourne, Australia, and Chair of the Board of the Australian Institute for Teaching and School Leadership, April 2018.

About the author

After taking a degree in engineering, Geoff helped form a soft rock band that won a national competition and gained a Warner Brothers recording contract.

But, even as a schoolboy, Geoff was puzzled that some teachers used methods that helped students learn, while others did not. He trained as a Physics and History teacher, teaching Physics in a 13–18 Comprehensive school and a Further Education college, where he also trained teachers.

The teachers Geoff trained complained that books on teaching were not practical enough, invariably ignoring the details of teaching methodology that were the trainees' (and Geoff's) main interest. So he published *Teaching Today* in 1994, which became a best-selling teacher-training text. This book established Geoff's reputation for explaining issues concerning learning and teaching, in a practical, down to earth, but lively and inspiring way. It has 140 5* reviews on Amazon (at the time of writing).

In Sutton Coldfield College, as 'Learning Development Manager', he used evidence to improve teaching across the College, which eventually achieved one of the best value added scores in the country.

Geoff's *Evidence-Based Teaching* was published in 2006. Using multiple sources of evidence in their most authoritative form, he describes the most powerful teaching methods, strategies and techniques, as well as how to use them in the classroom and why they work *How to Teach Even Better* builds upon, clarifies and simplifies that 2006 book

Geoff's books have been translated into eight languages, including Chinese and Russian His training sessions for colleges and schools have become legendary; after which teachers conduct 'supported experiments', working together to try new teaching methods, perfect them and help and learn from each other.

www.geoffpetty.com contains lots of free downloads, and Geoff can be followed on twitter @**geoffreypetty**.

Contents

What this book can do for you

Teaching is impossible to do perfectly: you are incredibly busy, but teachers touch students' lives forever. Consequently, this book offers practical advice about how to improve your teaching, so as to have the greatest effect on your students' achievement, with the least time and effort on your part. It focuses on teaching methods, strategies and techniques suggested by the most reliable research. I just call these 'methods' throughout the book. Teaching methods have more effect on achievement than any other factor we can change. There is more to teaching than student attainment, but the methods that work best are almost always those that students enjoy, that motivate them most, that challenge them yet make them believe in themselves, and create intrinsic interest in your subject.

This book summarises the advice gleaned from my many years of reading research on how to teach. However, it will not attempt to provide a comprehensive coverage of all the evidence for what constitutes high-quality teaching. Chapter 14 deals with the research on how student achievement can be improved, explaining that this is best done by referring to summaries of research from multiple sources of evidence so that conclusions are as reliable as they can be. In essence, if all or most of the schools of research say 'do this' in their summaries, and none say don't do it, then it's worth trying in your own classroom or workshop as a trial. This 'triangulation' of evidence is the basis for the advice in this book. At the end of each chapter, Evidence boxes give summary evidence for each chapter.

A word of warning. The methods you find in this book probably won't work the first time. You won't be used to them, nor will your students. The best methods often make great demands on your students, in fact. You will need to try a method five times to discover whether it is likely to work for you and your students, and about 25 times to get most of the power from the method, and to feel really comfortable with it. That might seem surprising, but research on teacher improvement is emphatic that teachers need to repeatedly trial methods that are new to them, reflecting and improving each time. These trials need to be done in a 'community of practice'; in other words, you need to talk with colleagues about their and your attempts to improve – doing what I call 'supported experiments'. There is more detail on this in Chapter 14. If your institution hasn't set this up, you can create your own informal community of practice.

Rather than start with the scholarly details of evidence sifting, I will fast forward to the conclusions. If you prefer the justifications before the findings, begin with Chapter 14, then return to reading the rest of the book in order. Of course, you can just dip in to what interests you – many chapters are self-explanatory.

Many people think that the best teachers have been born with special gifts. But there are hundreds of thousands of experiments where experienced teachers were chosen at random to trial highly-effective teaching strategies like those in this book. These methods greatly improved student learning. So it seems the key to great teaching is not the teacher as a person, but their effective use of high-performance teaching strategies. You can become an outstanding teacher if you learn to use outstanding teaching methods well.

Much of this material first appeared in my book *Evidence-Based Teaching: A Practical Approach,* but it has been substantially updated and improved. Some of the material is adapted from articles that first appeared in *InTuition*. Thanks in particular to Liz Singh for her patience, her editorial skills and so much else.

Part 1: What is learning and what helps it?

Chapter 1

You must ensure students make meanings: co-constructivism

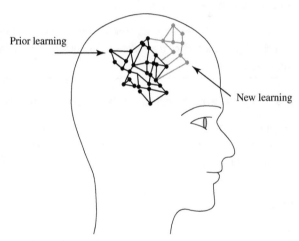

Figure 1.1: Prior and new learning

We know from research reviews that learning is usually a trial-and-error improvement process. It is rare for learning to be an immediate light-switch *'Oh, I've got it'* process (though this can happen, for example when a student restructures what they already know).

Students learn by encoding the *meaning* of what they have learned in a little cluster of interconnected brain cells – neurons. This learning won't be perfect first time and will need to be improved. This cluster of brain cells is called a construct. (The word 'construct' can mean other things in other books, so beware.) Of course, the way learning is represented in the brain is much more complex than shown in my diagram, which is just for explanatory purposes and is nowhere near anatomically correct!

The learner needs to connect this new construct (new learning is shown as grey in the diagram) to what the learner already knew when the lesson started (shown as black in the diagram). Familiar knowledge and skill is black in the diagram, unfamiliar new learning is grey.

This construct is the *learner's version* of what they have learned. Typically, it will be incomplete and will contain some misconceptions. Each of your students will have different prior learning and will form different constructs for the new learning. Sadly, students do not simply and faithfully record your explanations and store these in memory. They make it all up.

 Just so you know

Co-constructivism is NOT the same as 1960s 'constructivism'; the latter called for minimal guidance from the teacher. Co-constructivism calls for careful teacher direction.

Learning is not just remembering – it is meaning-making

If students simply remembered what they were told, they would never make mistakes or have misconceptions. The only fault in their learning would be omissions. We would never hear them make statements like these, which all come from genuine student exams:

Name a common disease in cereal crops.

'wheat germ'

How do mammals keep warm in cold weather?

'They wear cardigans.'

How does an amoeba feed?

'The amoeba picks up its food using a false leg.'

'Worms hold themselves together by the suction power of their little legs.'

'During the birth of a baby, first of all the mother becomes pregnant... later her hips will dislocate.'

'The mother experiences labour pains because the baby is turning itself round and getting in position for its head-first exit.'

I'm not arguing that all howlers are misconceptions, sometimes they are simply word confusions:

'We worked it out by a process of illumination.'

'We held the crucible with our thongs.'

Other times they are simply spelling mistakes:

'The early Britons made their houses of mud, and there was rough mating on the floor.'

However, the first list of howlers above makes it clear that students make up their own meanings. When you think about it, what else could they do? The brain is not a tape recorder.

Students learn what they think about

The highly influential cognitive psychologist Dan Willingham wrote that 'memory is the residue of thought'. He means that we learn what we *think about*, and the harder we think with the new material, the better we learn it. When students think about the material you have taught them, the neural links between the construct and their prior learning are created and strengthened, and the construct itself becomes more firmly embedded in the student's brain.

If material is just presented to students, and they don't think about it much, then the material will not be well connected to their prior learning, so:

- students won't understand the material well
- students won't be able to recall the learning as the links to it will be weak
- students won't spontaneously think of the new learning when it is relevant and useful.

Let's look at an example to make this clearer.

We need to develop relations between constructs    **Case study**

Research on SATs found that 80% of 12-year-olds with calculators could do this:

$225 \prod 15 =$

But only 40% could do this:

If a gardener has 225 bulbs to place equally in 15 flower beds, how many bulbs would be in each bed?

Most of the failing students did not know which mathematical operation to use.

Students need to establish relationships between concepts. Consider Jo:

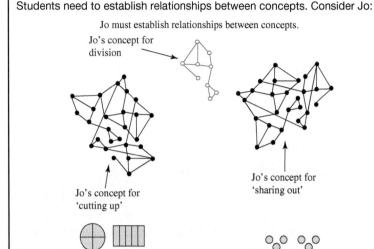

Figure 1.2: Conceptualising division

Students have trouble conceptualising division, but we know how to fix this.

Imagine Jo, a young girl, is learning division for the first time with a teacher who adopts co-constructivist methods to encourage deep learning. Rather than teaching her to punch numbers into a calculator without understanding, he tries to build Jo's understanding out of what she already knows.

Before starting work on division, he uses a method called 'relevant recall questions' (see Chapter 6). He asks Jo to recall her experiences of 'cutting things up' and he starts to relate this to division. *'So if you cut up the cake like this, how many pieces would you divide it into?'*

In a similar way he relates 'sharing out' to division. *'If there were six sweets to divide between two children, how many would each child get?*

Jo already has constructs for 'sharing out' and for 'cutting up', and the teacher is getting her to construct her concept for division out of and onto this existing learning. The teacher gives Jo some activities to cut up paper and share out bricks, and asks Jo to use the term 'divide' and to link it with 'cutting up' and 'sharing out'. Without these links to previous experience her concept of division would probably not be connected to her prior learning. These links between constructs are most important for two reasons. First of all they create 'meaning'. When we understand something it means we can explain it in terms of something else. If you looked up division in a children's dictionary, it would probably say something about 'sharing out' and 'cutting up'.

Second, these very links make our learning functional. When we problem-solve we think along these relational links. If Jo learned division well, building it firmly on her existing learning and experience, then when she was asked a question like *'If a gardener has 225 bulbs to place equally in 15 flower beds, how many bulbs would be in each bed?'*, she can think for a bit and say, *'This is a cutting-up question so I divide'* or *'This is a sharing-out question so I divide.'*

The links between new learning and her previous learning and experience have made her learning both meaningful and functional. In contrast, students just taught to do division questions will often not know when dividing is useful or necessary, or even what division is.

The need for challenging tasks

Another lesson we can learn from this example is that students need challenging tasks that require reasoning, rather than exclusively 'rote' tasks where they follow a drill or procedure. I will return to this issue in later chapters. There is nothing wrong with learning something by heart; it's the only way for much learning. However, what has been learned must be understood if it is to be of any use to the learner.

Given that learning is so tenuous and subject to error, it is not a surprise that one of the most effective ways of increasing achievement is checking and correcting students' learning. This is sometimes called 'formative assessment', 'feedback', or 'Assessment for Learning', but the meanings of these terms have become corrupted, so I will stick to the term 'check and correct,' as it says what it does on the can. Check and correct can be done by the student themselves, by peers, through dialogue, or by the teacher. In general, the quicker errors are found and corrected, the better. Check and correct can be done verbally, in discussion, or it can be assisted by you marking your students' work However, in each case the student must understand the check, must realise and understand their mistake, and change their construct. This all happens in a flash usually:

Student: *The biggest fish will be a whale.*

Peer: *No, that's not right. A whale is a mammal.*

Student: *What?*

Peer: *It breathes air and spouts and everything. It's not a fish, is it?*

Student: *Oh yeah!* (This student then improves their construct of 'whale' and reminds herself that not everything fishlike in the sea is actually a fish.)

Of course some constructs need more work to correct than the above example.

The Quality Learning Cycle

The Quality Learning Cycle diagram below summarises an effective teaching and learning process to teach a topic.

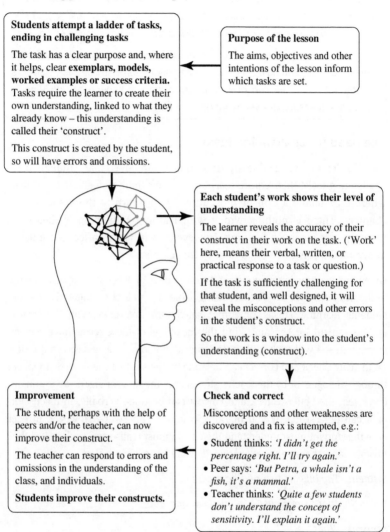

Students attempt a ladder of tasks, ending in challenging tasks

The task has a clear purpose and, where it helps, clear **exemplars, models, worked examples or success criteria.** Tasks require the learner to create their own understanding, linked to what they already know – this understanding is called their 'construct'.

This construct is created by the student, so will have errors and omissions.

Purpose of the lesson

The aims, objectives and other intentions of the lesson inform which tasks are set.

Each student's work shows their level of understanding

The learner reveals the accuracy of their construct in their work on the task. ('Work' here, means their verbal, written, or practical response to a task or question.)

If the task is sufficiently challenging for that student, and well designed, it will reveal the misconceptions and other errors in the student's construct.

So the work is a window into the student's understanding (construct).

Improvement

The student, perhaps with the help of peers and/or the teacher, can now improve their construct.

The teacher can respond to errors and omissions in the understanding of the class, and individuals.

Students improve their constructs.

Check and correct

Misconceptions and other weaknesses are discovered and a fix is attempted, e.g.:

- Student thinks: *'I didn't get the percentage right. I'll try again.'*
- Peer says: *'But Petra, a whale isn't a fish, it's a mammal.'*
- Teacher thinks: *'Quite a few students don't understand the concept of sensitivity. I'll explain it again.'*

Figure 1.3: The Quality Learning Cycle

Let's look at the cycle in the diagram being used in practice. Then I will look at the cycle in more general terms. Here is an example of one of many teaching sequences that follows the cycle. It is adapted from the excellent: *Assessment for Learning: Putting it into Practice* by Paul Black et al. (2003).

I'm assuming in this example that students have been taught how to create mind maps as described in Chapter 3:

1 Students are warned what is about to happen, by describing the sequence below. Relevant prior learning is checked (this is black on the diagram on page 9).

2 The teacher explains some new material.

3 Students are asked to create a mind map that summarises the topic. (Making the mind map requires the student to create a construct – grey in the diagram – and to *think* about what is most important in it, and how it relates to what they already know.)

4 When their mind map is nearly complete, students leave it on their desk, and move around to look at everyone else's mind maps. The aim is to learn how to improve your own mind maps. (This activity provides students with a check and correct of their current understanding (construct).)

5 Students improve their mind maps, which improves their constructs.

6 Students are given assessment criteria to self-assess (or peer assess) their mind maps, for example a list of things that should appear on their map. (This self- or peer assessment, which students were warned about, improves the students' constructs again.)

Notice that students improve their constructs at least twice, during steps 4, 5 and 6 above. For example, a student might think when looking at a peer's work in step 4 above:

'Oh, I had forgotten that.'

'Oh, that's a good way to describe it.'

Then students go through this same improvement process when they self- or peer assess their mind maps against the teacher's checklist or mind map. See Chapter 3 for a fuller explanation.

It's important to realise that teaching sequences often do not have these check-and-correct sequences in them. For example, students would not learn as well if the teacher taught the new content, and then gave students notes on it. Students would not then be required to form a construct, or to improve it; neither need they think much about the topic. Also, the teacher would not know if students had understood the topic and would therefore be unable to check and correct misunderstandings, or adapt their teaching in any other way.

The Quality Learning Cycle diagram is not anatomically correct of course. It is very 'diagramatic'; but it does explain what happens when we learn.

The Quality Learning Cycle in general terms

If students must make their own meanings, linked to what they already know, and will create misconceptions and other errors while doing so, constant checking and correcting of their learning is necessary. You, however, are too busy to do all the checking necessary. Later, we will see some good ways to drive students around this cycle that require little effort from you.

You use the purpose of your lesson to choose, or to design, a task or sequence of tasks that will require the learner to form a construct for what you will teach. Strong evidence suggests students are often more successful in this task if they are given:

- exemplars (examples of good practice), worked examples, and perhaps success criteria to show students what is expected of them in completing the tasks

- goals or tasks in advance of your presentation; this also helps students to grasp what is expected of them

- a check on prior learning vital for understanding the new material.

The task, or sequence of tasks, could require the students to make practical, oral, or written responses; crucially, these responses will make it clear how well the student understands. Much more than that, if the lesson is well planned, any mistakes will help improve the students' learning that is required for the students to improve their constructs. Errors made by a significant proportion of the students can be attended to by you, by for example reteaching.

Checks and corrections of students' work should be frequent.

How fast?

The cycle can operate on fast, medium and longer time scales.

- **Immediate**: for example, discussion between the teacher and the student(s) can illicit information on each student's understanding, and can correct it.

- **In the lesson**: a sequence of tasks can be set during a lesson that requires students to create an understanding, and then check and correct these understandings.

- **Between lessons**: teachers can monitor learning after the class, and set corrective work, extra practice, and other action plans that operate over days, weeks or months to fix errors and omissions in learning.

Ideally, we act on all these timescales if they are all necessary, as they nearly always are.

What we hope to achieve with teaching methods

While you read through this book, bear in mind that a good teaching method should ensure:

- students focus with some intensity on at least the vital content of the topic you are teaching

- a high participation rate: every student thinking hard, not just some of them

- a check and correct for students: spontaneous or planned self-checks, peer checks, and opportunities for dialogue between students so they can correct any errors or omissions in learning

- a check and correct for you: opportunities for you to discover the strengths and weaknesses in students' learning, so you can fix any problems and praise progress

- an enjoyable learning experience

- an insight into the way your subject works, if possible.

Quality Learning boosters

 Try this in the classroom

How can you make sure every learner is going around the Quality Learning Cycle while you present them with new material or while they are working on a task? Students need to be deliberately driven around the Quality Learning Cycle with a sequence of tasks including at least some of these:

Pair check: mutually checking and correcting their partner's draft work, with dialogue.

Snowballing: where students work individually first, then improve their work, first in pairs and again after pairs have combined into fours, to gradually arrive through discussion at an agreed best piece of work (see page 91).

Self-assessment or peer assessment: these can be done against answers, worked solutions, checklists or assessment criteria provided by you.

Assertive questioning: there can be class discussion of model ideas/solutions, or of ideas/solutions suggested by students.

Teacher check: for example, *'When you have completed questions 1 to 4, tell me and I'll mark them.'*

Formative quiz: understanding of vital content is checked and corrected (see Chapter 11). Students can prepare for this quiz in small groups and the groups can compete against each other if you like, or better, compete against a target to get, say, 8/10 in the quiz. Crucially, the groups and teacher then help fix any misunderstandings found.

When presenting new skills to learners you can use:

Active listening tasks: for example, a task set before your explanation to answer a question or to explain part of your presentation to a peer after they have had your input (see Chapter 8).

Models: students are shown 'models', that is model solutions, exemplar work, worked examples, videos of expert performance, etc. The aim is to show how. They then study, annotate, and/or peer explain these models in pairs (see Chapter 7).

Spoof assessment: models like those above can be imperfect, in which case students can assess, improve, complete or comment on those models (see Chapter 7).

I call such methods 'Quality Learning boosters' because they drive students, in the nicest possible way, around the Quality Learning Cycle to create continual improvement. All the methods above can be adapted to work in almost any teaching situation, including learning online, or e-learning. Indeed, in e-learning the check-and-correct processes offered by these methods are particularly important as there is usually no teacher to notice if a student is having difficulties. These methods all drive continuous improvement in students' learning. As they are boosting learning, these methods make your marking easier, as students' errors were corrected in class.

You need to set both reproduction and reasoning tasks

Tasks fall into two types: reproduction tasks and reasoning tasks. We need them both.

Reproduction tasks

Here, the student repeats back knowledge or skills that have been directly taught by the teacher or directly explained in resources. For example:

- copying a labelled diagram
- recalling a definition or a simple explanation given earlier
- completing a calculation in a way shown earlier.

These tasks are a useful starting point. However, they do not require the learner to process the material fully, just to reproduce it. Neither do students have to apply the learning in new contexts, or even understand it well. Such simple tasks ensure all students can, with practice, be successful. But they have the disadvantage that they do not require learners to firmly connect their meaning to their existing learning in order to create a secure functional understanding.

Typical verbs for reproduction tasks are: state, recall, define, list, describe, draw a diagram that shows… and so on.

Reasoning tasks

Assuming the answers to the following questions have not already been given, then the following tasks are reasoning tasks.

For students of lower attainment:

Which of these six knives would be best for slicing the apples, and why?

How could we make sure we don't forget something when we go shopping?

For students of higher attainment:

How could this business plan be improved?

Which of these factors most influenced Harold Macmillan's political thinking and why?

What happens to the product if you square a number less than 1? Why?

Here, the student must process and apply what they have learned, linking it with existing learning and experience. They must think with it. As a consequence of the reasoning involved, the task requires all learners to form and improve a construct linked with their existing learning.

Teachers who must cover a great deal of material in little time, or who teach students whose reasoning skills are weak, often stick to reproduction tasks. The problem with this is that students do not create their own meanings.

There is more detail on this in my book *Teaching Today* (2014), where I show that a student can get correct answers to questions on a piece of nonsense text such as Lewis Carroll's 'Jabberwocky' poem, without of course understanding it.

Reasoning questions are required for differentiation

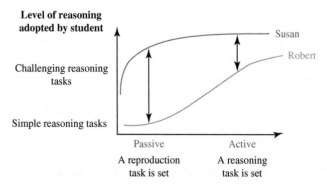

Figure 1.4: How tasks affect cognitive engagement

John Biggs (2011) imagined two students sitting next to each other in the same class: Susan, who is academic and a good learner, and Robert, who is not. Let's assume they are both reasonably well motivated.

If their teacher used a passive method, such as teacher talk, giving a demonstration, or showing a video, Susan would reason during this presentation, asking herself *'Why is it like that?'*, *'But what would happen if …'*, *'How could that be used in practice?'*, and so on. In order to answer her own questions she would have to make a meaning for what she was being taught and relate it to her previous knowledge. Robert, however, would just be trying to remember what he had been told. He would not be trying to make rigorous personal sense like Susan.

The reason Susan learns well, and Robert badly, may not necessarily be to do with intelligence, or even prior learning or motivation. The difference is that Susan habitually tries to make sense of what is being presented. *She goes through the cognitive processes required for good-quality learning*: making meanings related to what she already knows and reasoning with this. She has the habits and skills that create deep learning.

By contrast, Robert only learns deeply when he is set reasoning tasks, or other tasks that *require* him to go through these cognitive processes. There are Robertas as well as Roberts of course!

Differentiation requires that learners are set reasoning tasks, whatever their attainment. Then all students will go through the cognitive processes required for good learning.

 Reflection

What is surface learning and deep learning?

Surface learning is the *what*. It enables the learner to recall important facts and skills, but understanding is limited and can be non-existent.

Deep learning gives meaning and understanding. It involves the *why*, *when* and *how* as well as the *what*. It can recognise and use the learning in different contexts. Deep learning makes links between related concepts, thus creating meaning and enabling the learner to explain the learning well and to know when it is relevant.

Build ladders of tasks

Many problems in learning and teaching can be traced back to the nature of the tasks that students were set, or should have been set. It is active tasks and reasoning tasks that create understanding and deeper learning, especially for the 'Roberts' of this world. These tasks can be of any kind; they may be verbal questions or class discussions, as well as tasks requiring students to work practically or on paper.

In summary, reasoning creates student involvement, deep understanding, and learning that is functional. So, we must set reasoning tasks as well as reproduction tasks. We need both surface and deep learning. A good way of ensuring this mix is to build a ladder of tasks. This will be considered in detail in Chapter 9. In order to learn a topic well, students must start with simple reproduction tasks, then move onto simple reasoning tasks, and finish with challenging reasoning tasks, including tasks that strive for transfer of the learning. The lower tasks are carefully designed to prepare students for the later tasks, and the last tasks achieve the objectives for the topic. They also transfer the learning so it is available whenever it might help the learner.

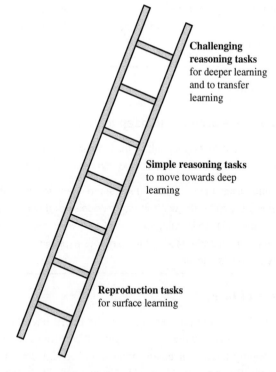

Challenging reasoning tasks for deeper learning and to transfer learning

Simple reasoning tasks to move towards deep learning

Reproduction tasks for surface learning

Figure 1.5: Build a ladder of tasks

If we set ladders of tasks for students, and use the 'boosters' mentioned above to ensure their learning is continually checked and corrected as quickly as possible, most students should learn very well.

What does Quality Learning require?

So in outline, Quality Learning requires the following:

- We ensure that the relevant prior learning is firmly established and correct before we teach the new material. This is so the new learning can be attached to firm foundations.

- We set some challenging tasks so that students think hard about the new learning: this makes them link the new learning to their prior learning more firmly. The thinking also more strongly establishes the new construct. The more learners think with new learning, the better it is understood and remembered.

- When students first form their construct it will likely be incomplete, contain misconceptions, and not be attached to as much of the prior learning as it should be for full understanding. So the construct, and its connections to prior learning, needs to be checked and corrected. This can be done by the students themselves, by peers and/or by you.

- Even if you do the above brilliantly, students will soon forget this new learning unless they reuse it on about six other occasions. The brain has an automatic system to ensure it doesn't get cluttered up with unnecessary information; it works unconsciously and brilliantly, and it's called forgetting. So you need to ensure that your students recall and reuse the new learning and preferably have it checked and corrected, but not necessarily by you. This is called 'spaced practice'. There is detail on this in Chapter 12.

 Reflection

The approach to learning described above is sometimes called 'co-constructivism' because the teacher, student and peers *co*-operate to create good *constructs*. This is not to be confused with a 1960s theory of learning that many call 'constructivism', which advocated that students should only get minimal guidance and work out new learning pretty much by themselves. Not surprisingly, students learn better with well-judged guidance than without it.

This 'co-constructivist' model of learning is summarised in the Quality Learning Cycle.

We need both surface learning and deep learning

Surface learning is an important first step towards learning a new topic; it has occurred if students are able to recall key content such as:

The divide sign on the calculator looks like this: $\div$. If you type 17 $\prod$ 3 = into your calculator, then it does the division for you.

12 divided by 2 is 6...

Or for the topic of salads on a catering course:

Salads might contain leaves such as lettuce, cabbage, and herbs.

Salads need to be prepared fresh from washed ingredients...

Such surface learning is vital, and occurs in every subject; without it the learner has no hope of making any progress with the topic at all.

Surface learning enables the learner to recall important facts, and perform simple skills. However, it's not enough to create a real understanding, or to make the learning functional. Also, it is quickly forgotten unless deep learning follows.

You can think of surface learning as being a construct that is not sufficiently connected to other relevant constructs. We have seen that division needs to be well connected to constructs such as 'cutting up' and 'sharing out' in order to create meaning, and a functional understanding. A mathematician will realise that division is also related to multiplication, ratios such as sines and cosines, and other concepts. Students with surface learning see division as a topic almost entirely separate and unrelated to other concepts – a little self-contained silo of knowledge. In the worst case, surface learning is not understood, just remembered.

Deep learning requires relations between concepts

Deep learning creates a meaning for the concept by connecting it to other concepts, rather like a dictionary explains a word you don't understand by explaining it in terms of words that you do understand: *'division is sharing out'*. Deep learning is assisted if students see the concept in different contexts, and look at it from different perspectives. It is also helped if the concept is represented visually and concretely, and informally as well as in formal academic language, as explained in the next chapter.

For example, a surface understanding of the concept of 'salads' on a catering course might include a list of foods often contained in salads: lettuce, cabbage, tomatoes, cucumber, chickpeas, and so on. This creates a disconnected silo of knowledge. A deeper understanding of salads, from a catering point of view, would be obtained by considering salads from different perspectives such as:

- *the costs of different salad ingredients*
- *when these ingredients are in season*
- *the time taken to prepare these ingredients*
- *how long the ingredients can be stored*
- *the food miles involved in buying salad ingredients*
- *the nutritional value of the different salad ingredients*
- *the colour of salad ingredients and means of presenting them.*

Note that this links 'salads' to other concepts such as seasonality and cost, for which the student will already have a construct.

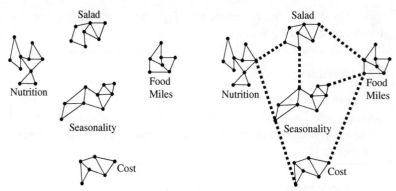

Figure 1.6: Surface learning of 'salad'

Figure 1.7: Deep learning of 'salad' with relational links

Relations between concepts make learning functional and better remembered

These *relations between* the constructs deepen the learning further. For example, food that is in season, with low food miles, tends to be cheap and nutritious compared to imported foods. Only a student with a deep understanding of salads could be expected to tackle a question such as: *'Devise a salad of low-cost for the winter months with a high nutritional yield'* or *'What factors cause the cost of salad ingredients to fluctuate?'*

It's *relating* the concept of salad with seasonality, with cost, with nutrition and so on, that enables the student to answer such questions. Relational thinking makes for deep learning, which is functional learning allowing the learner to make productive and independent use of their learning.

Relations work both ways. If a student is asked, in real life or in an exam, how to reduce the running costs of a restaurant, then they should come up with: *'Make sure you use salad ingredients that are in season and have low food miles'.* But they will only come up with this if they have deep learning. The common complaint that a student can't 'make the link', or can't 'see the connection', is a request for relational thinking, which requires deep learning. These links and connections are physical links made in the student's brain, by the student, as a consequence of good teaching.

Every subject is a complex of interrelations like this, and the more connections between concepts (constructs), the deeper the learning, and the more functional the learning and the better it is remembered.

With surface learning, the concepts of salads, seasonality, cost and nutrition are largely unconnected bodies of knowledge – the concepts are separate silos of surface learning. In this case, many students can't make the links required to answer real-life questions. They won't necessarily see the relevance of seasonality to nutrition, or road miles to cost.

 Consider

The Internet has many 'hyperlinks' for you to click on; these link one webpage with another. The brain also has such links between concepts. Imagine how limited – and diminished – the Internet would be without these relational links.

How deep learning can be transferred

Learning in one topic, can sometimes be transferred to other topics that have similar characteristics. For example, having taught students about salads, nutrition and seasonality, a teacher might ask:

Have we seen these issues before? Are there other topics where seasonality, cost, road miles and nutrition come up?

Students might not see these links, but the teacher can point out that fish and meat, which students studied earlier, are also at least partly seasonal, and when meat or fish are in season they are similarly nutritious, and less costly. They are also affected by road miles. This is called 'transfer'. A useful activity for transfer is to look for similarities and differences between salads and fish, or salads and meat. Venn diagrams can help (see Chapter 3).

In a similar way a mathematics teacher can, at an appropriate time in the future perhaps, point out the similarities and differences between:

- division and multiplication
- division, and ratios or fractions
- division and sines and cosines.

Again, *similarities and differences* help establish this transfer, along with the *'Where have we seen this before?'* question.

Transfer helps students to see your subject as a coherent, meaningful whole with repeating patterns, rather than as a seemingly random collection of discrete and disconnected facts. Transfer also helps your students to see your subject as intellectually more satisfying as well as more meaningful.

Explaining relations is not enough – students must learn to think with them

Of course, a good teacher will present these relevant relations, but unless the students have to *think* with these relations then the relations are likely to be quickly forgotten. Students will need to think about, indeed think functionally with, the relationships between concepts repeatedly, and on different occasions, to embed these relationships into their brains. It's important to recognise that what is happening here is that we are making a physical link within the student's brain. This won't happen without repetition. If memory is the residue of thought, then students must carry out thought-provoking tasks to embed the constructs and the links between them. Then we have deep learning.

Committed learners like the Susan we considered above, will tend to create at least some deep learning without a teacher's help, but the Roberts and Robertas usually don't. This is an equality, as well as a quality issue.

 Reflection

Deep learning is produced by the following overlapping experiences:

- Seeing and using the concept in many different contexts.

- Seeing and using the concept from multiple perspectives or points of view.

- Using the concept on many separate occasions.

- Relating the concept to other relevant concepts or, what amounts to the same thing, relating the topic to other relevant topics. (This means connecting one construct with another, e.g. relating 'salads' to 'seasonality', or division to ratios.)

- Actively reasoning with the concept and with relations with other relevant concepts, for example solving problems and answering questions.

- Having this reasoning checked and corrected.

Transfer of learning is produced by these overlapping experiences:

- Examining similarities and differences between similar concepts and similar relations.

- Looking for 'patterns' common to different but related topics.

- Noticing 'where we've seen this before'.

- Noticing that the same overarching principles can affect in different topics, e.g. keeping costs down, customer satisfaction, ratios, conservation of energy or fitness for purpose.

Transfer of skills, rather than knowledge, is considered in Chapter 13.

Teachers have an overcrowded curriculum, limited time, and sometimes we have high-stakes exams that only require simple recall. Consequently, many teachers succumb to the temptation of teaching topics in surface learning silos. They hop from topic to topic in a rush through the curriculum without showing the rich interconnectedness of their subject. Then they are disappointed when students can't answer what seems to the teacher to be a pretty simple question:

'Devise a salad of low-cost for the winter months with a high nutritional yield.'

We saw this issue above with the question: *'If a gardener has 225 bulbs to place equally in 15 flower beds, how many bulbs would be in each bed?'*

If there is no deep learning, arguably, there is no real learning at all.

The consequences of the co-constructivist model are profound

The capacity of the brain to create constructs and to create links between them is called neural plasticity, which continues late into life. The consequence of this neural plasticity is that learners are much more educable than some teachers realise. If we teach well, the Roberts and Robertas we considered above will learn almost as well as our Susans. As long as the prior learning is in place, as long as students are required to form a construct, as long as constructs are well related, and as long as all this learning is well checked and corrected, most students placed on an appropriate course will learn well. The limit is not the student, or the teacher, but the teaching.

Evidence for Chapter 1 on co-constructivism

 **Evidence**

Chapter 14 establishes that the most reliable sources of evidence are summary evidence, and we should triangulate three sources.

Evidence from summaries of qualitative research: The idea that learning is encoded in neural connections that are built by learners themselves on what they already know is almost universally accepted by all the disciplines that study the brain or the mind: neural physiology, psychology, sociology, philosophy, brain surgery, and so on. The idea that feedback or 'check and correct' is necessary to improve students' constructs is accepted by all the principle references, which start on page 284. The Quality Learning Cycle rests on these two assumptions.

Co-constructivism is NOT the same as 1960s 'constructivism'; the latter called for minimal guidance from the teacher, co-constructivism calls for careful teacher direction.

'We learn what we think hard about' is almost uncontested in cognitive science. The idea that students need to develop relations between, and within, concepts to understand them deeply is mentioned by all the research. The progress, while teaching a given topic, from memorising (surface learning), to in-depth structured understanding (deep learning), and then to transfer of learning is explicitly emphasised in Bransford (2000), see 'Conclusions' pages 233–247. It is implied in all qualitative references starting on page 284, except perhaps Rosenshine, but his paper is short.

Evidence from summaries of quantitative research: The Hattie Donoghue conceptual model (2016) was devised by reference to Hattie's massive database of summarised quantitative research. It explicitly requires learning to go from surface learning, to deep learning, to transfer (see Chapter 15 for a summary).

Evidence from research on the most effective teachers: Ayers (2004) explicitly noticed that the outstanding teachers he studied, while teaching a topic, used a sequence from closed questions/tasks on surface learning, towards individual or group work on open tasks that required challenging reasoning; this was followed by students making their own notes. Hattie's expert teachers set deep learning tasks much more frequently than experienced, but less effective, teachers.

Further reading

See also the principal references in Chapter 15 Further reading and references.

P. Adey and J. Dillon (Eds), *Bad Education: Debunking Myths in Education* (Buckingham: Open University Press, 2012).

P. Ayres et al., 'Effective teaching in the context of a Grade 12 high-stakes external examination in New South Wales, Australia' (*British Educational Research Journal*, Vol. 30, No. 1 February 2004).

J.D. Bransford et al., *How People Learn: Brain, Mind, Experience and School* (Washington: National Research Council, 2000). This book is the result of more than 20 academics working for two years on a large national project to summarise what is known about learning.

J.A.C. Hattie and E.M. Anderman (Eds), *International Guide to Student Achievement* (New York: Routledge, 2013). This contains more than 150 short essays on the major factors that affect student learning, each written by an expert in that research field.

J.A.C. Hattie and G.M. Donoghue, 'Learning strategies: a synthesis and conceptual model' (*NPJ Science of Learning*, 2016). Available free online, search for the title and author or follow: https://www.nature.com/articles/npjscilearn201613

R. Marzano, D. Pickering and J. Pollock, *Classroom Instruction that Works* (Alexandria: ASCD, 2001).

R.K. Sawyer (Ed), *The Cambridge Handbook of the Learning Sciences* (Cambridge: CUP, 2006). This is a most authoritative collection of essays by experts, summarising almost every aspect of research from a mainly qualitative point of view.

D. Willingham, *Why Don't Students Like School? A Cognitive Scientist Answers Questions About How the Mind Works and What It Means for the Classroom* (San Francisco: Jossey-Bass, 2010).

Chapter 2

Teaching the hard stuff: concrete to abstract and multiple modes of representation

Both weak and very effective learners learn every new topic from concrete to abstract. They also learn from known to unknown, because they link new learning to prior learning to make sense of it.

Many teachers still believe in the idea of 'learning styles' such as VAK (Visual, Auditory, Kinaesthetic) or 'left-brain' and 'right-brain' learning styles. A review of the research on learning styles summarised by Frank Coffield and colleagues has debunked this idea: they summarised evidence to show that teaching a student in a 'learning style' that is supposed to suit them does not in fact help their learning.

What does work is almost the opposite: students and teachers using lots of different styles. This is summarised in the diagram in Figure 2.2 on page 34, which shows a specific form of 'multiple representations'. The idea is that when first learning a difficult concept or idea, students benefit if the teacher starts from the student's concrete experience, explains the new learning in ordinary language, helped by visual or diagramatic representations of the new material. Once this is understood, students can be taught the more common academic way of describing the knowledge, using abstract and symbolic representations. Look at Figure 2.2, multiple modes of representation, before reading on.

Many teachers tend to use just one or two representations of the new material that they are teaching. Fatally, they are often drawn to the abstract, symbolic, general forms of representations usually found in textbooks. But these are an end point – they forget that their own understanding was first developed using the other modes of representation.

For example, a mathematics teacher might introduce the idea of division to a primary school class using abstract reasoning only, '15 divided by 5 is 3', while another teacher might use all the modes of representation. (We considered the 'existing concrete experience' of cutting up and sharing out in the previous chapter.) The multiple representation approach has been shown to be much more effective, not just in mathematics.

Explaining arithmetical division with multiple representations

 **Case study**

Existing experience: Teacher explains that 'cutting up' and 'sharing out' are examples of 'dividing'.

New concrete experience: The teacher asks students to use counters to do tasks such as 'share out', say, 12 counters between four children.

Ordinary language representations: The teacher does not use phrases such as '12 divided by 4', which is an abstract representation; instead she begins with expressions such as *'We have 12 sweets, let's share them out fairly between four children. How many sweets does each child get?'*.

Visual (non-verbal) representations: The teacher shows images on slides, posters, animations, and in handouts that visually show, say, 12 counters being sorted into four piles.

Abstract and symbolic representations: Eventually the teacher shows 12 being divided into four piles and describes that as *'We have 12 and we're sharing this out between three children; in other words we are dividing 12 by four. We write it like this: 12 $\prod$ 4.'* The abstract and symbolic representation might start after many hours of tuition on division, and might not be used exclusively until many hours after that.

The important point to remember is that the brain represents the concept 'division' in a number of different ways simultaneously, in particular visually and verbally. It is well accepted that the brain makes use of this 'dual coding' and not just in mathematics. Students who learn well may provide these multiple representations for themselves, but if the teacher provides them, or even better, requires her students to use them, all students get a deeper understanding.

To stay with mathematics for one more short example, students often have trouble with algebra The abstract and symbolic expression '$2a - 3 = 45$' seems paradoxical to many. How can you subtract a number from letters? How can something be 'unknown' and yet be part of a calculation? But many students are familiar with unknowns, for example with the challenge of guessing how many sweets there are in a jar. What if one jar had 'a' sweets in it, and another jar 'b' sweets in it?

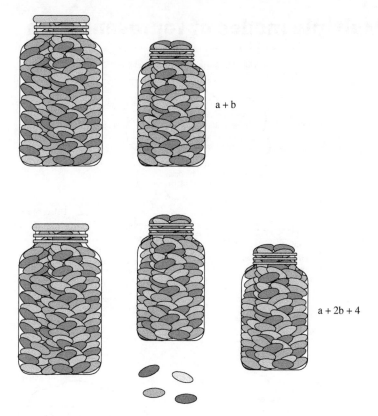

Figure 2.1: Algebra can be easier to understand when grounded in a concrete situation

Students can now express a concrete situation using algebra's abstract representations. The diagrams are from an excellent blog 'Sweet Algebra: A Model' by Tom Sherrington at https://teacherhead.com.

Multiple modes of representation

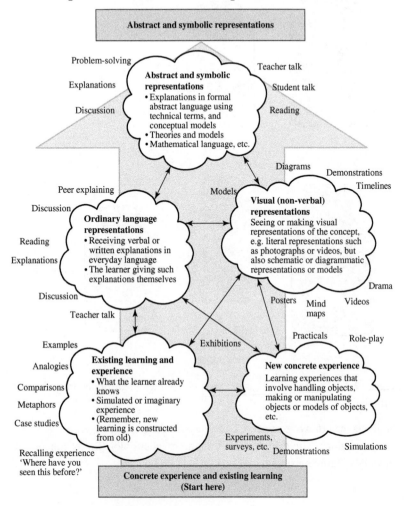

Figure 2.2: Multiple modes of representation

Explaining with multiple modes of representation

As the diagram in Figure 2.2 tries to show, if a concept or topic is hard for students, it can help them to see a number of concrete examples of it and to reason with these examples. The more varied the examples the better. The learner then begins to express the new learning in terms of their *existing learning and experience*.

It can also help to provide a *new concrete experience* (such as a game or simulation, or a teacher demonstration of a scientific experiment).

It helps the learner to express these ideas, or to hear them expressed in terms of 'everyday' language: *'voltage is the push on the electrons'* rather than *'electromotive force produces a potential gradient'*. These *ordinary language representations* help to fix the concept before it is 'labelled' in academic language. *Visual representations* both illustrative and diagrammatic can help greatly here. This allows the ideas to be represented in the brain in both a verbal and a visual way.

If the learning goes well, and if links between these representations are stressed, then the learner is eventually able to understand *abstract and symbolic representations* of this new learning.

Teaching abstract concepts in non-mathematical subjects

It is not only in mathematical subjects that students encounter difficult concepts. Suppose, for example, that some students have trouble understanding the concepts of the UK parliament, and the Congress of the USA. Students often suffer the misconception that parliament or Congress are the same as government, the executive, or the political party in power at the time.

Another concept students might have trouble with is that of imperialism. Students often assume that imperialism inevitably follows any simple military conquest. Students' understanding of the concepts of 'parliament', 'Congress' and 'imperialism' can be improved if the concept is presented in many or all of the multiple modes of representation in the 'Try this…' examples below. Another useful strategy is to challenge their ideas by showing a direct contradiction of their erroneous belief. This is called 'cognitive conflict' and it's a great way to dislodge student misconceptions. Some examples are shown just below.

 Try this in the classroom

Example 1: Improving the concepts of 'parliament' or 'Congress'

Concrete examples and non-examples: Examples of bills passing through both Houses of Parliament or Congress with opposition parties successfully resisting the bill. Examples of both successful and unsuccessful bills will help show the workings of parliament or Congress. It will also show the difference between the ruling party and parliament or Congress.

Analogies: Comparing parliament with the way a family might make a decision about whether or not to go on a holiday. Democratic and autocratic families could be considered.

Visual representations: Flow diagrams and other 'infographics' showing how laws are made, the role of government and the Opposition. Overlapping Venn diagrams comparing parliament or Congress with the government, and the leading political party.

Ordinary language representations: Ideally, explanations begin with ordinary language, for example *'The party, or parties in power can suggest a new law, but not all politicians may like it. If there are enough politicians against the suggested new law, they can effectively gang up and use parliament to stop it becoming law.'* Which later is expressed using terms like 'bill' and 'the Opposition' and 'second chamber'.

Cognitive conflict: The difference between ruling party and parliament could be shown by studying the fate of a bill that failed, despite government and ruling party support.

The difference between government and ruling party can be shown by stressing that only some members of the ruling party are chosen to be in the government, for example by being made ministers.

'Decisions-decisions' card-sorting games (Chapter 3) and 'diagnostic questions' (Chapter 11) can use cognitive conflict to dislodge misconceptions. Same-and-different diagrams with their overlapping Venn diagrams tease out the differences between concepts that overlap, and so are commonly confused.

Example 2: Improving the concept of 'imperialism'

Concrete examples and non-examples: Short accounts of the Roman Empire and the British Empire could be used as examples of imperialism. These would then need to be compared with a straightforward military defeat.

Analogy and ordinary language: If a thug beats you up and steals your wallet, that's a military defeat. If he beats you up then makes you join his gang, wear the clothes he likes, listen to the music he likes, and join his religion, that's imperialism.

Ordinary language: Students are asked to frame a definition of imperialism working in pairs or threes. These are then shared with the class and you manage the discussion in assertive questioning style, until the class agrees its definition. Then, or later, you can give a more formal definition relating it back to the class's definition.

Visual representations: Mind maps and illustrations that show imperialism by the influence the conquering nation has on those nations in its empire, for example on architecture, religion, judicial systems, government systems, and education. The aim being to show that imperialism is more than a military conquest.

Cognitive conflict: Discussing why the British Empire was more than a collection of military defeats, and its influence on nations after their independence.

Teaching a difficult concept using multiple representations and cognitive conflict

 Case study

First, I will describe an approach to teaching cash flow, which is a difficult concept or way of thinking. Then, I'll generalise this teaching strategy so you can use it to teach other difficult concepts.

A Business Studies lecturer teaches the concept of 'cash flow forecasting' with a spreadsheet activity. But her students just don't 'get it'. Cash flow is the flow of money into and out of a business. It needs to be forecasted so that managers will know how much cash will be available in the bank for purchases and wages over a period of time. The teacher finds her students confuse cash flow with profit and loss, and they don't turn to cash flow to solve problems unless directed to. They just don't think cash flow forecasting is necessary, especially for a profitable company.

The teacher realises her students use a 'profit and loss' schema instead of 'flow of cash over time' schema when making their mistakes. (A 'schema' is the name given to the concept or way of seeing that students use, whether erroneously or not, when thinking of something.) The teacher abandons her spreadsheet activity (abstract to abstract) and thinks of *examples, metaphors and simple models* of cash flow forecasting.

She shows students a simplified model or analogy for cash flow: a bath being filled with the plug out.

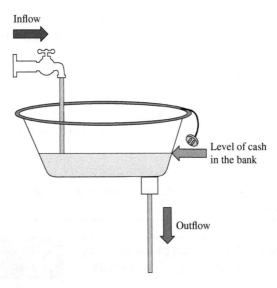

Inflow

Level of cash
in the bank

Outflow

Figure 2.3: Conceptualising cash flow

Her lesson starts with 'concrete preparation', which involves asking these questions of this model:

What provides inflow? Students suggest: receipts from customers.

What provides outflow? Students suggest: wages, purchases of materials and machinery.

What happens if inflow is greater than outflow? Students suggest: water level rises, i.e. money in the bank increases.

What happens if outflow is greater than inflow? Students suggests: water level falls, i.e. money in the bank decreases.

The teacher realises there is no point teaching cash flow schema without 'unteaching' the erroneous use of the profit and loss schema that most of her students are demonstrating.

Then she describes a joinery firm that very profitably makes oak tables and chairs – inflow has been greater than outflow for some time so the tank is half full. Then she creates 'cognitive conflict' with this highly simplified scenario. The company obtains a big order from a large company. The director calculates that this very large and urgent order will create a large profit. But the joinery company went bust – why?

Students are asked to discuss in pairs. They are very puzzled at first: using their profit and loss schema there seems to be no problem, and they suspect 'a trick question', but slowly they begin to work out that to meet a large urgent order the company must purchase a lot of materials, maybe purchase another machine, and hire and train more staff to meet the order on time.

Class discussion is vivid and useful. Eventually students realise that it is vital to do cash flow forecasting, even when a company is very profitable. A student asked to sum up what the class had learned said, *'To get big inflows in the future, you first need new equipment and stuff. Buying that creates big outflows in the present, and you can only do big outflows if you have money in the bank today.'* If you look at the multiple modes of representation diagram, you will see that this was an 'ordinary language formulation', but eventually with prompting from the teacher the class managed a more formal description that meant the same thing. For the next few lessons the teacher used the formal and the ordinary language formulations alongside each other, and reminded her students of the 'bath with the plug out' diagram.

Preparing to teach

What was the approach used in the case study above?

1 Identify tough concepts in your subject, ones that students find difficult and which often generate misconceptions.

2 Identify, if you can, the schema students use when misunderstanding the topic.

3 Identify concrete situations that:

- are simplified *examples* of the situation (the oak furniture firm going bust)

- are *models or analogies* of the situation (the 'bath with the plug out' diagram).

4 Use your concrete example, model or analogy, to create a *cognitive conflict* between the naïve schema the students are using to misunderstand the topic, and the reality of the situation. The schema you are trying to teach should of course correctly resolve this cognitive conflict.

5 Show students the conflict, and ask them to discuss in pairs or small groups. Use class discussion to *listen* to their thinking. Ask students to comment on each other's thinking, for example: *'Who agrees with Toni, and why?'* or *'Who disagrees and why?'* (see assertive questioning, Chapter 5). Gradually get the class to discover why the naïve schema doesn't work, and what schema they should use. Accept gratefully an 'ordinary language formulation' from the class.

6 Now, for the next few lessons, use the ordinary language formulation alongside the abstract and symbolic representation you want them to adopt, reminding the class of concrete examples they have discussed. Then use the abstract and symbolic representation only, which should now be well understood.

The above approach is an adaption of the 'cognitive acceleration' method developed by Shayer and Adey (2002) and has very many applications in the teaching of difficult concepts.

Summary

Students learn from concrete examples and from prior knowledge, but learning is often expressed in textbooks and the like in formal academic language along with symbolic representations. The brain represents knowledge in a verbal and a visual way at the same time, but in much teaching the verbal mode is predominant.

We need to give explanations, especially of difficult concepts, that first make use of concrete, visual, and ordinary language representations, and tasks for students that involve these. Only when the concept is established in this way, should we and our students begin to express the learning using symbolic, formal academic language.

It greatly helps this process if we and the tasks we set our students require learning to be expressed visually, using 'graphic organisers' such as flow diagrams and mind maps, and the closely related card-sorting game 'decisions-decisions'. This is explained in the next chapter.

Evidence for Chapter 2 on multiple modes of representation 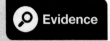 **Evidence**

Chapter 14 establishes that the most reliable sources of evidence are summary evidence, and we should triangulate three sources.

Evidence from summaries of qualitative research: The fact that the brain makes use of both visual and verbal/meaning representations, sometimes called 'dual coding,' or 'multiple modalities', is almost uncontested in cognitive psychology. Recently, it has come to light that the working memory of the brain has a visual and a verbal component, so using both representations for the same concept will put less strain on the working memory. See 'Cognitive load theory' (2017) in 'Further reading' below and Chapter 7. The idea of teaching from known to unknown occurs in all the qualitative references on page 284. Teaching from concrete to abstract is stressed in some of those references.

Cognitive dissonance helps students to form difficult concepts and corrects their misconceptions. Cognitive acceleration makes use of this, for example, and quantitative research reviews show that it is highly effective.

Evidence from summaries of quantitative research: Concept mapping, which displays information visually as well as in words and is described in the next chapter, has been found to be an exceptionally effective method for learning new material. 'Manipulatives', for example 'Cuisenaire rods' used to express mathematical ideas in concrete form, have been found to be highly effective. See Marzano (1998).

Evidence from research on the most effective teachers: I am not aware of any evidence from this sector that supports using multiple modes of representation.

Further reading

See also the principal references in Chapter 15 Further reading and references.

Free online resources

Search for 'dual coding' and 'multiple modes of representation'.

'Cognitive load theory: Research that teachers really need to understand' (Centre for Education Statistics and Evaluation, 2017). This is a free download, search for title and publisher. This paper summarises research on cognitive load theory. It suggests that working memory can be subdivided into aural and visual streams. The use of both streams reduces the strain on working memory. See also Chapter 7.

F. Coffield, 'Learning styles: time to move on' (National College of School Leadership, 2013). This provides a short introduction debunking the idea of learning styles.

R. Marzano et al., 'Nine Essential Instructional Strategies' (Adapted from *Classroom Instruction that Works,* Alexandria: ASCD, 2001). This shows that graphic organisers, a visual way of representing information, is very effective.

Prof. M. Sharma, 'Part I – Linear and Exponential Functions (6 Levels of Knowing)' (https://vimeo.com, 2012). A useful video on multiple representations.

T. Sherrington, 'Sweet Algebra A Model' (https://teacherhead.com, 2017). A concrete representation of algebra

Books and journals

P. Adey and M. Shayer, *Really Raising Standards* (London: Routledge, 1994).

J.C. Nesbit and O. Adesope, 'Learning with Concept and Knowledge Maps: A Meta-Analysis' (*Review of Educational Research* 76, page 413, 2006).

M. Shayer and P. Adey, *Learning Intelligence: Cognitive Acceleration Across the Curriculum from 5 to 15 Years* (Buckingham: Open University Press, 2002). This summarises research showing that concrete to abstract and visual plus verbal representations are powerful.

Chapter 3

Graphic organisers, card-sorting games and styles of analysis

We have seen that the use of both visual and verbal explanations (multiple modes of representation) help learners. Let's see how to make use of visual representations. These have been found to be highly effective in classroom trials.

To make use of visual representations of information, it first helps to understand that there are two ways to analyse information. The deliberate use of these two approaches helps students to plan extended writing, as we will see in Chapter 10. It also helps them to develop a deeper understanding of a new topic.

Atomistic and holistic analysis

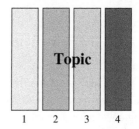

Figure 3.1: Atomistic analysis

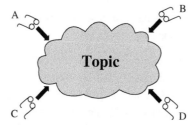

Figure 3.2: Holistic analysis

We need to get students to use both an 'atomistic' approach, and a 'holistic' approach to analysis. But many teachers and students only use the left-brain, atomistic method. Both are needed for a full and deep understanding. See Biggs and Collis (1982).

Atomistic analysis, or analysis by scissors: You can cut the topic up into discrete bits and look at these one at a time.

For example:

- looking at childhood diseases from the point of view of measles, mumps, whooping cough, etc.

- splitting a scientific experiment up into a sequence of tasks

- splitting the story in a novel, or an historical event, into a series of events to describe what happened.

There is often more than one way of analysing something by parts, for example a play can be analysed into a sequence of events (plot) and/or into a list of characters. Each of these can be considered one at a time.

Holistic analysis, or analysis by spectacles: You can look at the whole from different points of view, including different people's points of view, or with different questions in mind.

For example:

- looking at all childhood diseases from the points of view of immunisation or public health

- looking at a play, novel, or poem from the points of view of the different themes or issues it raises, or from the point of view of the author's influences, or their use of language

- looking at a scientific experiment from the points of view of criteria such as reliability, validity or methods of improvement, or from a 'what we learned' perspective. Also comparing the experiment with other experiments.

- looking at an historical event from the political, economic, religious, and social points of view.

Atomistic analysis, or analysis by parts, often produces what teachers disparagingly call a 'descriptive' piece of work When students have 'covered' all the parts one by one, they often think they have finished and so stop work If they are taught to analyse using spectacles as well as by parts, the quality of their work can improve greatly. When a student writes, *'Looking at King John's reign from the point of view of the barons...'*, we know we are reading a higher-quality piece of work than one that just lists what happened in the king's reign in chronological order. When a student looks at the role of the district nurse from the points of view of her patients, her family doctor, and from her cost benefit, we know we are getting a better piece of work than if the student centred on the district nurse in isolation.

Professor John Biggs has researched the characteristics of high- and low-grade work, and shown with his SOLO taxonomy that multi-perspective and relational thinking is a characteristic of high-grade academic work Students must see the big picture and the patterns and links in a subject to do very well in it. This requires a balance between atomistic and holistic approaches. It certainly requires 'spectacles' (Petty, 2009). I return to this issue in Chapter 10 when I consider how to help students plan writing. Some cognitive scientists seem unaware of Biggs' work and so do not regard 'spectacles' as helpful. But there is very wide acceptance of the importance of making use of the visual mode of representation, the subject of the rest of this chapter.

The danger of atomistic analysis being used alone – a common fault – is that the learner won't see how the topic relates to other topics, or see its meaning and purpose clearly. That is, they can't 'see the wood for the trees'.

You can teach students to overcome the following weaknesses in their use of spectacles:

- Not knowing which are the most useful and revealing spectacles.

- Not realising that one spectacle can't give the whole answer, and a spectacle can absorb us so much that we are blinded to the other points of view: 'every way of looking is a way of not-looking'.

- Not realising that you must balance the views from different spectacles.

Let's look at graphic organisers now; they provide powerful ways to represent knowledge visually, for almost any topic. As it happens, they can also help students use both atomistic and holistic analysis if you like that idea

Representing knowledge visually: graphic organisers

Flow diagrams, mind maps, and Venn diagrams, examples of which you can see in the next few pages, are all types of graphic organiser. If you *organise* information and then display this organisation in a *graphical* way, you have created a graphic organiser. A picture is not enough, the graphic must *organise* the knowledge.

Graphic organisers are most effective for learning when the students create them and then check and correct them; see the end of this chapter for a good way to do this. The meta-study by Nesbitt and Adesope (2006) gives a huge 'effect size' for better-designed experimental studies on graphic organisers, which shows that this is one of the most powerful teaching strategies we know of. It is so adaptable that you could use it in any subject.

Graphic organisers are often better than summaries or notes because they structure information more clearly and make the central ideas more apparent.

Relationships between concepts are often more clearly represented than in text too. They are an excellent aid for planning writing.

Graphic organisers fall into three categories according to Oliver Caviglioli and Ian Harris, and it is important to use the appropriate one for the task at hand.

- Some organisers, such as simple mind maps, **describe**.

- Some, such as an overlapping Venn diagram, **compare** one thing with another.

- Others, such as a flow diagrams, show a **sequence** or a **cause and effect**.

I describe some examples of graphic organisers for each of these three categories are described in the next few pages. Then I will discuss how you decide which organiser to use and when, and look at how to use these organisers.

Graphic organisers that describe:

Mind maps

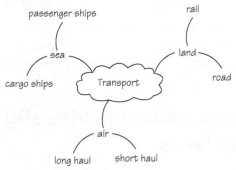

Figure 3.3: Holistic mind map (scissors)

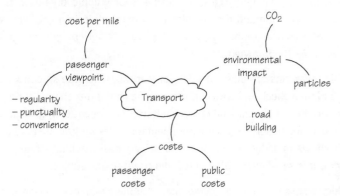

Figure 3.4: Atomistic mind map (spectacles)

You and your students will probably be familiar with atomistic mind maps, which cut a topic into subtopics. But making use of the styles of analysis at the start of this chapter, there can also be holistic mind maps, which look at a topic as a whole from different points of view or with different questions in mind (see Figures 3.3 and 3.4 above).

Tree diagrams

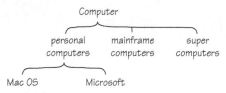

Figure 3.5: A tree diagram

These are very like atomistic mind maps, often used to show a hierarchy in organisations or in concepts.

Venn diagrams

Figure 3.6: A Venn diagram

Venn diagrams are a circle or other closed shape showing the boundary of a concept. For example, you might remember from your biology classes that snakes and lizards are reptiles, but frogs and toads are not (they are amphibians). Also, reptiles have scales on their skin and are cold-blooded. A Venn diagram for a reptile shows examples of reptiles inside the circle or other closed shape. Defining characteristics of reptiles can also be placed inside the circle, for example 'scales on the skin' and 'cold-blooded'. Indeed, anything pertaining to reptiles can be placed inside the circle, for example images, exam questions, etc. Clearly, the Venn diagram could be much more detailed than my example in Figure 3.6.

But what makes Venn diagrams really useful is that they can correct misconceptions. As many students think frogs and toads are reptiles when they are not, these can be placed outside the circle. Also, many students think reptiles have damp clammy skin, so this characteristic can be placed outside the circle to show it is *not* a characteristic of reptiles.

In this way Venn diagrams can show what something is, but also, what it is not. This is vital for concept formation.

Labelled diagrams

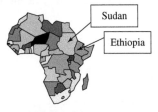

Figure 3.7: A labelled diagram

Labels on diagrams can describe either the names of the parts, or functions or other characteristics of the parts, for example 'oil-rich state', or 'dictatorship'.

Description table

Childhood diseases	
1 Measles	Students write here
2 Mumps	Students write here
3 Whooping cough	Students write here
A Immunisation	Students write here
B Doctors' views	Students write here
C Parents' views	Students write here

Figure 3.8: A description table

A description table summarises the key points in a topic under carefully chosen headings; it is useful for summarising a topic in notes, but also to prepare for writing. Using the 'styles of analysis' at the beginning of this chapter, a description table can include descriptions of *parts*, for example what happened first, second, etc.; or in the case of the topic 'childhood diseases' the parts might be measles, mumps, and whooping cough. The table can also include holistic 'spectacles', which are points of view that look at the topic as a *whole*: immunisation, doctors' views, parents' views, etc.

 How to

For this, and indeed all graphic organisers:

- it is best if you introduce it by creating one on the board for students, thinking aloud to model how a description table is produced (see Chapter 7)

- the real benefits come when students devise their own, because it requires students to create a structured, summarising construct.

Description tables are a useful form for notes; further explanatory detail can be added if necessary, and they can easily be created in a word-processing program using a table format. If large enough, they can be displayed on classroom walls for further reference.

To use a description table, which can be A3 in size, students work alone or in groups to write bullet-point summaries under each of the headings on the left of the table. These headings might first be given by you, but eventually students should devise their own headings, and then hear what other students have chosen as their headings. Class discussion can then reveal how to analyse atomistically and holistically: *'Which spectacles did you choose and why?'*, *'Why is that a good spectacle, Alice?'*

The table shown above is a very simple one; more detailed tables (when completed) can provide useful summarising notes showing the structure of a topic.

If you add rows at the top and the bottom for an introduction and a conclusion, students can use this as a plan for descriptive writing. They may change the order of the rows 1, 2, 3 and A, B, and C, so as to deal with these in a logical order. All students need to do now is expand each summary bullet point into a paragraph or two and they will eventually have a well-structured piece of descriptive writing.

Graphic organisers that compare

Same-and-different diagrams

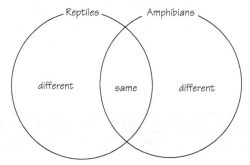

Figure 3.9: Same-and-different Venn diagram

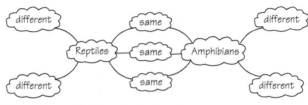

Figure 3.10: Same-and-different mind map

	Different	Same
Fractions		
Percentages		

Figure 3.11: Same-and-different table

Same-and-different diagrams can help prevent confusion between concepts that have similarities, such as 'reptile' and 'amphibian'. Figure 3.9 is an overlapping Venn diagram where the similarities are shown in the overlap and the differences on either side of the overlap. The same-and-different table in Figure 3.11 has the same structure, but is easier to use in a word-processing program.

Mind maps can be combined to show similarities and differences, as shown in Figure 3.10.

These diagrams are demanding to create. It is usually best for students first to create simple descriptive graphic organisers such as a mind map for each of the two concepts to be compared. Then they can use these to produce a comparison organiser. As ever, model how to do this, as described in Chapter 7. Search online for Venn diagrams to compare three or four topics.

In Chapter 10 we will see these organisers being used to plan essays of the 'to what extent' type, such as *'To what extent did the Treaty of Versailles cause the Second World War?'*

Comparison table

Changes created by the Communist Revolution in Russia		
'spectacle'	Before the Revolution	After the Revolution
Government		
The life of a peasant		
Industrial development		

Figure 3.12: Comparison table

Comparison tables compare two or more things using the same criteria. This is useful for evaluative thinking as fair comparisons usually require the same criteria to be used.

You can compare more than two things if you provide more columns, for example five computer printers could be compared using criteria such as cost, print speed, and colour capability.

As well as for *before and after* comparisons, these tables can be used to compare:

- *with and without* – for example stocktaking with and without a computer
- *strengths and weaknesses* – for example the strengths and weaknesses of three health policies.

Comparison tables can therefore help students to plan essays of the forms *compare and contrast*, *with and without*, *before and after*, and *strengths and weaknesses*, as explained in Chapter 10.

Continua or spectrums

not sugary   sugary

Figure 3.13: A continuum

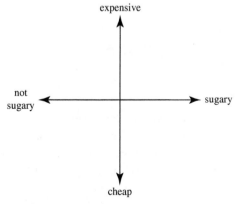

Figure 3.14: Crossed continua

	Not sugary	Sugary
Expensive		
Cheap		

Figure 3.15: A crossed continua table

Figure 3.16: A timeline showing years

A continuum or 'spectrum' (Figure 3.13) can compare different drinks by their sugar content, compare trees by their rate of growth, or compare political parties by how libertarian they are. Timelines (Figure 3.16) can display changes over time.

Continua can cross. Figure 3.14 compares drinks on the basis of both cost, *and* sugar content at the same time. A drink that appears in the bottom right-hand quadrant of Figure 3.14 will be both sugary and cheap. Graphs in mathematics and science are crossed continua of course, but the idea has a much wider application. Similarly, crossed continua could compare political parties on the basis of libertarianism, *and* attitude to abortion. The crossed continua table in Figure 3.15 is a similar organiser that compares more crudely, but sometimes more clearly.

It's well worth thinking of some topics where your students could make use of continua or crossed continua to organise information.

Graphic organisers that show sequences or reasoning

Flow diagram

Figure 3.17: A flow diagram

A flow diagram usually shows a process, for example the process of assembling a car in a factory. But it can also show cause and effect, or a reasoning sequence. For example, a flow diagram could show the chain of reasoning that justifies public spending on education within the UK economy.

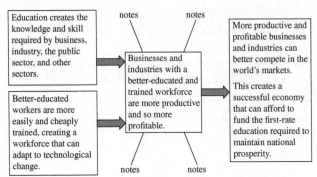

Figure 3.18: A flow diagram with notes to show reasoning

Notes can be added to a flow diagram as if each box in the flow diagram were the centre of a mind map.

Visual essay planning

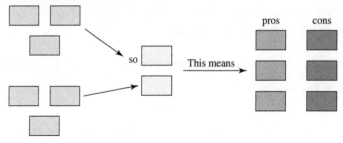

Figure 3.19: Planning visually

This is a way to help students plan writing, and works well as a summarising activity in class with students working in small groups.

🎯 Try this in the classroom

- Give students a question, assignment task, or essay title.

- Students work alone to write down 'ideas', i.e. pertinent issues, points or subtopics, each on separate sticky notelets or pieces of paper. The ideas should be as wide ranging and comprehensive as possible, but not detailed. Just headings will do.

- Students share their ideas one at a time. They place similar ideas from different students on top of each other, and discard ideas that don't get agreement. Also, they place ideas that are related close to each other.

- They then structure their chosen ideas by putting them into meaningful clusters.

- They name the clusters, and even cluster these clusters if it helps.

- They look for relationships between the clusters: these are often logical relations.

- They rearrange the clusters of ideas into a coherent and logical sequence.

- This can be copied or photographed and used as a plan for writing. They need only expand each idea into a sentence or paragraph moving from left to right across their flow diagram of ideas to get writing that is comprehensive and well structured.

The above process could of course be done digitally by creating, and then dragging and dropping, boxes of text. It works best for planning writing about cause and effect, or for explaining an argument, or a time sequence.

This is an excellent way to summarise a topic as well as to plan writing (see Chapter 10).

To prepare students for this method you could model the process on an interactive whiteboard, thinking aloud, as described in Chapter 7. This would be a good way to summarise a lesson.

Which graphic organiser should I use when?

The organiser you use must suit the topic. Some topics, or essay titles, that would suit each category of graphic organiser are given below.

- Organisers that **describe** (e.g. simple mind-map) are suitable for topics such as:

  'What are the main characteristics of a viral infection?'

  'Outline the management structure for a small hotel.'

- Organisers that **compare** (e.g. an overlapping pair of Venn diagrams) are suitable for topics such as:

  'Contrast the campaign for women's rights with the campaign for Black Power.'

  'Should immigrants be allowed immediate and full access to the National Health service?' (for-and-against comparison)

  'What contribution can computers make to hotel booking?' (hotel booking with computers compared to booking without them)

  'What important effects did the Black Death have on agriculture?' (comparing agriculture before the Black Death with agriculture after it)

  'To what extent did New Labour adopt Thatcherite policies?' (see page 188 on 'To what extent…' questions).

- Organisers that **sequence** (e.g. sequence an industrial process, a story, or a reasoned argument) are suitable for topics such as:

  'Describe how a bill passes through parliament.'

  'Outline the plot of Act 1 of Hamlet.'

  'Why is an effective education system important to the economy?'

Sometimes more than one organiser could be used, for example the effect of the Black Death could be given as a string of causes and effects or a 'before and after' comparison. It could also be seen as a simple descriptive topic.

Caviglioli and Harris point out that it is usually best for students to describe first, *then* compare or sequence as is necessary, for example describe reptiles and amphibians first, then compare them.

Why graphic organisers work

Graphic organisers work when they challenge students to structure information in their own heads, link it with what they already know, and then correct this structure and so their understanding. This creates much better learning than simply studying an organiser. If students do study organisers, the best results come from checking their recall of the organiser (see Chapter 11).

How to use graphic organisers

Familiarise students with graphic organisers first

Teach students how to use specific graphic organisers first by creating one in front of them while you think aloud and explain the process (see Chapter 7 on modelling). For example, you could create an organiser to summarise or review a topic before a test, so killing two birds with one stone.

As the process of creating each type of organiser is new to most students, be sure to create the organiser from content that is familiar to them. Then provide students with guided practice in creating this form of organiser, again using familiar content.

Once students are familiar with a few different types of organiser, explain the three kinds of organiser to them. Then get them to select the appropriate organiser for a given task or topic. There is an exercise on this on page 57 that you could adapt for your students.

Using organisers in the classroom

It is a great activity for students to create an organiser either alone or in groups. They work as a class activity, for homework, as part of an assignment, or to help plan writing. Here is an approach from Black et al. (2003):

1 Present students with new material in your usual ways.

2 Ask students to create a suitable organiser to summarise the topic or answer a question about it. You can either stipulate the type of organiser or later leave them to choose the most appropriate type.

3 When their organiser is nearly complete, ask students to leave them on their desk, and to move around and look at everyone else's. The aim is to learn how to improve their own organiser.

4 Students improve their organisers.

5 Students self- or peer-assess their organisers. Give them your own model organiser, a checklist, or some assessment criteria to do this.

You can do this electronically too, as shown in Figure 3.20.

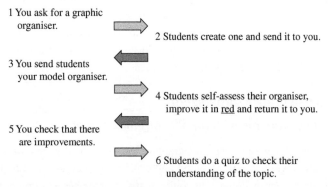

1 You ask for a graphic organiser.

2 Students create one and send it to you.

3 You send students your model organiser.

4 Students self-assess their organiser, improve it in <u>red</u> and return it to you.

5 You check that there are improvements.

6 Students do a quiz to check their understanding of the topic.

Figure 3.20: Graphic organiser ping-pong

Other uses of graphic organisers

Other uses of graphic organisers include the following:

• To summarise what a class *already* knows about a topic before you teach more of it.

• To create a summary of what they are *about* to learn, called an 'advance organiser' (Ausubel, 1968). Students can add their own notes to a copy of this during the class.

• Students can create flip-chart-sized organisers that can be posted on the classroom noticeboard, to be referred to later.

• Organisers can also be used as the basis for card-sorting games, as described later in this chapter. For example, statements such as 'has dry skin' or 'lays hundreds of eggs' could be placed on a 'same-and-different' diagram comparing reptiles and amphibians. This approach is great for using on an interactive whiteboard.

• Groups can record and report their findings to the class using organisers.

• They are also useful for your presentations and displays.

• Students can create their own notes in organiser form, e.g. summarising a chapter from a book

Some students may be resistant to using graphic organisers initially: tell them that research shows they help almost everyone, and ask them to give organisers a fair try. Most people convince themselves of their value after five to ten uses. If a student remains unconvinced, require them to use the same structures as the organisers above, but just in writing with very clear headings. It is the structuring of information that is the greatest benefit of graphic organisers.

Groups can produce graphic organisers

Students can take a part of a topic, or a spectacle, and do an individual graphic organiser that can then be assembled on a noticeboard. They can then present part or all of this to the class.

 Preparing to teach

Which graphic organisers would be most appropriate for the following tasks?

Here is a task for you, or you could adapt this task for your own students. Decide which organiser you would use for each of the following topics. First consider if it is a describe, compare or a sequence organiser you need, then choose a specific organiser of this type.

1. Brainstorm the main advantages of stocktaking in a small shop.

2. Distinguish between a viral and a bacterial infection.

3. Explain the main events leading up to the Second World War.

4. Describe and critically compare the main methods of presenting numerical data.

5. How much does funding of education affect educational attainment?

6. Consider common teaching methods from the point of view of whether the teacher or the student is most in control, and how challenging they are for the student.

7. What reasoning is used to justify having a Department for Trade and Industry?

8. Critically review the main types of computer printer.

Preparing to teach

Answers to the above task. Sometimes more than one organiser could work well, but here are my choices:

1 Holistic mind map showing the advantages from the point of view of the customer, manager of the shop, supplier, etc.

2 A comparison table, an overlapping Venn diagram, or a 'same-and-different' diagram.

3 A flow diagram, perhaps on a timeline.

4 Comparison table.

5 (This is a hard one!) A same-and-different diagram (see the end of Chapter 10).

6 Crossed continuum, for example with teacher or student in control on the x-axis and degree of challenge on the y-axis.

7 A flow diagram.

8 A comparison table.

Card-sorting games: 'decisions-decisions'

Graphic organisers can be adapted to produce a highly versatile learning game. You give students a set of cards that can contain text, diagrams, formulae, computer code, photographs, drawings, or a combination of these, indeed almost anything.

You then set students a task to sort, group, sequence, or rank the cards, or to place them appropriately in a diagram. (Text boxes can be dragged and dropped to appropriate places for a digital version of this game.)

Have a quick scan through the diagrams below to get the general idea I just searched for 'card-sort activity geography' on the Internet and got over a million hits; most of the games were free to download, often in forms that you could adapt. Your own subject will have similar free resources, and you can of course make your own. The table feature in your word-processing software will help make cards all the same size if you want that.

We will see later that 'decisions-decisions' is an exceptionally effective teaching activity. This is not surprising, as it requires students to form a construct and then check and correct it. That is, it takes students around the Quality Learning Cycle we saw in Chapter 1.

Cards or text boxes can establish a single concept

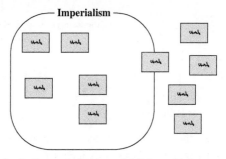

Figure 3.21: A single Venn circle can establish a single concept

Here, the students have in effect a single Venn diagram (described earlier in this chapter) and are asked to place cards either inside the circle or outside it. For example, suppose a teacher was trying to develop the concept of imperialism in history. Cards could contain examples of imperialism, characteristics of imperialism, etc. However, other cards have non-examples and non-characteristics of imperialism. Students must place cards to do with imperialism inside the imperialism Venn diagram and those not to do with imperialism outside.

The cards could contain illustrations or diagrams of imperialistic architecture. Other cards could contain exam questions that do not mention imperialism, but where imperialism would figure in the answer. Again, other cards could contain illustrations and diagrams of architecture that is *not* imperialistic, and still other cards could contain exam questions where imperialism would *not* figure, but that a confused student might think would.

If a student places a card incorrectly, it is best to ask *'Why did you put that one there?'*: this should reveal the misconception that caused the misplacement. You can show a correct card sort after the students have finished and students can self-assess, and class discussion can be used to clear up any problems.

Cards or text boxes can be sorted into groups

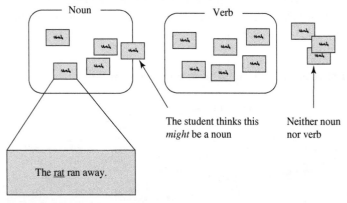

Figure 3.22: Sorting cards into groups

Concepts that might otherwise be confused like 'noun' and 'verb' can be developed in a similar way. Other examples include:

- the duties of a vice president and president

- metaphor and simile

- colon and semicolon.

'Same-and-different' card sorts

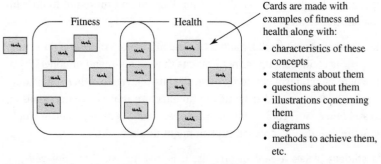

Figure 3.23: Sorting cards on a 'same-and-different' diagram

In some cases Venn diagrams overlap, and so represent the similarities and differences between concepts. The card-sorting game could be developed to tease out the similarities and differences between easily confused concepts such as, for example:

- health and fitness

- murder and manslaughter

- natural fibres and synthetic fibres.

This is a very powerful activity that untangles easily confused concepts.

Cards or text boxes can be matched

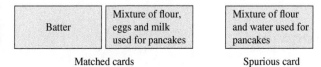

Matched cards   Spurious card

Figure 3.24: Matching cards or text boxes

Students can match technical terms with their meanings; questions with answers; parts of the heart with their function; or tools with their typical uses. Card-sorting games are highly adaptable because every subject can involve students in sorting, matching, grouping, sequencing, or ranking.

Examples of these are the matching games in mathematics suggested by Swann and Green (2002). Students are given cards on which there are algebraic expressions. They are also given other cards to match with these, which contain statements in English. Some of the statements in English have the same meaning as the algebraic expressions, but some do not, and the aim is to match cards with the same meaning.

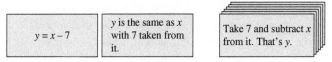

Figure 3.25: Matching cards can be used to determine mathematical understanding

There are 'spurious' cards that have statements in English which do *not* match any of the algebraic equations. However, some of them are very close. Students must look carefully at the algebraic expressions and the English expressions to determine which match.

The cards could also contain visual representations of algebraic expressions to match with their corresponding expressions, as shown in the diagram Figure 3.26 below. Students often confuse $3n^2$ and $(3n)^2$. This is an example of multiple methods of representation that we saw in Chapter 2.

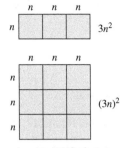

Figure 3.26: Matching cards can include visual representations to help overcome confusion

Cards can be sequenced

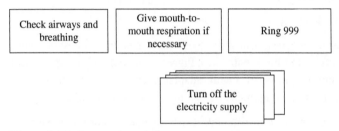

Figure 3.27: Sequencing cards

This method is best explained by an example:

Sequencing 🅣 **Case study**

I once saw students studying what to do if someone suffered a suspected electric shock. Instead of teaching by talking, the teacher put students in pairs and gave each pair a set of cards. Students were asked to reject cards describing what they would *not* do, and put the others in time order.

I was observing two students, one bossy, the other quiet. Their teacher had placed the cards in a thoughtful order. The bossy student picked up the first card suggesting that they ring the emergency number: 'Ring 999.' Despite protestations from the quiet student, the bossy student stated authoritatively that this card must come first. Then the quiet student picked up a card reading 'Give mouth-to-mouth respiration if necessary.' 'Hey,' said the quiet one, 'when you're ringing 999, he could be dying!' The bossy one was annoyed, but they agreed together to place artificial respiration before ringing the emergency number. Later, the crestfallen bossy student picked

---

up a card reading 'Turn off the electricity supply.' 'Hey,' he said, 'when you're giving him mouth-to-mouth, he's still *plugged in*!'

There were also spurious cards. One read 'Wear rubber gloves and wellingtons.' This, the students solemnly placed in order, until they encountered the card saying 'Turn off the electricity supply.' Then they both agreed they could do without rubber gloves and wellingtons. The teacher, of course, displayed to students the correct sequence of cards after the student activity and discussed difficulties with the class.

This is an example of where students, with guidance, had the capacity to 'discover' for themselves what they were expected to learn, and in a most vivid way. It shows the power of peer tutoring to check and correct learning too.

Here are some examples of where this sequencing approach could be used. In all of these games, spurious cards are helpful to develop the concepts concerned.

- English literature students place events in a novel or play in time order or in order of significance.

- Business studies students sequence activities that prepare for the launch of a new product.

- In a drugs education workshop participants place drugs in perceived order of danger to health and their addictiveness.

- Students with learning difficulties sequence digital photographs taken yesterday of them making tea, verbalising the process in time order.

- Plumbing students sequence the process of fitting a new central heating system.

Text cards can be sequenced

A very simple use of the above game is to take one of your existing handouts and cut it up into about six or more pieces, a few paragraphs for each piece. Students must now read the pieces and place them in order to create a meaningful handout. If this is done electronically, students now print off the text as a handout. This is surprisingly effective, and at least makes sure that students have read and understood the handout!

Cards can be ranked

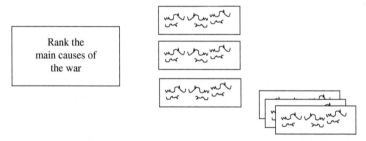

Figure 3.28: Ranking cards

Here, students put cards in order of importance, effectiveness, cost or time taken. For example, they might be given cards which describe the possible causes of a war that they have been studying to place in order of importance, rejecting those that are not causes. Or business studies students could be given cards that describe three different marketing policies designed for a given case study and be asked to place the policies in order of effectiveness. Then they could be asked to place the same policies in order of cost.

This game has very many applications in vocational education; useful factors for ranking include effectiveness, importance, cost, ease of implementation, efficiency, etc.

Graphic organiser games

Any of the graphic organisers we saw earlier in this chapter can be the basis of a card-sorting game, not just the ones I have shown above. For example, rather than presenting students with a complete mind map, they can be given its elements on cards, and then asked to arrange these into a coherent structure. Students may create slightly different structures, but this is fine and can be quite illuminating.

You could give students text boxes that describe a process, asking them to turn it into a flow diagram. Or give them statements to place in a decision tree.

Remember, these card-sorting games can be played with real physical cards, or cards can be created as text boxes to drag and drop into the appropriate place on a screen. This is a brilliant activity for an interactive whiteboard. Students can come up to the board to drag and drop text boxes into the place they think appropriate. Then you can test class understanding by asking *'Has Wolfgang put that one in the right place?'* Then you can use the assertive questioning procedure to develop deeper understanding, and to give you feedback on your students' understanding. Great fun too.

Evidence for Chapter 3 on graphic organisers and card-sorting games

Chapter 14 establishes that the most reliable sources of evidence are summary evidence, and we should triangulate three sources.

Evidence from summaries of qualitative research: The 'spectacles' approach is criticised by Willingham (2009), but the other references state that 'transfer is assisted by seeing learning in widely varying contexts'.

The evidence is the same as was given in the evidence box at the end of Chapter 2, see page 40.

Evidence from summaries of quantitative research: Concept mapping, which displays information visually as well as in words, has been found to be an exceptionally effective method for learning new material. 'Manipulatives', for example 'Cuisenaire rods' used to express mathematical ideas in concrete form, have been found to be highly effective. See Marzano (1998).

Evidence from research on the most effective teachers:

Two independent sources of evidence suggest graphic organisers and card-sorting games might be worth trying in your classroom.

Further reading

See also the principal references in Chapter 15 Further reading and references.

Free online resources

Search for 'graphic organisers' and there is a wealth of material available.

Search also for 'card-sorting games' or 'manipulatives' followed by the subject/topic you are teaching.

For cards being used in mathematics, search online for 'loop cards'.

Books and papers

J.B. Biggs and K.F. Collis, *Evaluating the Quality of Learning: The SOLO Taxonomy (Structure of the Observed Learning Outcome)* (New York: Academic Press, 1982).

J. Biggs and C. Tang, *Teaching for Quality Learning at University* (4th Edition) (Maidenhead: McGraw-Hill, 2011).

O. Caviglioli and I. Harris, 'Wiseguide to Model Mapping' (2008) and 'Wise guide to Visual Tools' are available if you search online.

R. Marzano, D. Pickering and J. Pollock, *Classroom Instruction that Works* (Alexandria: ASCD, 2001). This shows that students creating graphic organisers is an exceptionally powerful teaching strategy.

J.C. Nesbit and O. Adesope, 'Learning with Concept and Knowledge Maps: A Meta-Analysis' (*Review of Educational Research* 76, page 413, 2006).

G. Petty, *Teaching Today: A Practical Guide* (5th Edition) (Oxford: Oxford University Press, 2014).

M. Swann and M. Green, *Learning Mathematics Through Discussion and Reflection* (CD-ROM, video and print materials) (London: LDSA, 2002).

Chapter 4

The RAR model: structuring your teaching of a topic

I magine that you are about to teach a topic that takes up to about 90 minutes and that this teaching may range over more than one lesson. This topic requires the learner to form one or more constructs and build them on constructs already formed in their prior learning as described in Chapter 1 (see page 9).

Your challenge is to find a sequence of activities for both you and your students that will cause every learner to form a successful construct or constructs, well-linked to their prior learning. This is not easy! To be successful the teaching of a topic must be carefully structured to drive co-constructivism.

I will assume in what follows that you are teaching content of some kind in a classroom, but the methods can all be adapted very easily to almost any teaching situation: workshop, practical work, work-based learning, resource-based learning, and fieldwork.

What is RAR?

The basic idea of the RAR model is that, in order to learn well, students need to **Receive** new content, **Apply** this new learning by doing some tasks, and then **Reuse** the learning on a number of occasions, spread out over time to consolidate the new learning in long-term memory. Throughout, there needs to be a *check and correct* of the learning, as the RAR diagram on page 75 makes clear. The aim is to teach the topic in a way that moves from surface learning of the basics to deep learning, and then to transfer of learning as described in Chapter 1.

Have a good look at the RAR structure in the diagram on page 75 now. It is not a structure for a single lesson. It describes how students might learn a short topic: the receive and apply phases may take more than one lesson. In any case, the reuse phases will extend well into the future. There is no sense in just thinking in terms of a single lesson structure when learning requires repetition.

We need to focus on topic plans, not lesson plans, to ensure deep meaning is created and to ensure the learning is used often enough to get well established in long-term memory. See Hattie and Donoghue (2016) and Bransford (2000).

To receive the new content, students may get an explanation from you, or they might learn it from resources online.

The receive phase, whether the content is presented by you, or learned online, includes a preparatory 'orientation' phase where students are readied for the new material. The aim of the receive phase is to establish the main outline of the topic, which is the 'surface learning' described in Chapter 1. Students then need to **apply** their new learning in some sort of activity, in order to consolidate the surface learning and to deepen the learning (Chapter 1). The learning needs to be **reused** a number of times, to ensure it is not forgotten, and to deepen it further. Throughout, there needs to be a check and correct on learning in progress. In both the apply and reuse phases, the teacher should attempt to transfer the learning beyond the strict confines and content of the topic at hand, as described in Chapter 1.

The three-part sequence of the RAR elements is not a necessary one, and in practice the student may visit each of these phases many times. They may do a bit of receive, a bit of apply, then a bit more receive, and a bit more apply, then do a reuse, and so on. Whatever the sequence, however, it is difficult to imagine a topic being taught well without students visiting all three elements in the RAR model. So, we can characterise good teaching as being like a three-legged stool, and if a leg is missing the stool falls over!

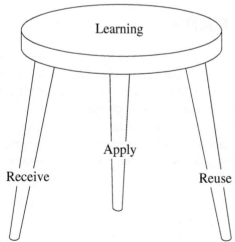

Figure 4.1: Learning is a three-legged stool

The RAR structure drives co-constructivism

The RAR structure ensures that the Quality Learning Cycle we saw in Chapter 1 is in full operation. Specifically, the RAR structure:

- requires the teacher and/or the learner(s) to check and correct any relevant prior learning, so that students have a firm foundation on which to build the new construct(s). This usually takes a little time but greatly improves learning

- requires each learner to form an understanding: that is, to form a construct(s) for the topic. (It *requires* this, rather than just allowing students to form a construct if they feel like it.)

- ensures the learner has linked their new learning to any relevant learning, in a way that creates a deep and accurate understanding

- requires a check and correct of each learner's construct(s), to correct as far as possible any errors or omissions in their learning

- enables the teacher to check and correct their teaching too, so they can adapt their teaching

- provides a periodic reuse of the learning, days, weeks and months later. These reuses are frequent enough to ensure that the learning is not forgotten.

Different elements of the lesson and different methods will be required to provide these activities and needs, not just for the class as a whole but for each individual student.

Characteristics of the best teaching methods

Soon we will look at some common teaching strategies for different parts of the RAR structure. In order to learn well, these teaching strategies should provide the following characteristics.

A high participation rate: All students should be engaged, or as many of them as possible at any given time. In order to achieve this, students need to anticipate that their learning will be held to account.

A check and correct of learning for you in real time, as well as later: As you teach, you need representative feedback on how well students understand what you are teaching so you can correct any errors and omissions in learning quickly and regularly.

Students need continuous checks and corrections of their learning: When peers talk about their learning, one peer often expresses an idea that is at odds with the conception of another. This conflict creates engagement, and there is a desire to resolve the conflict by persuading the peer of one's own conception, or by improving one's own conception. (When teaching methods are compared for their relative effectiveness, class discussion comes out exceptionally well – see Chapter 14.)

> '... the teacher who is openly receptive to incoming feedback about their interventions... is among the most powerful moderators in the learning equation.'
>
> *John Hattie, 'The Role of Learning Strategies in Today's Classrooms'*
> *(The 34th Vernon-Wall Lecture, 2014).*

Using RAR to teach the use of the apostrophe in a classroom

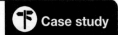 **Case study**

The receive and apply phases below could range over more than one lesson. The reuse phase necessarily involves short activities spread over some weeks.

Receive: Orientation: The aim of the orientation phase is to prepare students for learning by checking any necessary prior learning, making it clear what they will learn, what they will do with this learning, and what success looks like.

Advance organiser: The teacher explains that there are two apostrophe rules to learn.

Relevance: The teacher gives some funny examples of ambiguous sentences where the apostrophe has been misused. Discussion of the importance of the correct use of apostrophes, and the content and purpose of the lesson.

A goal is set: Students are shown the sentences that they must soon mark and correct in the 'apply' phase. These don't look easy! Students are told their work will be peer assessed – this makes them feel accountable. The success criteria are explained – get those apostrophes in the right place and be able to explain why they are where they are.

Prior learning: The teacher checks any important prior learning on plurals and possessives.

New material is received by learners: The teacher explains the apostrophe rules and gives a note summarising them.

Modelling: The teacher does some exercises on the board to put apostrophes in the right place, thinking aloud. Then he gets the class to direct him in similar tasks and ask questions to develop class discussion: *'Who agrees with Guy that no apostrophe is needed? Why do you agree, Safa?'* He uses assertive questioning (withholding the answer for some time, to encourage this discussion, see Chapter 5).

Monitored practice: The teacher gives students work to do in pairs to put apostrophes in the right place. The pairs mark and correct their own work using worked examples provided by the teacher (these are correct answers to similar tasks, with a brief explanation). The teacher discovers what students found hard, and he explains more carefully, including why the wrong answers are wrong. When the teacher judges the class is ready, he moves to the full apply phase.

Apply: Students are given a sequence of tasks of increasing difficulty, each requiring the student to use apostrophes properly. Groups of four compare and discuss differences in their answers. Then a whole-class discussion on the hard ones, assertive questioning style (see Chapter 5). Hard points are explored by some students doing some on the board for the class, thinking aloud. Class discussion. Students now punctuate a text using apostrophes where necessary. This reuses previous learning on other punctuation marks.

Reuse: Students are asked to write the rules for apostrophes in their own words, giving their own examples using a topic of personal interest. Groups of three check each other's work. The teacher gives a model note and students check that they have all the key points in their own notes. There are examples for homework for the next two weeks. A poster of the rules designed by a student is displayed in class, and every now and again the teacher asks pairs to explain a rule, each to the other.

Subsequent written work often requires the correct use of apostrophes.

Students prepare for and take a formative quiz at the end of that half term that includes some questions on the apostrophe. Students who do badly on apostrophe questions in this test do remedial work assisted by another student and then retake a similar test.

Notice that the above plan includes many of the Quality Learning boosters considered in Chapter 1, including: pair check, self-assessment, assertive questioning, teacher check, formative quiz, and models. These help check and correct the learning of each individual student, giving each individual the precise help they may need. This is unusual: in many lessons continual checks with corrections are absent, which allows misconceptions and weak learning to grow uncontrolled.

Designing a resource using RAR

 **Case study**

A new ICT teacher is writing assignments for her students to do in a resource centre. One assignment she inherited on 'Health and Safety for Computer Workers' has not worked well in the past. It has involved giving students links to websites on health and safety and requiring them to fill in a worksheet. She has decided to redesign the assignment using the RAR structure. Students log onto the assignment on the institution's virtual learning environment (VLE) or intranet, where students can save their work and upload some work for peer assessment.

This work is done in dedicated periods and as homework over about two weeks.

Receive phase: Orientation.

Advanced organiser: Students are given a mind map that consists of the main headings or subtopics for 'Health and Safety for Computer Workers' but with none of the detail.

Relevance: Some stories of computer workers getting repetitive strain injuries, which meant they could no longer work on computers all day, as well as suffering pain and other problems.

Goal: Students are told they are to create a summarising website on the topic; the best work will be used by a local business. Work will be uploaded for presentation to parents and other interested parties. (Students learned how to make a simple website last year.)

Prior learning: Quiz on any vital prior learning, which students mark and then correct themselves, informing the teacher of their mark so those who need help can get it.

Receive new material – first subtopic: Students are given websites, links to pdfs, and videos, etc. that provide the information they need at about the right level of detail. The teacher has checked that the reading age of the material is suitable. Students can search for other material if they want to. To learn each subtopic, students are required to print off some pdfs from the Internet, underline key points, and summarise. Then they meet in teams to discuss and improve their summaries.

Students grade some student-produced websites created for another assignment in a previous year. They compare their grading and discuss online. The teacher then provides her grades for the same work, with justifications. This reuses and checks previous learning on website design.

Apply: Students create their own webpage to explain the first subtopic. This is uploaded for peer assessment and improvement, followed by teacher feedback. Students then improve their websites.

The above process is repeated for the second and subsequent subtopics. That is, students study new material, summarise it, have it peer checked, improve it, design a webpage on the topic, upload this for peer assessment, improvement, and then teacher feedback and final improvement.

There is a diagnostic quiz on the main points, results go to the teacher.

Reuse: Students have six or seven questions and tasks on the health and safety aspects of computer use while studying other topics studied on their course. These are spread out over two terms.

It is useful to compare the above RAR process with the assignment that just involved students working alone to fill in a worksheet using websites on health and safety. That didn't work for a multitude of reasons: students had no support if they got stuck, their prior learning was not checked, neither was their progress, and the task was not broken down into bite-sized pieces. Also, entirely absent was the continual check-and-correct processes built into the RAR design.

With the RAR design, misconceptions were continually discovered and corrected. It is rare for blended learning, e-learning, independent learning or flipped learning assignments to be designed with sufficient checking and correcting, or with sufficient thought to the design and sequence of activities. The RAR structure helped all students to get the support and instruction they required.

Note that, as well as the RAR structure, there are a number of boosters in this assignment: pair check, self-assessment, peer assessment, teacher check, a formative quiz, and the use of models. These ensure that each student has the individualised help they need without unusual demands on the teacher.

I have been shocked to find that even commercial companies designing online courses simply present information to students and then skip directly to a formal assessment of this learning, with no student activity to process the learning and no check and correct as concepts are created.

How can we choose suitable teaching methods for each of the RAR phases? There are many methods that have been rigorously tested and found to greatly improve students' performance even without a RAR structure. They are likely to be even more powerful within a RAR structure. We look at these high-powered methods in the next few chapters.

Why is the RAR structure important?

RAR considers the whole topic, not just a lesson

Many teachers think in terms of lessons, but learning a topic requires a structure that moves from surface learning to deep learning and then to transfer, and requires students to reuse learning so it passes into long-term memory. We need to plan topics, not just lessons. See Hattie and Donoghue (2016), Bransford (2000).

Research shows that structuring learning works very well

RAR is a form of explicit instruction that updates well-researched methods such as direct instruction, and whole-class interactive teaching, among the most successful teaching strategies found (see Chapter 3). Despite their names, these methods involve a great deal of student activity, albeit closely monitored by the teacher. Their power comes from structuring the teaching of a topic very carefully, so students get everything that they need in order to learn effectively in a logical sequence. The RAR structure adapts and combines the most effective features of direct instruction and whole-class interactive teaching, and updates these methods by adding strategies, such as setting goals in advance, which are known to be highly effective (Petty, 2009).

Because the RAR structure is based on human cognition, it applies to almost any deliberate teaching situation, including students learning alone from digital resources – often called e-learning – or blended learning, although there are many other terms for this.

If teaching and learning are well designed and structured, every learner gets what they need to learn well, and attainment is very high. That's the aim of the RAR structure.

The RAR structure for teaching a topic. (This takes more than one lesson to complete)

Receive for surface learning · 35% of teaching time?

Orientation: Students are prepared for learning.
• Students recall relevant prior learning.
• There is a persuasive account of the relevance, importance and value of the learning.
• An advance organiser structures the new content.
• Challenging goals are set in advance or negotiated.
• Success criteria for the task are explained.

New material is presented: Knowledge, reasoning, theories, etc. are explained to students or learned in some other way. Abstract ideas are illustrated with concrete examples.
Modelling: Skills and methods are demonstrated, e.g. how to use a tool or formula, or how to punctuate a sentence. You show how on the board.
Students study 'exemplars' of good work. This stresses both process and product. Key points are emphasised.

Typical learning strategies:
• Listen to teacher talk or watch a video.
• Watch a demonstration.
• Study exemplars, e.g. spoof assessment.
• 'Teaching by asking' (rather than by telling).
• 'Teaching without talking' strategies, such as learning from ILT and other resources.

Check and correct for student and teacher:
Learning in progress is checked and corrected, e.g:
• interactive question and answer
• peer explaining and other 'presenting activities'
• students demonstrating on the board, followed by class discussion, etc.

Apply for deeper learning · 60% of teaching time?

Students work towards their challenging goal. The ladder of tasks from reproduction tasks, to **reasoning** tasks, to transfer, requires them to apply the knowledge, theories, skills, etc. that have just been presented. This involves them in reasoning, not just reproduction, e.g. problem-solving, making decisions, and creating things such as mind maps, etc.

Typical learning strategies:
When learning a practical skill...
• Practical task to carry out the skill.

When learning cognitive skills and knowledge...
• Answering questions on a case study in groups.
• Exercises, questions, worksheet, essay, etc.
• Class discussion to develop an argument or answer a question, etc.
• 'Decisions-decisions' game.
• Student presentations.
• Critical evaluation of exemplars, e.g. are these sentences correctly punctuated?

Check and correct for student and teacher:
This may not be a separate activity and may involve the students more than the teacher. The aim is to:
• inform students of what is good, and what is not ('medals and missions')
• provide support for those who need it
• check attention to task, quality of work, behaviour, etc.
Common strategies include: self-assessment; peer assessment; peer assessment; class discussion; teacher comments, etc.

Reuse · 5% of time?

Repeated reuse and reviews of learning to ensure the topic is well understood by all students: 'spaced learning'.
Summaries of what was learned, emphasising **key points** and the **structure** of the knowledge.

Typical learning strategies:
• Summary note-making.
• Creating a mind map to summarise key points.
• Create a same-and-different diagram to transfer learning.
• Class discussion.
• Advance organisers revisited and more detail added.
• Reviews at the beginning of a lesson with a short task.
• Peer explaining of key objectives followed by check by the teacher.
• Quizzes, tests, etc.
• Students setting themselves new goals for improvement.

Check and correct for student and teacher:
Learning is checked and corrected, e.g:
• question and answer in an interactive dialogue to discover and correct weak learning
• peer and self-assessment
• mastery learning to correct weaknesses in learning.

Figure 4.2: The RAR structure

Evidence for Chapter 4 on the RAR model: structuring your teaching of a topic

Chapter 14 establishes that the most reliable sources of evidence are summary evidence, and we should triangulate three sources.

Evidence from summaries of qualitative research: RAR is in effect an updated version of 'whole–class interactive teaching' (WCIT) and 'explicit teaching'; both are widely regarded as effective. RAR makes use of social constructivism and Vygotsky's zone of proximal development, both highly regarded in cognitive psychology.

The idea that learning should be built on previous learning, goals should be set, teaching should be well structured, students should actively use, and then repeatedly reuse new learning, and that learners and teachers need feedback to correct misconceptions and to confirm effective learning is hardly contested. Countries that do well in international comparisons of education systems have found that teaching there is structured in a RAR-like manner (WCIT).

Evidence from summaries of quantitative research: RAR is modelled on direct instruction and rigorous trials of this method have shown it to be highly effective, see page 262. The elements within RAR have all been found to be highly effective, for example relevant recall questions, advance organisers, challenging tasks and check and correct.

Evidence from research on the most effective teachers: Both Ayers and Lemov show that teachers use a similar highly structured approach to RAR. Hattie finds direct instruction that is very similar to RAR is highly effective.

Three independent sources of evidence suggest RAR is a structure worth trying.

Further reading

See also the principal references in Chapter 15 Further reading and references.

Free online resources

Search for 'direct instruction' or 'whole-class interactive teaching'.

Visit the National Institute for Direct Instruction at: https://www.nifdi.org/.

J.A.C. Hattie and G.M. Donoghue, 'Learning strategies: a synthesis and conceptual model' (*NPJ Science of Learning:* London, Vol. 1, August 2016).

Books and papers

S. Allison and A. Tharby, *Making Every Lesson Count* (Carmarthen: Crown House Publishing, 2015). Brilliant and highly readable book with lots of detail on strategy.

D. Mujis and D. Reynolds, *Effective Teaching: Evidence and Practice* (London: Paul Chapman Publishing, 2017). Great book with another slant on evidence-based teaching, good on direct instruction.

G. Petty, *Teaching Today: A Practical Guide* (5th Edition) (Oxford: Open University Press, 2014). See also www.geoffpetty.com.

Chapter 5

Classroom questioning and discussion: the self-correcting classroom

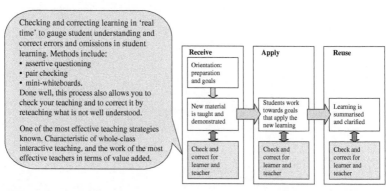

Figure 5.1: Prior learning and new learning work together in the Receive, Apply, Reuse (RAR) model

The diagram above shows where we are in the RAR process and gives an 'advance organiser' for this chapter. I start describing the RAR process here because good dialogue is central to each part of RAR, including orientation.

Improving this aspect of your teaching can create huge gains, but does take time and trouble. Questioning and discussion need to be used throughout the teaching of a topic to:

- require students to form a construct and to explore it in detail

- link students' constructs to prior learning and so generate real understanding

- inform the teacher of the extent and depth of students' learning, enabling the teacher to fill gaps in learning and to tackle misconceptions head on. Without this information you are teaching blind and likely to be too optimistic about the extent of learning. This last point is often missed or underestimated.

For the above reasons it is hardly surprising that the very best teachers make a great deal of use of questioning and class discussion. See Lemov (2010), Ayres

(2004). If used effectively, class discussion can be one of the most powerful teaching methods we know (see Hattie's review of research in Chapter 4).

Most questioning in most classrooms is far from optimal. Let's compare common practice with some best practice to see why. We will use our model of high-quality teaching to evaluate both approaches. I will assume in both cases that the teacher asks a substantial question, not one just requiring students to recall a fact.

Common practice: question and answer with volunteers answering

Students volunteer to answer questions posed verbally by the teacher. This is usually done with 'hands up', but sometimes students call out their answer. If more than one student puts their hand up, the teacher chooses who will answer.

You can usefully evaluate any teaching method with four questions: *Is there a high participation rate? Is there time for each student to work/think? Does each student get a check and correct? Do you get a check and correct on the level of student understanding so you can adjust your teaching?* Let's evaluate 'Q&A with volunteers answering' in this way.

Is there a high mental participation rate? No! Typically, only a few students put their hands up, usually the most confident. Often some students decide there is no need to listen to the questions, let alone answer them, as others will do this work for them. So they just keep their hands down and daydream.

Is there time for students to work/think? The thinking time between asking a question and the answer being delivered is usually less than a second here. If some students call out the answer, this reduces the thinking time of others. This discourages participation of the weakest students, the very ones who need help.

If students call out answers rather than put their hands up, then weak students are still thinking what to answer when the correct answer is called out. They may not understand why that answer is correct of course, as the teacher often just evaluates the answer as correct.

Do the teacher and students check and correct? Not much! The teacher gets to know what the best students in the class can do, the very ones they don't need to be worrying about. Students are not involved at all in check and correct here.

Some teachers try to improve this method by having a 'no hands up' policy, instead choosing a student to answer a question. This is an improvement, but there is a tendency for reluctant learners to think: *'I've just answered a question, so I won't be asked again for a bit – I can have a little sleep.'* Students are still not involved in the check and correct, and the teacher only learns what one or two students can do so they don't get a representative view of the learning of the class.

Let's look at a better method: 'assertive questioning', which has a near-identical variant suitable for mathematics and other teachers called 'student demonstration'.

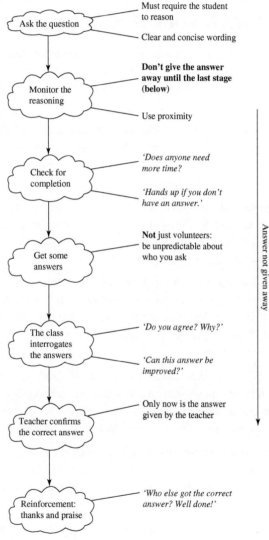

Figure 5.2: Assertive questioning

Assertive questioning

1 You ask a thought-provoking question and ask students to work on it in small groups. You warn them that **you** will be choosing who will answer for their group.

2 You ask:

'Does every group have an answer? Ask me for a hint if not.'

'Does anyone need more time?'

If a group does not respond to this offer of help, they are fair game for the next stages, and they know it. Don't give the answer away when you help a group.

3 **You choose** a student to give their group's answer and another in that group to justify it: *'What did your group think?'* ... *'Why did you think that?'* Then you say *'Thank you'* for the answer, **but crucially, you do not evaluate it**.

You could get answers from all or most of the groups one by one in the same way, but the following is often better with a larger class. After the first group gives their answer, ask *'Do any other groups agree with that answer?'* and if so, **choose** a member of that group to say why. Then you choose a group that did **not** agree with the first group's answer and again **you** choose a student to answer: *'I notice you disagree – what does your group think?'* and ask another student in the same group, *'Why?'* You ask if any other group agrees. In this or a similar way, all differences between groups are highlighted, ready for inspection. You have not yet given the answer away.

4 You summarise the various positions of the different groups, and point out inconsistencies. If all groups agree, perhaps the question could have been more challenging, though in early practice easy questions are helpful.

5 The aim now is to get the whole class to agree their 'class answer(s)'. You encourage the class to discuss and evaluate each other's answers, and to agree, and to justify their class answer. Minority views are allowed, but consensus is preferred.

6 Only when the class has agreed its answer do you 'give away' the right answer, and evaluate and comment on the answers given by the groups.

This method works whether there are right answers or whether different interpretations and answers are likely, for example in a critical appraisal of a painting or a poem. This method is excellent preparation for writing, though students will need time to make notes on the ideas suggested.

(See Figure 5.2 above and 'Whole-class interactive teaching' Chapter 24, Petty, 2014.)

Evaluating assertive questioning

Evaluate this method yourself before reading on, as it will be useful practice at evaluating other teaching methods, a vital and very difficult skill.

Is there a high mental participation rate? Every group must prepare an answer and its justification. Every student must prepare to explain and justify this answer, because *'she might choose me'*. This creates a very high participation rate, and there's a good chance you will know if a student is not participating: they will not take part in discussion and will answer badly.

Is there time for each student to think/work? There is usually plenty of opportunity for most students to think and discuss.

Do the teacher and students get a check and correct? When students discuss, they will check and correct each other's thinking and answers. For example during a card sort (as in Chapter 3):

Jerry: A whale is cold-blooded.

Alicia: No. A whale must be warm-blooded. It's a mammal...

Iqbal: ... Yeah that's why it has blubber, to keep it warm.

Jerry: Oh... Yeah.

As students might be asked to justify their group's answer they will want to understand it, and so will ask questions of their peers to clarify their understanding: *'What do you mean about blubber?'* Also, students will not want their group to do badly, so stronger students will tutor weaker ones until they can give a good answer.

There is strong accountability in this questioning method – usually students will want to understand and to help those who don't.

The teacher gets a good representative view of what students know and understand. What's more, the teacher knows which groups misunderstand.

Assertive questioning is not an easy method to use. If you have been teaching for some time using hands-up or a distributed questioning style, it will take quite a bit of practice to get used to this method. It took me a term. However, it absolutely revolutionised my classroom. As with most really effective teaching methods, students really enjoy the class discussion, and the cut and thrust of argument that this method produces.

Assertive questioning models how to think in your subject. It models how to question ideas, how to test them, and how to falsify and how to verify them. This is called the epistemology of your subject. It's the subject-specific knowledge of how to discover what's true and how we know what isn't true in your subject. This is a vital and precious legacy to pass onto your students. It models the process of creating and testing understanding in your subject. In other words, it models the thinking you want your students to go through as they create and improve their constructs.

No surprise, then, that classroom discussion has been found to have a very high effectiveness indeed, as we find in Chapter 15.

 Reflection

The criteria used to evaluate assertive questioning can be used to evaluate almost any teaching strategy from the co-constructivist point of view:

Is there a high mental participation rate?

Is there time for each student to think/work?

Do students get a check and correct?

Does the teacher get a check and correct?

The blame-free classroom

It's important to create a blame-free climate, especially when you are using questioning or class discussion. Here is an example of some ground rules you might like to establish with your students.

- *We will learn best if we all work towards a 'blame-free' classroom.*

- *It's okay if you don't fully understand a concept first time; learning takes time.*

- *What counts is whether you understand the question or task, and its answer eventually, not whether you get it right first time.*

- *I ask challenging questions, so it is not humiliating to make a mistake. We all make mistakes when we learn. Indeed, that is part of how we learn. If we don't make mistakes, the work is too easy for us to learn at our maximum rate.*

- *Mistakes are useful because they tell us where we can improve.*

- *If you make a mistake, you can bet your life that others in the class have made it too.*

- *It's good for learning (yours and other people's) to say 'I don't understand' and to ask for clarification.*

- *You should never ridicule another student for their mistakes, even in a joking way, because you wouldn't like it if you were ridiculed, and because it stops us learning.*

- *Peers should give 'medal and mission' feedback* (see Chapter 11), *which is forward looking and positive.*

- *You will only learn from mistakes if you find out how to do it without mistakes next time, and really understand this.*

- *Let's help each other! The helper learns at least as much as the helped.*

Ground rules and understandings like these are best established very early on, and are best developed Socratically by asking students for their ideas for class ground rules. *'We all want to enjoy ourselves and we all want to learn well, so what should be your ground rules?'* Note it is *your* not *my* ground rules! You will need to keep to these ground rules rigorously, so no laughing at silly answers!

The ground rules need to be vigorously enforced for the first few lessons; do this by pointing out to offenders that *'you have broken one of your/our ground rules'*. The blame-free culture can often establish itself quite quickly, especially if you stress why it helps – students are usually very grateful for it. Ground rules on bringing pens to class and turning up on time will also be suggested, and these can be enforced in the same way.

You need to adopt ground rules too. Never ridicule answers. Show appreciation of good answers: *'That's an interesting point'*, *'Good thinking'*, *'Thanks Anthony'*, and so on; try not to use the same appreciative phrase too often as it devalues it.

Here are some other questioning methods that also develop classroom discussion. If used well, most of these methods have a high participation rate and involve teachers and students in check and correct. Mark the ones you would like to try! Remember, however, it will take quite a bit of practice with a method before you are confident with it and use it well.

Ladders of questions

In Chapter 1 we saw that students need to climb a ladder of tasks or questions, from questions requiring the reproduction of basic key facts (surface learning) to more challenging questions, for example 'why', 'how' and 'which' questions, which require students to reason. There is more on this in Chapter 9. Assertive questioning is arguably most appropriate higher up the ladder with reasoning questions. Reasoning tasks are vital, as Chapter 1, and Marzano and Simms (2014) show.

Student demonstration

This is an excellent method to test and develop students' understanding of a simple skill such as mathematics problem-solving, punctuation, scientific reasoning or detection of imagery in a poem, to name a few. It is very similar to assertive questioning and is used in Eastern European countries and in Pacific Rim countries such as Taiwan and Singapore, which routinely achieve top ranking in international comparisons.

The method is used after a teacher demonstration of a practical or intellectual skill. The aim is to check and correct understanding of a skill before all students practise it. It is initially a bit daunting for students, but they will greatly enjoy the method when they are used to it. Use peer explaining first (see page 119): this prepares them for student demonstration very well. After they have learned to use peer explaining well, set them tasks to do in pairs followed by a student demonstration, perhaps asking for volunteers. Then move onto pair work followed by you nominating a student to demonstrate. Give them fair warning of any changes.

The basic procedure for student demonstration is found in the following stages.

1 **You set a task.** For example:

- *'Working in pairs, factorise $6x^2 - 6x - 8$'*

- *'In pairs, punctuate this paragraph.'*

- *'Working by yourself this time, can you see any personification or metaphors in the third or fourth verse of the poem?'*

2 **Students work on the task.** This can be done in pairs initially, but after a bit of practice students do tasks individually, perhaps checking each other's completed answers in pairs.

They strive to get the answer, with any justification, such as necessary reasoning or working. If students are in pairs, they make sure that either of them can provide this justification.

3 **You monitor the work.** You check attention to task and occasionally ask:

- *'Can everyone do this one?'*

- *'Can you all explain your answer?'*

Students who can't answer the question are required to own up and get help at this stage, otherwise they are fair game for the next stage.

4 **You choose a student to demonstrate their answer to the rest of the class.** If students are in pairs, you choose one student at random to give the pair's answer. The student gives their answer on the board, explaining each step and its justification to the class. You ask questions to clarify, but do not evaluate the answer yet.

- *'Why didn't you use 6 and 1 as the factors of 6?'*

- *'Why did you choose a full stop and not a comma?'*

- *'So how did you choose between personification and metaphor?'*

5 **You ask for a 'class answer'.** You ask the class if they agree with the student's answer and its justification, or whether either could be improved. The aim is not to criticise the student's answer, but for the class to agree a class answer. The student who did the demonstration becomes the class scribe, writing up any changes the class agrees to. You again facilitate without evaluating the answers or the arguments.

- *'Why do you think it should be plus four and not minus?'*

- *'How many think it should be a comma? Why?'*

- *'So why exactly is it not a metaphor?'*

6 **You comment on the class answer.** Praise any useful contributions, confirm any correct reasoning, and correct any weak reasoning.

7 **The process is repeated** with another task; after sufficient practice the students can do stage 2 as individuals rather than in pairs.

Students are often initially resistant to doing a demonstration if they are not used to it. So you could make use of volunteers to begin with, but try to move onto students nominated by you as soon as you can. They will be more confident of answers that they have produced in pairs than answers produced in isolation, so when you first start nominating students do it after pair work.

All the arguments in favour of assertive questioning apply also to this method. You might like to compare student demonstrations with other methods you use in similar situations, using the criteria in the Reflection box on page 83.

Suppose a student, Svetlana, lacks the confidence required to write her solutions on the board. You can first ask the class to tell Svetlana what to write down, line by line. Get class agreement for each line before she writes it. Then the class is responsible for what is written, rather than Svetlana

After doing this a few times, Svetlana may have the confidence to display one of her own solutions to a problem on the board and have it subjected to class scrutiny.

Using mini-whiteboards

This is another brilliant way to get answers, and so check and correct both learning and your teaching. It is possible to buy a class set of A3, A4, or A5 whiteboards very cheaply, each complete with a dry-wipe pen and eraser in a sealable plastic wallet. Or you can make your own sets by laminating card.

The idea was first invented in primary schools but they are used everywhere now, including university, where a hi-tech version is used, called clickers.

To use the mini-whiteboards

It starts off like a student demonstration:

1 **You set a task.** It works well to start with students working in pairs, and then later working individually. Tell them if you are going to do this, so they work towards their own independence.

- *'Working in pairs to begin with, factorise $6x^2 - 6x - 8$'*

- *'By yourself this time, punctuate this sentence: "Some people such as farmers work outside."'*

- *'Working by yourself this time, write down any phrase from verses three or four that involves personification.'*

2 **Students work on the task and write their answer on their board.** Students all write an answer.

3 **You check what is on the boards.** You ask students to hold up their boards all at the same time so that you can see their answers. They will crane their necks to see everyone else's answers!

4 **You ask students about their answers.** Students need to know not just whether they have the right answer, but whether they arrived at the answer using the correct reasoning. So you can ask students 'why' they have the answer they have, for example *'Phil, why did you decide to put the comma where you did?'* If you can, withhold your evaluation of the answers you can spark a class discussion: *'Well, some of you have a comma after "people" and others haven't. What do we think?'*

Also see

Training materials on questioning can be found at: http://geoffpetty.com/training-materials/questioning/.

'Champion teacher' strategies

Let's look at two strategies used by most of about 100 very exceptional teachers studied by Doug Lemov (2015). See Chapter 15 for the background on his study.

Right is Right

This technique can be used in conjunction with the No Opt Out technique (see below) or on its own.

The idea is that the teacher questions the class until they come up with a near perfect answer given in scholarly language. Earlier answers are used as stepping stones and are gradually improved to arrive at the near-perfect answer. Below is some text from Lemov's book (which he also provides in video form), showing the technique in action in a mathematics class.

> **Armstrong:** We're going to do a couple of things with volume today. Then we're going to practise volume and then surface area. Can someone give me a definition for volume to get us started? Mark?
>
> **Mark:** Volume is length times width times height.
>
> **Armstrong:** You're telling me how we're going to solve for volume. If you say 'length times width times height', you're giving me a calculation. What I want to know – and you probably know this too, Mark – is what volume is. What is that amount? Yeritza?
>
> **Yeritza:** Volume is the amount of square cubes that takes up something.
>
> **Armstrong:** Okay, but I want to refine what you said – 'the amount of cubes'. What should we say? What's the technical definition instead of just cubes? What were you going to say, Wes?
>
> **Wes:** The amount of cubic inches that a rectangle or prism or a three-dimensional figure takes up.
>
> *(Many teachers would have accepted this answer, or a previous one.)*

> **Armstrong:** Right, any three-dimensional figure. But I don't want to just say cubic inches because it's not necessarily inches. It could be feet; it could be centimetres; it could be yards...
>
> **Wes:** Cubic units.
>
> **Armstrong:** *(writing on the overhead)* So the amount of cubic units that an object takes up... and Donte, I know you know the other word. What's the other word for 'takes up'?
>
> **Donte:** Occupies.
>
> **Armstrong:** Yes. *Occupies*. Volume is the amount of cubic units that an object occupies.
>
> *From Doug Lemov,* Teach Like a Champion 2.0 *(Jossey-Bass, 2010)*

In that example of 'Right is Right' the teacher kept checking and correcting students' answers until a complete and correct answer had been produced. Many teachers are delighted by a nearly complete or nearly right answer and stop gratefully at this. But this prevents the improvement of the most-able students.

It's as though the class are being required to climb a ladder of inadequate answers, until they reach at the top an entirely adequate one. During the above interchange, weak students may only climb up one or two extra rungs before they lose comprehension. But if, in a later class, the same question and discussion takes place, the weak students will be able to climb another rung or two. If this discussion takes place often enough, most students will be able to 'climb' up to a very good answer.

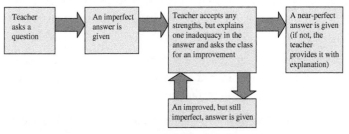

Figure 5.3: Right is Right technique in diagrammatic form

No Opt Out

Another strategy Lemov found to be common among his star teachers was in their response to a student who does not give an answer to a verbal question from the teacher, or who gives the wrong answer. Lemov's teachers asked other students the same question until a very good answer was given. Then they went back to the student who had 'opted out' or got the answer wrong and asked that student the same question again. Students who 'opt out' or get it wrong anticipate this, so they listen carefully to this class discussion. They nearly always get the answer right the second time. The main reason Lemov's teachers did this was to ensure that students eventually got it right and remain self-believing. *'Learning is about getting it wrong, then getting it right'* is the important message behind the strategy.

Note how both 'Right is Right' and 'No Opt Out' require students to form a construct, and then check and correct this construct. There are very high mental participation rates if you nominate students to answer rather than allow hands up.

Dialogue in the mathematics (and other) classrooms where answers are right or wrong

Here are some similar methods for mathematics teachers that can be adapted to many other subjects where students must problem-solve in some way on tasks with right and wrong answers.

Snowballing solutions to a challenging mathematics problem

Snowballing creates real dialogue, participation, and understanding. It needs to be done with supportive ground rules, where errors are accepted without blame and are seen as an opportunity to learn. In studies with underachieving youngsters in low-performing schools, this method greatly increased students' interest and enjoyment of mathematics, and improved their average standardised test results from 45% to 79%! However, this degree of improvement took time, about six years, but expect improvement of a sort quite quickly.

Explain your no-blame ground rules, as mentioned above. Then give students a challenging question, one they can attempt or get started on but which they often won't be able to finish by themselves.

1. Individuals write down their own answer, or their attempt, working alone.

2. Students then share what they have written in groups of three or four. Each student presents their attempt, justifying it to the others. The others give constructive criticism about the pros and cons of each approach after it has been presented.

3 Each group now decides which method is best and why, and presents it to the whole class.

4 There is class discussion on which methods are best and why; this can be done using the assertive questioning style, or student demonstration style as described above.

An alternative is to use conventional 'snowballing'

1 Individuals write down their own answer, or their attempt, working alone.

2 Students pair up and show each other their work. They give constructive criticism to each other, and decide on their best method.

3 Pairs form fours, which look at each pair's method and again give pros and cons and decide on the best method. Leave time for this dialogue.

4 The teacher chooses individuals by name from each group of four to present their solution/work to the class, and to justify it to the class.

5 The class as a whole now scrutinises each group's work, and decides which method(s) are best and why. You could now use assertive questioning, or student demonstration, to interrogate these answers further.

Ideas from
other groups

Figure 5.4: Snowballing

Evidence for Chapter 5 on classroom questioning and discussion

Chapter 14 establishes that the most reliable sources of evidence are summary evidence, and we should triangulate three sources.

Evidence from summaries of qualitative research: Look at the Quality Learning Cycle, which summarises some important aspects of the cognitive psychology of teaching (see page 14). Clearly, questioning, and especially discussion, provides the opportunity for the learner to improve their construct and the teacher to improve their understanding of any limitations in the learner's construct. What is more, this is done in real time, allowing the teacher to correct misconceptions and other weaknesses as they occur and before they become habitual.

Evidence from summaries of quantitative research: John Hattie's synthesis of research finds that classroom questioning has moderate to large effectiveness in improving attainment, but if the questioning leads to classroom discussion, it becomes almost twice as effective, and among the most powerful teaching strategies we know. The Education Endowment Foundation rates feedback as having the biggest impact on student progress, and both classroom questioning and discussion can give students and teachers feedback on present understanding in real time.

Evidence from research on the most effective teachers: Both Doug Lemov's and Paul Ayre's research on exceptionally effective teachers shows that these teachers make extensive use of questioning and discussion to probe and improve student understanding. See Lemov's 'Right is Right' on pages 88–89, for example. Ayre's research shows such teachers withhold evaluation of student answers in order to stimulate discussion.

Three independent sources of evidence suggest that questioning and especially discussion are exceptionally powerful tools, so some of the methods above might be worth trying.

Further reading

See also the principal references in Chapter 15 Further reading and references.

Free online resources

Search for 'questioning', 'class discussion', 'dialogic teaching'.

B. Yeung, 'Kids Master Mathematics When They're Challenged But Supported' (Edutopia, 2009).

Search for 'Geoff Petty training materials on questioning' to run a training session on this topic.

Books and papers

R.J. Alexander, *Towards Dialogic Teaching: Rethinking Classroom Talk* (4th Edition) (York: Dialogos, 2008).

P. Ayres et al., 'Effective teaching in the context of a Grade 12 high-stakes external examination in New South Wales, Australia' (*British Educational Research Journal*, Vol. 30, No. 1 February 2004). Shows that exceptionally good teachers use class discussion and withhold answers.

B.M. Gayle et al., 'How effective are teacher-initiated classroom questions in enhancing student learning?' from B.M. Gayle et al. (Eds) *Classroom Communication and Instructional Processes: Advances Through Meta-analysis* (Mahwah NJ: Erlbaum, 2006, pages 279–293). Shows that high-order questions are best for student achievement, suggesting a ladder of questions is necessary, as described in Chapter 9 of this book

D. Lemov, *Teach Like a Champion 2.0* (San Francisco: Jossey-Bass, 2015). This is an important book as it gives detail about strategies used by excellent teachers.

R.J. Marzano and J.A. Simms, *Questioning Sequences in the Classroom* (Bloomington: Marzano Research, 2014). Excellent resource that includes quantitative analysis.

G. Petty, *Teaching Today* (5th Edition) (Oxford: Oxford University Press, 2014). See Chapter 24 on whole-class interactive teaching.

Chapter 6

Teaching methods for the 'orientation' phase: setting the scene

The teaching methods in this book are arranged around the three phases in the RAR model shown in the diagram below and explained in Chapter 4. The RAR model explains how to teach a topic rather than a lesson. I will look now at methods suitable for the 'Receive' phase, which has two main parts: 'Orientation' and 'New material is taught'. This starts the new topic off. You need not cut your teaching up into the RAR phases; some activities combine its parts.

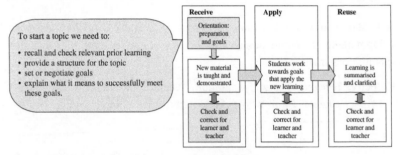

Figure 6.1: Orientation prepares students to learn

Orientation: the learners are prepared for learning

The purpose of orientation is multi-layered.

- It is to get students to recall relevant prior learning, including any relevant everyday experience that can help them understand the new material. This puts it in students' short-term memories, ready for use. It also enables you to check and correct this relevant prior learning. This checking and correcting of prior learning and the spaced practice of it is useful in its own right.

- It provides a structure for the new learning, built on what is already known. This involves prioritising the important aspects of the content, stressing the vital principles, concepts, and key points, but also showing how these are related, for example what causes what.

- In it you set or negotiate goals. To explain the challenging goal, usually in the form of a task that you will set the learners.

- It allows explanation of success criteria for the completion of this task or goals, and for the learning of this topic more generally.

- It motivates the learner, for example by persuading students of the purpose and value of the learning and the goals, and giving them a sense of belief that they can tackle the goal.

- You could also state objectives for the topic; this isn't particularly effective, but it takes little time.

Faced with a new topic, most teachers just state some behavioural objectives, such as telling students *'At the end of this lesson you will be able to multiply fractions'* and then get on with teaching it. But this is a huge missed opportunity.

Imagine a weak student in your class, one who might latch onto relatively irrelevant points and miss the key issues and principles. This learner experiences difficulty in structuring or organising this new learning, and building it onto what he already knows. This structuring is important: it creates meaning and understanding, helps distinguish the important from the noticeable, and gives a holistic overview of the meaning and purpose of the topic.

Methods for the orientation phase

Here are some methods to experiment with; hopefully, you will ring the changes rather than get into a rut with just one method. Consider using the most powerful methods for the hardest topics, though.

Methods that recall and check prior learning

Ask questions that recall and check relevant prior learning

This simple but remarkably effective strategy puts the foundations in place before you build on them. You ask students questions requiring them to recall the prior learning necessary to understand the new material before you teach it. Most teachers check recall of the previous lesson, but this goes further, to include any prerequisite or helpful prior learning or experience.

'We are about to look at a conflict between Henry VIII and the Church. Now, we have already seen conflicts between king and Church – can you give me some examples? ... Can you see any common factors in those conflicts?'

Or:

'We are about to use ratios to solve triangles. Where else have we met ratios?'

As well as preparing the learner, such introductions help your students see your subject as a coherent whole rather than a string of disconnected details.

If they have very little experience or prior learning that might help them, then try analogies. For example, a teacher trying to teach students about power relations might ask them: *'What would you think if a neighbour came into your house and started telling you how to run your home?'* Use assertive questioning for best effect (see Chapter 5).

Write down everything you know

Students are asked to write down everything they already know about a topic you are about to teach more about. Their prior knowledge could be presented in a non-linguistic form; for example, they could devise a flip-chart poster or mind map to summarise the key points. They could present these to the class.

Black et al. (2003) describe this method being used by teachers who were surprised to find that their students often knew far more than they expected. So the method saved much more time than it took! It would help to do this at the end of the previous lesson, to give you time to digest the findings before you teach the topic. (RAR shows the structure for teaching a topic, which is not necessarily all in one lesson.)

Check and correct methods for the orientation phase

Check and correct methods are teaching methods that enable either you or your students, and preferably both, to get feedback on the quality of students' understanding, in other words the quality of their constructs, as described in Chapter 1. When checking students' relevant prior learning you could use *assertive questioning,* or one of the other methods described in Chapter 5. You could also use *diagnostic questions* or many of the other methods described in Chapter 11 on checking and correcting.

We have prepared our students, they know what they are studying and why, they have been persuaded the topic is important, and they know they have some challenging goals to meet, and that their learning will be checked. They have the relevant prior learning checked and ready for us to build upon. In terms of the RAR structure, students are now ready to receive the new content, either by teacher explanation, by reading, or by online or other digital methods.

Methods that show the structure of what will be learned: the advance organiser

Having recalled relevant prior learning, you can now explain something of the structure of what students are about to learn. This is called an advance organiser because it shows the organisation of the content in advance. I have produced an advance organiser for this chapter, see the bottom part of Figure 6.2. It is in graphical form, which is often the most effective, but advance organisers can also be entirely verbal. There are many formats for graphic organisers in Chapter 5, so at least one of these should have the right structure for your advance organiser.

The advance organiser, whether graphical or verbal:

1 gives an overview of the topic, a short summary of the main sections, or subheadings in the content, stating how they are related

2 might also stress any general principles that will apply, for example *'Sines and cosines are ratios'*

3 can state any links with any related topics and show how it is related to the whole, for example *'Sines, cosines and tangents are the main trigonometrical functions we study in this unit on how to find unknown lengths and angles'*

4 can stress the importance, relevance, purpose, and value of what is about to be learned. This is linked with motivation, for example *'Sines help us find unknown angles and sides in trigonometrical problems.'*

You could just give a summary in advance, and this works well. But you can also do steps 2, 3 and 4 above. For example, if I were teaching the present topic, I would show the advance organiser for this chapter and talk about it for about a minute, summarising the key points I was about to cover. But after leaving the organiser to teach a subtopic, I would return to the diagram to introduce the next subtopic, and so on. I could use my advance organiser again to summarise at the end of the topic, and indeed to review it at the beginning of the next lesson.

Don't confuse an advance organiser with giving behavioural objectives. Advance organisers provide much more information. Let's look at some ways to provide an advance organiser.

The parable approach

This involves telling students a story that helps students make personal, real-world connections to what they are about to learn. The great books of all religions contain parables, as do many sermons. The speaker tells a story and then extracts a principle from it, or perhaps leaves the listener to do so. When a social studies teacher is about to introduce the idea of bias, for example, she might tell a personal story that showed bias from her family life, and then ask her students for other similar anecdotes.

The purpose of this technique in co-constructivist terms is, of course, to require the learners to recall relevant experiences on which to build the ideas in the lesson. It is sometimes called a narrative advance organiser.

Skim reading

When students are learning from text then you can ask them to skim it as the first task; this only goes some way to providing an advance organiser. The idea is to skim a few pages, paying attention to headings and first and last paragraphs to get the gist about what the text is going to say, and then go back and read it in detail.

Students add to an outline graphic organiser

The graphic organiser is an advance organiser in visual form, as described above. If students make extended use of these themselves, for example by adding to them extensively, they are exceptionally effective, as explained in the previous chapter.

Below are two graphic organisers for a lesson on Impressionist painters. One is at a higher level of abstraction than the content of the lesson, the other just summarises the content. It is not entirely clear from experiments which creates the highest achievement, but they both work well.

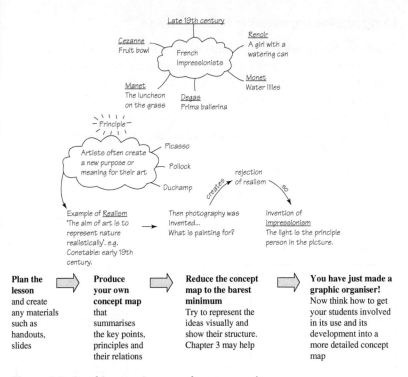

Figure 6.2: Graphic organisers as advance organisers

Using organisers in practice

The Marzano references at the end of this chapter find that organisers seem to have more effect for difficult learning. They are also thought to be particularly useful when the learning experience is not well structured, for example when students are searching the Internet, on a field trip, or visiting an exhibition.

You can refer to the organiser throughout the lesson, as this helps learners to see where they are in the structure of the topic at any given time.

Consider using organisers on:

- handouts and workbooks

- a board or smartboard

- a board or flip-chart, left up for the whole lesson and at the beginning of the next

- on an introductory screen for a new topic on a computer-based e-learning module.

Using graphic organisers in the next lesson

Recalling the last lesson will be covered in more detail later, but if the organiser is first presented in electronic form, on a smartboard say, or in a slideshow presentation, the detail added in the class can be covered up with sticky-note style text boxes, and the students asked to recall what is beneath. The sticky notes could have clues on them if that helps. Similar follow-up activities could be used with other orientating methods described in this chapter.

Curriculum maps and unit organisers

Another way of showing students where they are in their learning is a curriculum map or unit organiser. These are advance organisers for larger chunks of learning and can be used in the same way. Use them as well as, not instead of, advance organisers.

Unit organiser: The Industrial Revolution		
Key concepts		
Natural resources	Technology	Economic system
Waterways	Steam engine	Mass production
	Textile machines	Fair wage
Key questions		
• What caused the Industrial Revolution and why did it begin in England? • What impact did the Revolution have on the culture and society of England? • How did the technology of the Industrial Revolution lead to a new Age of Imperialism?		
Resources		
Sadler Commission: *Report on Child Labour* Engels: *The Condition of the Working Class* Marx: *The Communist Manifesto* Smith: *The Wealth of Nations* Primary source photos (Internet) Thompson: *The Making of the English Working Class*		
Assessment		

Setting goals

Setting goals in advance has much more effect on achievement than the more common behavioural objectives.

Behavioural objective: Students will be able to describe the main symptoms and complications for childhood measles.

Goal in advance: *'You will create a mind map for the main symptoms and complications of childhood measles, check it with peers, and then self-assess it against a list of key points that I will provide. Aim to get all my ten key points on your diagram – we did 'ten key points' when we studied the heart. How did you do? Can you do better this time? Remember we want reasons, not just facts. This is the success criteria for the task.'*

Goal setting takes very little time, less than a minute or two in many cases, and yet it has a more marked effect on achievement than the more commonly used learning objectives. We shouldn't be surprised that what they *will* do has more impact on students than what they *should* be able to do.

Goals show your high expectations and they give students a reason to listen to your teacher-talk. Ideally, a task is set along with success criteria, as in the example above where students are challenged to get all ten key points.

Most teachers don't set goals until they set the students an activity, which can be quite late into a topic. Even then the goal is only implied by the activity and may not have success criteria. Also, it does not usually involve the student setting themselves goals, the setting of which is highly effective.

In all cases below, remind students of their goals from time to time in the lesson, and revisit the goals at the end of the lesson to see if they have been met. Here are a few ways to set goals at the beginning of a new topic.

Setting goals at the start of the topic

We should set students goals before they receive new information. If the goal is challenging and requires reasoning, this will ensure that students attend.

You could set the goals very informally, for example by asking a rhetorical question:

'What was the effect on the people who used to weave these garments by hand, now that they could be made so quickly by machine?'

'How could we measure this atmospheric pressure? Let's find out.'

Rhetorical questions like these, if there is enough emphasis on them, can effectively set a goal and can create curiosity and interest in your subject, as it begins to be seen not as an interminable list of important facts to memorise, but as a subject that asks interesting questions and answers them.

Keep reminding students of these rhetorical questions during the lesson. Consider displaying them on the board, or in running headers on presentations and on handouts.

Question Exploration Routine

 **Case study**

Lenz et al. (1994) devised a method of questioning called the Question Exploration Routine:

The teacher poses a guiding or 'critical' question to students that is central to the topic. The students, with teacher help, then:

- Identify what information is needed to answer this guiding question, and so generate the sub-questions that can lead to its answer.

- Answer the sub-questions and then the guiding question.

- Transfer the learning, by seeing how it relates to earlier learning or other experience.

This works well for students of any ability: Lenz et al. found that the achievement of students with learning difficulties doubled. Search for 'Lenz et al. 1994 question exploration routine' on the Internet, for more information.

Setting goals for teacher-talk or other explanatory input: peer explaining

Suppose, for example, a teacher is about to teach students about the role of the district nurse. She could give the students specific goals for the receive phase and for the main activity phase of the lesson.

'When I have told you a bit about district nurses, and we have seen the video, I will ask you in pairs to work out answers to the two questions here on the flip-chart:

- *What are the main roles of the district nurse?*

- *How does her role fit in with those of other health professionals?*

So, during the first part of the lesson listen carefully and begin to think through your answers to these questions.

Your other task today will be to work out what a district nurse would do in a few specific cases. The case studies are there in front of you. You will have to present your ideas to another group, so be really clear about how her role works in practice, not just in theory. Do we all understand these two goals?'

Goals by exemplar

This involves showing students what they will be able to do at the end of the lesson. A computing teacher might show students a good example of a desktop-published document and say, or write in the workbook, *'At the end of this module you will be able to create documents like this.'* Trainee chefs could be shown photos of the dishes they are about to create.

Teachers of any subject, including practical or academic skills, can use good-quality work in this way and it can be very inspiring for students, as long as they believe they can do it! Chapter 7 goes into the detail.

Goals by setting problems

'Here is a geometrical problem that we can't solve using any of the methods we have seen so far. But it is possible to solve! Let's see how we could do it.'

'Delegating to your staff empowers them, but as their manager you remain responsible for what they do. What if they begin to make a mess of it? Let's see how we can have it both ways: delegation and control.'

Goals by cognitive dissonance

A cognitive dissonance is provided when students' expectations are up-ended. This helps 'unteach' a misconception while teaching something new. It can also create curiosity.

'The mass of the glycerine has increased overnight. Yet nobody has added anything to it! How can that be? It's your job today to find out!'

'Yesterday most of you thought that if you tossed a coin and got a head, then tossing a tail next was the most likely. But look at the figures from your experiment. It just isn't the case. You found the chance of tossing a head was always fifty-fifty. What is going on?'

'Shakespeare wants to show that Romeo is really in love with Juliet. You might expect him to do this by describing his previous relationships as failures. In fact, he does the exact opposite. Let's see.'

Goals by challenge

Challenges are much more motivating than competitions as, in principle, everyone in the class can meet a challenge, but only one can win a competition.

'Can you make a really persuasive case for this business plan? At the end of the lesson I am going to play the role of a speculative investor, like in the TV programme Dragons' Den, *and you will be the entrepreneurs with this plan. Will you be able to persuade me to invest?'*

'I am going to explain a commonly used method of budgetary control that some managers are very critical of. I will explain it very positively, but I want you to think of its weaknesses. See if you can get all four of its main weaknesses!'

'Have a look at the marks you have had for exercises like this in the last month. What is your personal best mark? Well, your challenge today is to beat that!'

Students can also set themselves personal goals

The Marzano references for this chapter show that goals were most effective if students set them for themselves, as well as getting goals set by the teacher.

Personal goals can be:

- **very informal:** Students can be asked at the end of a lesson to set themselves goals for the next lesson. Or at the beginning of the lesson you can say:

  'Look at our ground rules for being a good student. Set yourself a goal now; write it on the top of your sheet. Think of something you want to improve about your work...'

- **set by the teacher as well as, or instead of, the student:**

  'Think back to the personal goal I set you at your last one-to-one tutorial. Find it in your file if you can't remember it. This can be your personal goal for this lesson.'

Negotiated goals

You can negotiate a goal with a group, trying to find a goal that meets their needs. One way of doing this is to get the class to pose questions after the advance organiser; this works particularly well with adult or more-able groups. For example a business studies lecturer could give an advance organiser on decision-making and then ask the class for some goals/questions on this topic. Those with some experience of decision-making might have questions that can be shared and then answered by the class or the teacher during the topic.

Learning-loop goals

Goals can be diagnosed from a self-assessment. For example, after assignment 1, one of your students can self-assess on a competency questionnaire consisting of a set of 'learning to learn' competencies like the example below. She might decide that her main weakness is that she doesn't ask for help when she needs to, and so set this as her goal for assignment 2. You remind the class of this self-assessment at the start of assignment 2 and ask students to set themselves a target. Your student could then self-assess again on the same competency sheet after assignment 2 to see if there was any improvement and to set a goal for assignment 3, and so on. (The 1 and 2 in the competency form below refer to the two assignments.) Learning loops are explained more fully in Chapter 11.

Learning to learn	Study skills		
	Never	Sometimes	Usually
Ask others for help	1	2	
Underline key points		1, 2	

Figure 6.3: Using competencies to set goals

Clearly, learning-loop goals can also be based on teacher assessment rather than a student self-assessment, but involving students in self-improvement is usually worthwhile.

Competency questionnaires can be devised for almost anything, student behaviour for example. In which case, base the questionnaire on your class ground rules (search online for 'classroom management Geoff Petty' to download a document that gives the detail). This provides personally set and personally diagnosed goals such as *'I'm not going to talk when Mr Petty is talking.'*

However you set goals, it is worth returning to them at the end of the lesson to decide whether or not they have been met.

Are your goals challenging enough?

Students learn best if goals are challenging. The main goals for a topic should involve reasoning, and ideally they should be open rather than closed so that every student is stretched but every student can respond (see Chapter 9 on ladders of tasks).

Once we have orientated our students we are ready for the 'New material is taught' phase in the RAR model, which is greatly assisted by modelling, the subject of the next chapter.

The vital first five minutes

The research on the methods suggested above show they are unusually effective, and you have hardly started teaching the topic! The first five minutes teaching a topic are important, and conventional practice is weak

---

Evidence for Chapter 6 on teaching methods for the 'orientation' phase

Chapter 14 establishes that the most reliable sources of evidence are summary evidence, and we should triangulate three sources.

Evidence from summaries of qualitative research: All of the principle references on page 284 et seq. stress that new learning needs to be built on relevant prior learning and experience, and that learning needs to be checked and corrected (feedback). This is summarised in the Quality Learning Cycle on page 14. Most sources stress that challenging goals help students learn; Bransford (2000) is very explicit on this. The idea that new learning is more easily understood and remembered when it is structured is widespread, but is not mentioned in the shorter references on page 284 et seq.

Evidence from summaries of quantitative research: Marzano states that the following are highly effective: checking and correcting relevant prior learning; giving students an advance organiser; and setting goals in advance. See Marzano (2001). Hattie (2009) stresses that challenging tasks should be set with clear success criteria, and finds advance organisers to be moderately effective. He finds direct instruction to be highly effective, and this method includes at least the checking of prior learning and an advance organiser.

Evidence from research on the most effective teachers: Ayres (2004) found that exceptionally effective teachers established and corrected prerequisite prior learning before setting more challenging tasks.

At least two sources of evidence suggest orientation methods might be worth trying in your classroom.

Further reading

See also the principal references in Chapter 15 Further reading and references.

Free online resources

Search for 'advance organiser' and 'setting goals in the classroom'; note though that goals do not need to be 'SMART'.

R. Marzano *The Art and Science of Teaching: A Comprehensive Framework for Effective Instruction* (Alexandria, Virginia: ASCD, 2007). See also the 'Learning Map' of the Teacher Evaluation Model based on this book

R. Marzano et al., 'Nine Essential Instructional Strategies' (Adapted from *Classroom Instruction that Works*, Alexandria, Virginia: ASCD, 2001).

Books and papers

D.P. Ausubel, *Education Psychology: A Cognitive View* (New York: Holt, Rinehart and Winston, 1968).

P. Black et al., *Assessment for Learning: Putting it into Practice* (Buckingham: Open University Press, 2003).

R. Marzano, D. Pickering and J. Pollock, *Classroom Instruction that Works* (Alexandria, Virginia: ASCD, 2001).

Chapter 7

Modelling: demonstrating physical and intellectual skills

Teachers need to show how, in other words to model or demonstrate, intellectual skills such as how to solve a mathematical problem or how to write a critical appreciation of a poem. They also need to model good work by showing students exemplars or worked examples. The importance of modelling has always been appreciated by the best teachers, but thanks to research on working memory it has rocketed up the priority list.

Our small working memory means modelling is vital

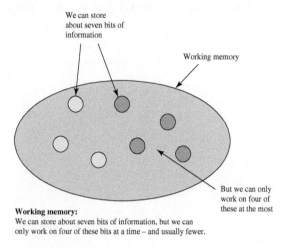

We can store
about seven bits of
information

Working memory

But we can only
work on four of
these at the most

Working memory:
We can store about seven bits of information, but we can
only work on four of these bits at a time – and usually fewer.

Figure 7.1: Working memory

Did you ever experience the following when learning mathematics at school? The teacher showed you how to do something on the board, and you thought you understood it. Then the teacher said, *'Now you do some similar questions by yourself'*… and you got stuck. What had seemed simple when the teacher was doing it was hard when you were working alone.

We've all had this experience, which occurs in all subjects and at all academic levels. I will look at other subjects later, but let's stick with mathematics to explain the problem, and its fix.

When you are learning something very new, you tussle with different aspects of the topic in your 'working memory'. But your working memory is small. It can only store about seven bits of information at a time, and can only *work* on four of these, usually fewer. So it is easy for a teacher to overload working memories while students are trying to conceptualise something for the first time.

Mathematics teachers usually use a two-step approach to teach how to solve a particular type of mathematics problem. They first do a few examples on the board, explaining the process, and then ask students to do similar problems by themselves. This is shown on the left in Figure 7.2.

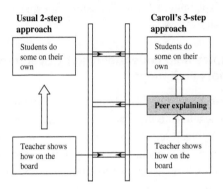

Figure 7.2: Two-step and three-step approaches compared

Figure 7.3: Peer explaining

William Carroll saw a weakness in this two-step approach. When students are working on the mathematics problems alone they are trying to do two things at once: *understand* the mathematical process, and *apply* this process.

For many students this double task swamps the working memory, and there is 'cognitive overload'.

So Carroll developed a three-step approach. After the teacher has explained how to do the problems on the board, the students are given worked examples very similar to those just explained by the teacher. These are problems with the solutions fully and correctly worked out for the students to study. A useful activity here is to get students in pairs to study a couple of different worked examples each, and then to explain their different examples to each other. (They have to *explain* them, not just read the solutions out.)

It's best to show students varied worked examples of the skill you are teaching. The more varied the examples, the easier it will be for students to adapt what they learn to different contexts – that is, transfer the learning.

After using peer explaining, tell your students that explaining to themselves is a great way to study.

Worked examples help understanding by overcoming working-memory limitations

In Carroll's three-step approach, students first hear the teacher explain the mathematical process to gain the basic *knowledge* of the approach. Then the peer explaining requires that each student *understands* this process. Only then do students have to *apply* the process by doing problems on their own. The working memory is not swamped by students trying to understand and apply at the same time.

Carroll found that students learned well in less time with the three-step approach, even though there was an extra step. Also, they made hardly any errors in the 'apply' phase, and they found the learning easier than with the two-step approach.

It's not surprising that the study of worked examples works well. As we saw in Chapter 2, we learn very naturally from 'concrete examples' to 'abstract generalities', and we also learn very naturally by imitation. Peer explaining is only one thing you can do with models of good practice. I suggest many other activities to try below, but it is often best to use peer explaining before these other activities.

Using verbal and visual modes of representation

The multiple modes of representation we saw in Chapters 2 and 3 put less strain on the working memory. See the first reference in the evidence box on page 125 for more detail.

Reflection

Terminology

Terminology overlaps greatly in this chapter, and indeed the first three concepts below are often interchangeable. Only the first two concepts necessarily include the *process* students should go through to create good work. Models and exemplars may just show the nature of the product the teacher wants students to create, not the process they must go through to create it.

Worked example: This phrase comes from mathematics and science, where it is used to describe a problem solved correctly with all the working shown.

Demonstration: A performance showing how to do something properly. As well as explaining what they are doing, teachers often 'think aloud' while giving demonstrations to model the thinking processes they want students to use.

Model: A product produced by the teacher or a student with at least some positive characteristics. This may not show the process used to arrive at the model.

Exemplar: An example of a piece of work done very well.

Assessment criteria: General statements that describe the characteristics and qualities of students' work that the teacher wants to see.

When and how can you use modelling?

If you don't teach mathematics, you will still have problems with cognitive overload and can still teach with models of good practice or worked examples. You can also explain how on the board like mathematics teachers, thinking aloud to 'model' (show and explain how to do) any intellectual skill, such as looking for metaphors in a poem.

Suppose your students aren't very good at:

- critically analysing a poem
- evaluating a marketing plan
- punctuating a sentence

- writing an 'if-then' loop in a computer program

- justifying an historical argument

- analysing a design

- reflecting on a lesson the student teacher has just taught

- solving trigonometrical problems of a certain type

- writing paragraphs in essays that are well structured to maximise marks, using for example the 'PEE' (Point, example, explanation) structure.

In all these cases, and many more, you can find a worked example, model of good practice, or exemplar to help your students understand 'how to do it'. You could also 'do one on the board' for students while thinking aloud.

Let's now look more generally at how you can show your students how to do something in a clear and vivid way, which also conveys all your hopes and expectations for the way you want your students to work and the quality of work you want from them. This is called 'success criteria'.

The main approaches, which can be used in combination, and can overlap to some extent, are:

- **demonstrating or modelling:** for example, showing how on the board – a concrete example of how to do it

- **exemplars and models:** for example, showing good pieces of work – a concrete example of what to aim for

- **assessment criteria:** a generalised description of good work or expectations.

I will now look at these three approaches in detail.

Demonstrating or modelling to the class while you think aloud

Widely used by mathematics teachers, this approach can be used by a teacher of any subject.

If you wanted to teach how to do a certain type of mathematics problem, or how to punctuate a sentence, you might show how on the board, or perhaps in a video presentation. You break the task down into a sequence, and explain why each step is necessary.

While you show how on the board, you think aloud to show the thought processes you want your students to go through. Having done this successfully, you can demonstrate again with a different task, but this time it helps to ask students or the class as a whole what to do next, and why. This both involves the students and informs you whether the students are ready to try the skill or procedure on their own. Here are some case study examples.

Study 1: Modelling while thinking aloud

 **Case study**

If you are not a mathematics teacher, you can still learn a lot from how mathematics teachers model. Below, a teacher is demonstrating how to solve a type of trigonometrical question on the board; they give a running commentary on their thought processes.

*'So far we've solved questions like this using right-angled triangles, sines, cosines, Pythagoras and so on. But we're stumped here! There **is** no right-angled triangle! What am I to do? Any ideas?'*

*The teacher waits, but gets no offers. 'Well, how about if I make my **own** right-angled triangle? Is there a line I could add to the diagram that...'*

A hand shoots up. 'Yes, Muhammad?'

Muhammad: *'If you join D and E, I think you get a right-angled triangle.'*

'Do I? Let's see.' (She joins D with E, then turns to the class).

'Is Muhammad right? Where is the right angle?' Almost the whole class puts their hand up or calls out the answer, and the teacher continues. 'Yes, okay, so what's next?' (Lots of hands go up). 'Tracey?'

Tracey: *'The question's changed. Now it's just the same as the ones last week.'*

Teacher: *'It is! And how did we solve those, Mabel?'*

Mabel: *'Just, sine, cosine, tangent, Pythagoras, inside the right-angle triangle.'*

Teacher: *'Exactly! So, any ideas for my next step?...'*

When the teacher has finished she summarises the problem and its solution, or gets the class to do so.

'There were no right-angled triangles so what did I do? I looked for somewhere to add a line so that I made a right-angled triangle. Then I solved the problem in the usual way, with sine, cosine, tangents, and Pythagoras. Okay, time for you to do some!'

Notice that the teacher explains the thinking required, especially at the beginning, and she showed what to do if she were a student stuck with such a question. She would not have needed such thought processes herself: she was modelling what she hoped a weak student would think.

However, she only explained what to do until students in the class could take over and explain for themselves. This engages the students more and develops a sense of 'we can do this' among the class (self-efficacy). But it also provided the teacher with an insight into what at least some of her students might be able to do alone. This helped her to make the judgement about when to stop modelling and when to get her students working on such problems independently.

You might need to model once or twice, with different but related tasks, before students can begin to tell you what to do next. The best check on student readiness is to model another example, but this time 'leading from behind'. That is, you ask the class as whole or individuals in it for each step in solving a similar problem. After each step is explained by a student you ask: *'Why should I do that?'* and other questions to clarify the process and its justification. If the class can talk you through an example, it gives you confidence that they might be ready to work independently. In the end it is this independent work, preferably on a 'ladder of tasks' of increasing difficulty, that will ensure students learn, so this needs more time than the modelling.

Study 2: Modelling while thinking aloud

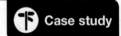 Case study

A teacher has taken some time to explain the concept of power to her science class and now intends to summarise the concept in a note. Some teachers would write a note for the class. However, this teacher knows that students need to improve their explanations of concepts, partly because exams often require this, and partly because if the students struggle to explain a concept well, this will help to improve their understanding. She will also use this class note-making activity to get an insight into the class's level of understanding of what she has just taught.

'Right, let's do a note on power now. Where should I start? First sentence anyone?' (Some hands go up.) 'Henry?'

Henry: *'Power equals the energy you've used, divided by the time it took to use it.'*

'Well, that's a useful explanation, but we'll use it later I think. You have

*explained how we **calculate** power, but before that we need to say what power **is**. So, what is power?'*

Mia: *'It's the energy you've used in a second.'*

'It is. And what's the scientific way of saying that?'

(It takes a few stabs from various students to arrive at: 'Power is the rate of doing work'.)

'Very good, but there's just one thing missing.'

(The students are stumped so the teacher explains that the unit used to measure power must be given.)

'So what have we got now?'

Andrew: *'Power is the rate of doing work in joules per second.'*

'Spot on! Why is that a good first sentence, Amy?'

Amy: *'Well, it's like, a definition.'*

'A definition, exactly. A short, precise description, and in what sort of language?'

Elsie: *'Science language.'*

'That's it. Okay, I liked Henry's sentence explaining how we calculate power, so Henry could you give it to us again now?'

Henry: *'Power is the energy you use, divided by the time you've taken to use it.'*

'Can you get rid of the 'you' for me, please? We write science in the passive, without using 'I' or 'you' or 'they' and so on.'

(There are a variety of suggestions adapting this sentence before the teacher is finally happy with it.)

'Okay, now let's write that down: 'Power is the energy used, divided by the time taken. Right! Now what?'

(The students decide that the note should now state the equation for power, which most students can recall.)

Notice that the teacher leads the students towards defining 'power' first of all, and also models the use of scientific language showing how to change student speak to science speak. But she does also give an ordinary language explanation (see Chapter 2).

Notice also that the teacher asked *'Why is that a good first sentence?'*, in order to stress the sort of writing she wanted from her students when describing a scientific concept.

At the end of the note the teacher summarises power, but she also summarises the note-making process.

*'We wanted to explain a scientific concept. We started with a **definition** in scientific language. We then explained it in everyday language. Then we put down the equation. If you are asked in an exam what does something mean, that's a really good way to answer. The definition in scientific language, an explanation in everyday language, and then the equation. If you're short of time, you can omit the explanation in everyday language. But never miss out the scientific definition and the equation.'*

This teacher was modelling how to write in the scientific context. We all need to develop writing skills appropriate to our subject, and note-making with the class is an excellent opportunity to model this process, while clarifying what you have taught.

Modelling the process of planning writing

Allison and Tharby (2015) make a persuasive case for modelling the process of planning writing on the board while thinking aloud. They say that this should include all your dithering and uncertainty. For example:

'Okay, so I want to mention photosynthesis in the leaves, and transpiration, and the idea that roots provide water. But which should I mention first? Well, if I go back to the question it says... So it would make sense to start with the transpiration.'

Assessment criteria to describe the product

Assessment criteria are usually very general descriptions of the characteristics of the work you want your students to produce. For example, assessment criteria for an essay may include:

'There is evidence that an imaginative range of appropriate resources have been consulted.'

'The material is organised into a coherent structure with an introduction, argument with evidence, and conclusion.'

'A high level of critical analysis and independent judgement is evident.'

Criteria like this are very vague, however carefully they are written. They have to be general in order to apply to a wide range of essays. But what is an 'imaginative range of appropriate resources'? What is a 'coherent structure'? Is having an introduction, argument and conclusion enough, or does it mean more than that?

When shown such criteria students often ask point-blank, *'What do you mean?'* Some will request examples. Research shows that they are right, and this is the focus for this chapter.

The best way to make use of assessment criteria is to explain them first in student language and show exemplars that demonstrate a number of different ways of meeting the criteria in practice. When this has been done ask students to comment on work that is weak, moderate and good in terms of the assessment criteria. Spoof assessment (see below) is an excellent way to do this. Then use 'learning loops' that require students to identify their weaknesses and work on them during their next piece of work.

Even if the assessment criteria could explain what you want with clarity – a well-organised essay, for example – they do not explain to students *how* to organise an essay. Models, however, can show what you expect and hope for in a finished *product* – that is, what an organised essay looks like. But if you explain or annotate a model, you can often also show a *process* that will best achieve this organisation, for example how to organise an essay: *'Notice that this model keeps going back to the essay title to maintain focus.'*

So, with care models and exemplars can be used to demonstrate both *product* and *processes*, and for difficult skills we need to show both.

In general, students benefit if more than one model is shown, exemplifying different ways to achieve the same high standard. You can of course use demonstration, modelling, *and* assessment criteria – indeed that would be advisable for skills that students find hard.

See Christodoulou (2016) for the detail on the weaknesses of assessment criteria or 'descriptor-based assessment'.

Making use of models and exemplars

Examples of good pieces of work show students what you want them to be able to do. These can be analysed and annotated so that students notice key features of the good work, for example *'Notice how the student uses quotes from the text to illustrate her arguments.'*

You can of course make up exemplars yourself, which is often the best way. You might start by showing perfect or near-perfect exemplars. Later you could give students work with deliberate mistakes in, to create weak, moderate and good work on the same task. Then you can ask students to rank or mark these three pieces of imperfect work, giving their reasoning: *'She should have given an example to illustrate her point.'*

Your own students' work can provide useful models, as they can inspire other students – because *'If a classmate can do it, so can I.'* By contrast, a model you produce is not inspiring – they know *you* can do it.

You can copy students' practical work by using a tablet or smartphone to photograph or video a performance. Why not create a library of the good work and make it available on the Internet to share with your students and perhaps with other teachers who could be encouraged to contribute to the resource?

More simply, you can read out students' work or ask students to write up a calculation or a sentence or two on the board (see student demonstration in Chapter 5). Alternatively, you can ask students to get out of their seats and look at each other's work

Reading from students' work as they write can be useful too:

'Clive has written: "We took corresponding readings of time and temperature as it cooled." That's neatly put: "corresponding" is a useful word there.'

'Lucy has written: "Consequently, Martin Luther felt betrayed." "Betrayed" is a great word – who knows what it means?'

Exemplars will not always make clear every aspect of *how* to produce such work; thinking aloud or peer explaining is usually necessary to explain the *process* of creating a good product. *'Okay, I've put all the full stops in, so now I'm going to look at the sentences I've created and decide what commas and other punctuation are needed within these sentences.'*

Some uses of models or exemplars

Models or exemplars can require students to apply their learning while clarifying success criteria – that is, what is expected of students and how to create it.

Completing a model of good practice

'I've put the full stops in this paragraph for you, but I want you to put the commas in.' (The next model for completion has all the commas and students must provide the full stops.)

'This computer program has the last few lines missing. Study the program, then complete it to make it work.'

'This analysis of our poem needs a section on the poet's intentions. Read the analysis then add the missing section.'

Improving an imperfect model

'Here is an evaluation done by a student last year. She got a merit. Improve it to distinction standard.'

'Here is a paragraph punctuated by a student last year. Explain what's wrong with the punctuation and then improve it.'

'Here are some algebraic rearrangements, but they contain some deliberate mistakes. Find the mistakes, explain why they are mistakes, and then do the rearrangements properly.'

Annotating a model

'Have a look at this assignment. Please point to sentences or paragraphs with numbered arrows to show where assessment criteria 1 to 4 are met.'

'At the end of each line of this computer program, write an explanation in ordinary English describing what the line does.'

Assessing an imperfect model

'Here are three justifications for the same historical argument done by students last year. Please mark these using the mark scheme provided.'

'Here are three marketing plans for our Red Lion Inn. Working in groups, put them in order of effectiveness, and explain your ranking.'

Peer explaining

'Here are two correctly punctuated paragraphs. In pairs, study one each, then explain and justify each punctuation mark in your paragraph to your partner.'

'Have a look at this well-justified historical argument. How does the writer justify her views? What use does she make of primary and secondary historical sources?'

Some teachers mistakenly argue that students should not be shown imperfect work as this will confuse them. The trouble is that students see imperfect work all the time – their own. They don't need protection, they need to develop the skill of recognising errors and omissions and then correcting them. Careful use of imperfect models can 'inoculate' students against common misconceptions and common errors.

It is very important to recognise that working-memory overload occurs most often when students are *first* learning a new concept or process. Once they have an initial understanding of this concept or process, you can stretch them with more challenging tasks. Indeed, you *must* finish a topic with challenging tasks to get high-quality learning (see Chapters 1 and 9).

Marking against models or exemplars

Rather than marking students' work yourself, you can provide model answers or worked examples for the work they have just completed, and then ask students to mark their own or each other's work against this. This enables students to compare their performance against an excellent performance, which often makes clear how to improve. By contrast, your marking may not show so clearly what needs to be done to improve. Marking against models works especially well with past paper questions. It will save you some work too, though you will usually still need to mark some of their work

Anonymous or spoof assessment (in groups, pairs or individually)

A 'spoof' piece of work is one created by the teacher to give students practice at assessing work It could be a piece of work done by a student in a previous year, with their name removed, though the student's permission is still required to meet copyright law. If students present work electronically, it is not difficult to save work for this purpose. Alternatively, you can create work with deliberate errors yourself for students to assess.

An advantage of spoof assessment is that all students are marking exactly the same piece of work, which makes class discussion easier than with self- or peer assessment. Also, you can have control over the deliberate errors to make the teaching points you think most important.

Spoof assessment is best done in small groups first so that students can provide each other with support. As ever, snowballing is useful to develop independence, while still providing support. Then students should be able to spoof assess alone, checking their judgements during class discussion The sequence just described is excellent preparation for self- and peer assessment.

Assessment criteria may or may not be given If they are not given, students can be asked to come up with their own criteria before using these to assess the work

A useful strategy is to give students two pieces of work: one is good and looks bad, and one is bad but looks good (Gibbs, 1981). Below are some examples.

The first time you use spoof assessment it is fun to tell students that one piece of work is an A grade and one is a D grade and ask them which is which When they get them the wrong way round, as they usually do, ask them as homework to go away and work out why.

Example 1

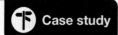 **Case study**

A mathematics teacher gives his students two pieces of work on trigonometrical calculations, along with the worked solutions, including answers to these questions. Students are asked to mark two pieces of work using their own criteria.

- One piece of work has all the right answers, but the methods are not explained or justified, some are overlong, and any working or reasoning is not clear.

- The other piece of work has some wrong answers, but the methods are good, fully explained and justified, and the working is well laid out and easy to follow.

If they are not given criteria, most students will give the worst work the best mark, because they believe the goal is to get the right answer, while methods and working are of little importance. Students can experience useful 'cognitive dissonance' when they learn that the work they thought worst gets the best marks! Class discussion can then be very productive: *'Why do you think this work got such low marks despite getting the answers right?'*

Example 2

Students of economics are given two essays. One is well presented, long, has many technical terms and impressive diagrams and is written in long sentences with quite complex grammar. But this student does not answer the question. The other spoof piece of work is short, only uses technical terms where necessary, but answers the question very well and very concisely. Again, without criteria students usually give the worst work the best grade. Some will do this even with criteria, especially if they do not understand them well enough.

In both cases there is class discussion after students have given their judgements. *'Look at work X – did they justify their answer as question 3 required? What does it mean to justify an answer? Let's look at how Y did this…'*

If no assessment criteria are given to students, it helps to conclude discussions on spoof work by stressing what the criteria are. However, students will benefit greatly from being given criteria for later attempts so that they can practise interpreting criteria and so learn what they mean.

Reflection

Many students believe that 'describe', 'explain', 'analyse' and 'evaluate' all mean pretty much the same thing: 'write about'. Spoof assessment can really help them to understand assessment language and assessment criteria – and importantly *how* to meet these criteria. Another useful method is to use 'decisions-decisions'. Students are given phrases or short paragraphs of text to classify as descriptions, explanations, analyses and evaluations.

Alternative approaches to spoof assessment are explained in Chapter 11, along with self- and peer assessment, all of which help students to determine what they are aiming for.

How to ensure students learn from (rather than just copy) exemplars

Sometimes students copy models slavishly, even irrelevant characteristics of them, showing that they haven't really understood. Rather than simply copy, we want them to learn from the models. How can we ensure this?

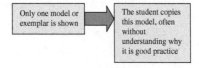

Figure 7.4: Copying

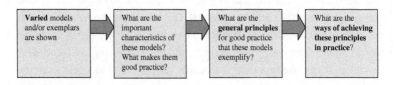

Figure 7.5: Learning

As Figures 7.4 and 7.5 show, we must give students a *variety* of models of good practice. Then we can establish what these models have in common. This should lead to some general principles of good work, and the models should provide alternative ways of achieving this. (If indeed there are any alternatives.)

Once students have gone through the learning process outlined in Figure 7.5, students should now understand what they are trying to achieve and have a 'repertoire of moves' in order to get there. For example, they now know that they must justify their arguments and that one way to do this is to bullet-point relevant evidence.

Another way to discourage copying and encourage learning instead is to give examples or models that are slightly distant from the work students will soon attempt by themselves. For example, if students are about to write a critical appreciation of the use of metaphor in a soliloquy by Hamlet, the model could be an appreciation of a soliloquy by Romeo.

If students are about to write a note on power, they could examine a note on energy.

After examining a model, some good questions to ask are:

'What can we learn from these?'

'What do the models have in common?' This can lead to conclusions such as *'All the definitions are in scientific language, give a unit, and are short.'*

'How do each of these models achieve X...?' e.g. How do these essays justify their arguments?

Developing independence

It is common to find that your students are successful with a skill immediately after examining a model, but unsuccessful at a later date without it. As with all learning, your students may need to re-examine models a number of times on different occasions: see spaced practice in Chapter 12 on reusing learning. It may make sense to make models available to students online in a library of good practice so they can see them when they need them.

Modelling is a form of scaffolding (Bruner, 1966) and like all help it needs to be removed at an appropriate time to encourage students to develop their abilities to work independently. Don't worry if the quality of your students' work dips a little without the models. All teachers experience this. Only sufficient independent practice will develop the skill, and this practice will be much more time-consuming than the modelling. You need to fade out your use of models and follow up with unaided problem-solving so that the learning is transferred as much as possible. Ayers (2013) gives a summary of research on worked examples in this respect.

Demonstrating physical skills

It helps you to demonstrate an intellectual skill if you study how physical skills are commonly demonstrated. All the following strategies can be used to demonstrate either physical or intellectual skills.

Conventional teacher demonstrations

In a conventional teacher demonstration the teacher carries out a task and explains what they are doing and why at the same time. But in this approach students are not required to listen or to create their own understanding. How would we do a demonstration using a co-constructivist approach? Let's look at a few approaches.

Teacher demonstration co-constructivist-style

Demonstrating using a 'receiving task'

You could of course demonstrate while using a 'receiving task' such as peer explaining (which I will explain in full in Chapter 8). You tell students in advance that they will be explaining in pairs either what you did in order, or why you did it that way. You don't tell students which. Then you do your demonstration explaining what you're doing and why. Then you split students into pairs, giving one of the pair the task to explain what you did in order, and the other in the pair the task to explain why you did it that way. When students have completed their peer explanations, you could repeat your demonstration quickly, giving your explanation and then ask students to self-assess: were their explanations accurate and complete?

Here are some other approaches:

The silent demonstration

You tell students you are about to demonstrate how to do something without an explanation and that when you have finished you will ask students *what you did (in order)* and *why you did it that way*. This works best if the technique is a bit puzzling. This method could be used with a video demonstration of a skill.

When you finish the demonstration, use assertive questioning (see Chapter 5) to get students to explain what you did, why you did it that way, and so on.

Teacher: What did I do first? Iqbal?

Iqbal: You heated up the frying pan.

Teacher: Yes: why did I do that first? Philip?

Philip: If the oil had been cold, the batter might stick to the pan.

Teacher: Good. Then what did I do?

To get the full advantage of this approach, you need to warn students in advance that you will use assertive questioning after your silent demonstration. Then students will realise that they might be called upon to explain.

You can of course use this assertive questioning approach after doing a conventional demonstration that includes teacher-talk. Indeed, this will prepare students for later silent demonstrations. Again, a warning that you will use assertive questioning will encourage them to pay attention.

Demonstrating by asking

You tell students that you are about to, for example, prune a plant, or load up a trailer and secure the load. But you play dumb (yes, I know you will find this very difficult). You ask the class to tell you how to accomplish the task step-by-step. *'What should I do first?'* When a student makes a suggestion, you say *'Why do you want me to do that?'* If the suggestion and reason is sound, you do this, and then ask for the next stage: *'What should I do now?'* and so on.

'Isn't there something else I should do first?' is a useful question.

You can also ask 'dumb' questions:

'Why do I need pruners? Can't I just take a chainsaw to it?'

'Can't I just drive away now? I don't need the lock for a short journey, do I?'

Evidence for Chapter 7 on modelling: demonstrating physical and intellectual skills

 **Evidence**

Chapter 14 establishes that the most reliable sources of evidence are summary evidence, and we should triangulate three sources.

Evidence from summaries of qualitative research: The limitations of the working memory or short-term memory are almost universally accepted by cognitive scientists and are stressed in most of the summary references on page 284. The use of worked examples, models, and exemplars are often suggested by cognitive scientists to overcome these limitations. A recent summary of research is free to download: search for the title: *'Cognitive load theory: Research that teachers really need to understand'* (2017).

Evidence from summaries of quantitative research: Modelling is part of 'direct instruction' which is highly effective. Worked examples have been found to be only moderately effective; peer tutoring, which would include peer explaining, also has a moderate effectiveness.

Evidence from research on the most effective teachers: Lemov has examples of modelling, e.g. the 'I/we/you' approach.

At least two sources of evidence have good evidence that modelling is worth trying in your classroom.

Further reading

See also the principal references in Chapter 15 Further reading and references.

Free online resources

Search for terms such as: 'modelling teaching', 'worked examples', 'teacher thinking aloud', 'working memory'.

'Cognitive load theory: Research that teachers really need to understand' (Centre for Education, Statistics and Evaluation, NSW Government, 2017). This is a free download, only 12 pages long; authoritative and practical. Recommended by the Institute for Effective Education.

W.M. Carroll, 'The use of worked examples in teaching algebra' (ED353130, 1992). A brilliant paper.

Search for 'Ron Berger Youtube Austin's Butterfly'. This video shows a teacher modelling success criteria and a 'growth mindset'. He is working with nine-year-olds, but the principles can be adapted to any age.

Books and papers

S. Allison and A. Tharby, *Making Every Lesson Count* (Carmarthen: Crown House Publishing, 2015). Brilliant book with lots of detail on strategy including modelling.

R.K. Atkinson et al., 'Learning from examples: Instructional principles from the worked examples research' (*Review of Educational Research* 2000, 70, 181 DOI: 10.3102/00346543070002181).

A. Ayres and J. Sweller, '8.18 Worked Examples', pages 408–410 *International Guide to Student Achievement*, J.A.C. Hattie and E. Anderman (Eds) (Routledge, 2013). A highly authoritative and very short summary of research on worked examples.

J.D. Bransford et al., *How People Learn: Brain, Mind, Experience and School* (Washington: National Research Council, 2000). This is a report from a massive government project in the USA to summarise what we know about learning and teaching.

J.S. Bruner, *Toward a Theory of Instruction* (Cambridge, Mass.: Belkapp Press, 1966).

D. Christodoulou, *Making Good Progress* (Oxford: Oxford University Press, 2016).

G. Gibbs, *Teaching Students to Learn* (Buckingham: Open University Press, 1981).

J.A.C. Hattie and G. Yates, *Visible Learning and the Science of How We Learn* (Routledge, 2014). See Chapter 16, 'The impact of cognitive load' particularly.

R. Sadler, 'Formative assessment and the design of instructional systems' (*Instructional Science*, 18, 119–44, 1989). A short paper on what students need to know in order to learn well. A work of genius, born out by all research reviews on feedback and modelling. See 'guild knowedge' in this paper.

D. Willingham, *Why Don't Students Like School?* A Cognitive Scientist Answers Questions About How the Mind Works and What It Means for the Classroom (San Francisco: Jossey-Bass, 2009). A highly regarded cognitive scientist answers questions about how the mind works and what it means for the classroom

Chapter 8
The 'receive' phase: presenting new content to students

You will recall from Chapter 1 that students must create their own meaning encoded as a 'construct' (see page 9). This new learning must be built onto relevant prior learning, as shown in Figure 8.1. When students receive new information, how do we ensure that each student in our class creates a meaning, that they understand it, and how do we check and correct this understanding while they learn it?

Chapter 7 considered how to model or demonstrate a skill, and this chapter considers how to teach new content, whether you present it with teacher-talk, reading, or some other approach such as e-learning.

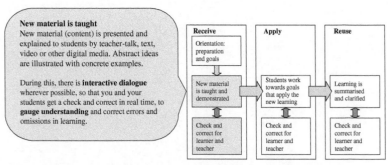

Figure 8.1: The method for new content delivery is important

Whatever the learning, the content can be delivered to students by involving them in one or more of the following:

- **Listening:** to teacher-talk, podcasts, radio, video, etc.

- **Reading:** text and graphics in any form, for example handouts, books, but also websites, online pdfs, etc.

- **Watching:** a demonstration, video, TV programme, film, animation, etc., which usually involves listening too.

More rarely, new content can be learned by the following:

- **Experiencing:** making or doing something – visiting a museum or gallery, or role play, for example.

- **Thinking:** the student can work out some content for themselves.

By far the most common activities are listening, reading and watching, and these are often received passively by at least some students. This need not be the case. You can set an 'active attention task' that requires the learner to make sense of the content being delivered, as I explain below.

I have often observed poor teaching and I expect you have too. In such lessons the teacher is often working their socks off trying to make the lesson clear and interesting, while some students daydream or worse. Some students may try to form an understanding, but it's not being checked and corrected by the student, the teacher or a peer. So learning contains errors and omissions that the teacher is unaware of. We can do better than this – let's see how.

Peer explaining: an example of an 'active attention task'

The teacher is about to teach a new topic, the role of the district nurse, but wants students to attend actively.

1 The teacher sets a task in advance of their explanation of the new topic, warning that students in pairs will soon explain to each other two aspects of the explanation she is about to give. Students are told they will need to either: *Explain the main roles of the district nurse* or *Explain how her role relates to other health professionals*.

Students are *not* told at this stage which of these two explanations they must give; consequently, they must prepare for both.

2 The teacher explains this new content on the district nurse using teacher-talk, video, presentation software, and so on, in the usual way: concrete to abstract, and known to unknown, as described in Chapter 1. Meanwhile, students are preparing to give their explanation, perhaps taking notes, perhaps asking questions to clarify their understanding.

3 Having finished the explanation, the teacher puts students into pairs and then assigns an explaining task to each student: *'Those nearest the window in your pair please explain to your partner the role of the district* *nurse. Those furthest from the window, please explain how the role fits in with other health professionals.'*

4 Students are given one minute (timed) to prepare their explanation, working alone. They are asked to note down the key points for their explanation.

5 Students take turns to explain their subtopic to their partner, helped by their notes. They have one minute each, say, timed by the teacher.

6 Students are given a minute or two to improve their partner's explanation. They might be helped by the other's notes. Was there anything missing? Anything wrong? What was done well? The teacher asks students to give more strengths than weaknesses during this peer assessment.

7 The teacher displays key points for each explanation on the screen: *'Here are my key points, Did you get them all?'* Students, still in their pairs, self- and peer assess against these.

Unlike pure teacher-talk, this approach *requires* the learner to make a meaning, to form a construct. It also checks and corrects this meaning. Indeed, this is done at least twice, once in the peer assessment, and then again by self- and peer assessment against the teacher's key points. Setting a peer-explaining task before presenting new material gives students a good reason to listen to your presentation, and the method holds students accountable for their understanding. Students really enjoy this method too.

Remember the graph on page 20 in Chapter 1. Active attention tasks like these can make your Roberts and Robertas learn like your Susans – they pay real attention and think about the content being delivered.

 Try this in the classroom

Peer explaining works in any subject:

'While I explain how to find the unknown length in these triangles listen carefully, because you will have to explain a similar one to your partner straight after.'

'Watch this video about how to take a penalty kick. When you've finished you will explain one of the two approaches to your partner. But I'll tell you which one.'

I remember setting a peer-explaining task for the first time, and with some trepidation. Halfway through my prior explanation, which of course sizzled with searing clarity, a student at the back of the class, who I knew to be weak, put his hand up and said, *'Could you explain that bit again? I didn't quite get it.'* I had been teaching for 15 years and this was the first time I had received such a request during teacher-talk. Other students were nodding. I reeled for a second or two. I explained it again. *'Got it,'* said the boy at the back, and the others with trouble nodded in agreement. Peer explaining gives students the responsibility for making sense of what you are explaining.

Peer explaining is only one 'active attention task' – there are many more, a number of which are given below. Remember that the purpose of an active attention task is to ensure students listen attentively and create their own personal meaning (construct) and to check and correct this.

When to use an 'active attention task'

There is of course no necessity to use an active attention task for every explanation. As ever in teaching, you must use your judgement. These tasks don't only work for teacher-talk, they work if content is to be delivered by computer, video, or film, etc. and if you are doing a demonstration of some kind.

Some people object to active attention tasks because they take time away from the presentation of new material – they are 'losing' 3 to 5 minutes. This means the teacher is unable to say everything they know about the topic in the time available. Unfortunately, you know too much, and there is hardly ever enough time to say everything you would like on a topic. Your challenge is not to give all the information you have, or even all the information that the course requires: it is to give as much vital information as your students are able to make sense of, in the time that you are allowed. There is no point delivering what cannot be understood, if only because it will almost certainly be forgotten. If students emerge from your explanation with a clear understanding of *the most vital points, structured in a meaningful way*, you will have done as well as you can.

And what about the detail you courageously omit? Well, detail can easily be added later if the student well understands the key points that you had time to explain. For example, you could set a reading homework specifically to add this detail. Even if this homework is not done, and so the detail is not added, the student will still have a well-understood outline of the most important parts of the topic. This is usually enough to pass comfortably. If you had instead presented everything you knew, or everything you think the student should know, they would likely be swamped by data, and many would not understand your presentation well at all. There is a limit to how much students can learn in a given time, not least because of the limits of working memory or short-term memory (considered in Chapter 7).

It is not easy to decide what content is vital and what content students can do without for now, while ensuring that your students make a good sense of the outline of the topic. It requires a steely nerve to teach only what is vital and to leave time to check and correct this, rather than to cover everything you can. Indeed, this is often the hardest decision most teachers face. If there are past paper questions, study these; if this content supports later topics, consider that too. What can you leave for top-up activities and revision?

I remember visiting the history department of a college that got some of the very best A-level history results in the country. They adopted this 'teach for deep understanding of the key material' strategy to a degree that many teachers would consider reckless. I asked what happened to students who did not do the background reading that was designed to top up their understanding of the detail missed out in very active learning lessons. The head of department shrugged, and with a sigh said, *'They get B grades.'* I had seen the results, and unlike almost all schools and colleges at this time, all their students did get As or Bs. They did so well because they understood what they had learned in class very well indeed, and this was all vital material, even if some students had not learned everything they should. We need to prioritise deep understanding of the vital, rather than superficial coverage of the detail.

In the RAR structure the active attention task is set before the presentation of the new content, and the task with its check and correct is completed just after this explanation. However, the active attention task is almost never enough to establish full understanding of the new content. It makes a start on surface learning – a vital first stage (see Chapter 1). There must be a more substantial and different task for students in the 'Apply' phase, or better, a ladder of tasks, as explained in Chapters 1 and 9. This will create a fuller understanding linked to other learning, which is 'deep learning' (see Chapter 1). Students learn best when they think hard and long with the new content, and active attention tasks are only designed to make students actively engage with new content while it is being explained.

So have a go with some active attention tasks such as peer explaining, which only need a few minutes. Try it with a topic that is not easy for students to understand and, if you need to, add the detail with a reading homework, using an active reading task as explained later in this chapter. Below are some other active attention tasks to try; students enjoy a bit of variety, so don't use the same type of active attention task in every lesson.

More 'active attention tasks' to try

Set a mini-task

You can set a short task before the new material is presented, for example:

'While I describe these three marketing strategies, I want you to work out whether any or all would be useful for your case study.'

'While you watch the video, listen out for the main functions of a health centre: you should find five. See if your group can get them all. I'll check with you later.'

'What do you think Henry II would be thinking during this episode? I'll ask you this again after I have explained it.'

Of course, you will have to remember to set these tasks after your explanation, or students won't take any subsequent active attention tasks seriously.

Note-making

This is like peer explaining, except students write notes instead of explaining to a peer. In both cases there is a check and correct. This method goes back to Aristotle and before, but cognitive science shows that even the best students can't listen and write at the same time; instead, they switch attention between listening and writing, missing some of the input as a result. Also, their notes will have errors and omissions. Here's a way to overcome these and other difficulties:

1 You give students a warning that they will have to write their own notes on the subtopic you are about to explain, and that they won't get a note written by you. You warn them that their notes will be checked in pairs and self-assessed against your key points.

2 You teach the subtopic for, say, five to ten minutes. You write key words and new terms on the board. You don't allow students to try to write down everything you say. They may make short notes, but then must put their pens down and listen.

3 You stop talking for, say, a timed minute (you may find this hard). Students write notes of key points only, leaving gaps between paragraphs and down the side of their page. They might create mind maps instead.

4 Students check each other's notes in pairs for, say, a timed minute, and then improve them, using the spaces between paragraphs to add material where necessary.

5 You go through the really key points that ought to appear in the notes, either verbally or by displaying a list of key points. Better still by class discussion assertive questioning style (see Chapter 5).

6 Students improve their notes again where necessary, again using the gaps left in their original notes.

You will probably not be greatly impressed by your students' notes, but the cognitive engagement with the material should be pretty high. The aim of the method is not to create brilliant notes, but to require students to make sense of the presentation. Rigorous experiments with note-making have shown that it is outstandingly effective at ensuring students learn content.

If you expect students to find note-making hard, show them some model notes for topics you have just explained and point out the features, for example that they are very short or they only give key points.

If you want students to learn note-making skills as well as the content, read Chapter 13 and follow the advice there.

Other ways to present new content actively

Teaching by asking

There are times when you must teach something that is very like something you have already taught, or something that is so easy that students can work at least some of it out for themselves. In this case, you can use 'teaching by asking', which first finds what students can work out for themselves, corrects this where necessary, then teaches what they don't know. This can be preferable to boring students by teaching it all.

 Consider

McKinsey & Company analysed data from the Program for International Student Assessment (PISA), and in a 2017 report found that students performed best when taught through a mix of teacher-directed and inquiry-based instruction. However, 'students cannot progress to inquiry-based methods without a strong foundation of knowledge, gained through teacher-directed instruction.' If you use teaching by asking, make sure students have the background knowledge to be successful.

Rather than 'teaching by telling', you start the topic by asking students a question that leads to what you want to teach. For example:

'What methods are used to market food products? Think of as many as you can.'

'Why do you think managers value staff training?'

'Who would have supported Cromwell, who would not, and why?'

'Here is a mathematics problem you can't solve with the methods we have seen so far. How would you solve it?'

Students work in pairs or small groups (buzz groups) to answer your question(s) using common sense, experience, and their prior learning. This group discussion can last for literally a minute or less, or for 20 minutes or longer. This group work can be strengthened by snowballing, as described below.

Ensure each group has a scribe. Check the group's attention to task, and the quality of their work, by checking what the scribes have written down. Ask them if they need more time. If they have finished, ask each pair or group for one idea they have had, ensuring that each group offers something. Write the strong ideas on the board, saying a little in support of each idea if you wish. Allow the class to discuss any points of disagreement until they have agreed a common answer. This gives you a very thorough understanding of students' prior learning and experience.

When the class has its common answer, 'top up' the answer with any additional points the class has missed, and correct any misunderstandings. If students get half of the answer, it saves half of the teacher-talk, and the question that you asked has generated interest and thought. It works well with snowballing (see below), and can be assisted by resources if this helps, but these mustn't give the answer to your question away directly.

Of course, there is a good deal of judgement in deciding which topics can be taught in a teaching by asking way, and which need to be explained in full.

See 'Effective management of active learning strategies to maximise participation' on page 152 for more detail on how to manage this activity, and the activities that follow.

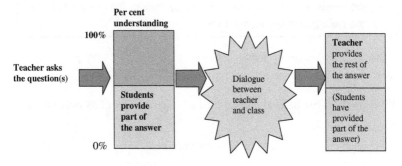

Figure 8.2: Teaching by asking

Variations on 'teaching by asking'

Class brainstorm

The teacher requests as many ideas as possible from the whole class by asking questions such as:

'You are a child just admitted to hospital – how do you feel? What do you need?'

'What are the advantages of prior booking a hotel?'

'What diseases are common in childhood?'

'Why might Hamlet not have taken revenge straight away?'

The teacher or a student compiles the answers on the board, classifying them if necessary by writing them in groups. It is usual to be non-judgemental at this stage.

This method involves the whole class and can enliven a dull session. Optionally, you could ask students to brainstorm in groups and the session then becomes like 'teaching by asking' above.

Round

This method is useful for small groups if the experiences of the students are a particularly useful resource. For example, managers on a part-time management course sharing experiences of how new staff are inducted into their organisation.

Each person has a minute, say, to describe their experiences on a given topic and to express their point of view while others listen. Students can 'pass' if they wish. This method mines useful experience, elicits a range of viewpoints, and builds a sense of safe participation. It also informs you of your students' prior learning and experience.

Snowballing

This can be used with any of the methods above, indeed with almost any task or activity. It creates the best dialogue of all these methods and so has the potential to work best. It requires full participation, provides a check-and-correct discussion, and involves an interesting way of collecting ideas on almost any task.

Like the methods above you don't *tell* students, but ask them a question that leads to what you want students to learn. For example: *'Why do you think we use stocktaking? Think of as many reasons as you can.'* Then:

1 each **individual** writes down their thoughts without reference to others

2 students share what they have written in pairs or threes

3 optionally, the pairs or threes pair up to create larger groups, which again compare their answers, and then agree a group answer with its justification. Leave time for this dialogue.

4 the teacher asks individuals by name from each big group in turn for **one** idea their group has had. She then asks for a justification from a member of the same group, for example *'Why did your group think that?'*; and then writes the useful ideas on the board. Or better, a full assertive questioning style can be used.

As in 'teaching by asking', the teacher then tops up and corrects the class answer, 'unteaching' any misconceptions. Snowballing involves more student interaction than brainstorm, round, or thought experiment. The teacher can classify the ideas from the groups in columns on the board, or as a concept map.

Mnemonics

If you want students to remember something tricky like the colours of the rainbow, mnemonics are very powerful. For example, **R**ichard **O**f **Y**ork **G**ave **B**attle **I**n **V**ain gives the colours of the rainbow in order: **R**ed, **O**range, **Y**ellow, **G**reen, **B**lue, **I**ndigo, and **V**iolet. Students can be asked to create their own mnemonics. This is fun, but be prepared to be shocked!

Your explaining skills

Don't expect active attention tasks to do all the work. When explaining, fully orientate your students first, including a check on relevant prior learning, an advance organiser and goals in advance, and then:

- explain the new material from known to unknown, and from concrete to abstract, asking questions along the way to create dialogue and check understanding

- use multiple modes of representation in your explanation (see Chapter 2)

- check and correct student understanding with questioning (see Chapter 5).

See G. Petty, *Teaching Today* (5th Edition) Chapter 12 'The Art of Explaining' for more detail.

Teaching without talking

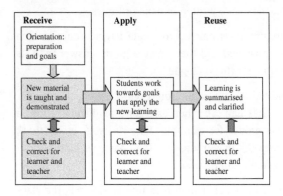

Figure 8.3: Teaching without talking in the RAR structure

At the beginning of this chapter, I pointed out that students can learn new content by listening, reading and watching. I've described how to make learning by listening an active experience with peer explaining. But how do we make students attend actively when learning by reading and watching? This has become increasingly common, for example during:

- **e-learning, online delivery, distance learning,** and so on. Typically, students read websites, pdfs, and watch animations or videos

- **blended learning**, where some learning is done without the teacher, online or with other resources, and some learning is done under the direct guidance of the teacher

- **flipped learning,** where students learn the basics of a topic online or with other resources, without the teacher, and then learn the rest of the topic with teacher help

- **homework tasks,** to learn a topic unaided

- **independent learning,** where a whole topic is studied by students without teacher explanation, though the learning is assessed by the teacher. See Petty, 2014.

- **an in-class activity**. This is rarer, but there is no reason why you shouldn't ask students to learn part of a topic from resources without your explanation. This is an excellent way to teach students skills such as underlining key points in a handout or writing a summary.

In my experience, when students are asked by their teacher to learn directly from digital media, the pedagogy is poorly designed, if it is designed at all. Consequently, students simply skim read text that is often too difficult for them, or listen with half an ear to the videos they are directed to, and so poor learning results. This is a design fault, not the students' fault: the teacher should have set an active attention task that required the student to make sense of the material and to check and correct their understanding. Then students need to apply the learning. In short, students need to be taught as the RAR structure suggests.

The active attention tasks below are easy to set, and get much better engagement and higher-quality learning as they encourage students a round the Quality Learning Cycle (see Chapter 1).

These are demanding ways to learn, and the topic must not be too conceptually challenging until students' learning skills have been developed by practice with these methods.

How to

Calculating readability with the FOG index

There are sites online that will find the reading age of text for you. But it is well worth understanding how reading age is calculated. The 'reading age' of text is the age at which the average person can read it. This means that about half of people of that age would have trouble reading it of course! So the reading age of your material usually needs to be considerably lower than the chronological age of your students.

To find the readability:

1 In a representative section of the text, select five to eight complete sentences. Find the total number of words **'n'** in the **'s'** complete sentences.

2 Calculate the average number of words per complete sentence: **'A' = n ÷ s**

3 Select a passage of continuous text of exactly 100 words within your sample. Find the number of words of three or more syllables, **'W'**, in your 100-word sample. Don't count the 'ed' or 'es' endings of verbs, so that the word 'compounded' counts as only two syllables, despite being three syllables.

4 Calculate the reading age as follows:

Add **A to W**, then multiply your answer by 0.4. Now add five years. This is the reading age of the material. For mathematicians:

Reading age = 0.4(A + W) + 5 years

For somewhat greater accuracy, select three or four passages from the book, find the reading ages of these, and then average them. This is called the FOG index, which stands jokingly for the 'frequency of gobbledegook'.

The average TV guide has a reading age of about six years; 17 years is very tough reading indeed, and only suitable for postgraduates.

To reduce the reading age, simply shorten sentences, simplify grammar, and 'translate' difficult words into more common language, adding the formal word later if this helps, for example '... *makes them feel they can make a difference, that is, empowers them...*'

Teaching without talking: using resources that explain the topic

These methods work best when you can find appropriate resources with a low reading age. Tabloid newspapers often have a reading age of about ten years but are designed for adults. You will need well-written material such as handouts, books, and Internet sites, etc. A combination of resources is ideal, and this is what I mean by the 'resources' and 'materials' described below. Ask librarians to help you find materials, as they are the world's experts at this, but do give them sufficient notice. Students may find materials on the Internet, and the links can be kept for the next cohort of students learning the same topic. The methods are described as if students are working out of class, however, these methods can easily be adapted for use in class.

When students learn on computers they learn more if they share the computer than if they work alone (Hattie, 2009). This is at least partly because sharing a computer creates dialogue, mutual support and informal peer assessment. Try to build dialogue, peer helping, and peer assessment into your 'teaching without talking'.

You will remember from Chapter 1 that 'boosters' are very useful to ensure students go a round the Quality Learning Cycle. I have suggested some boosters in the methods below, but you could adapt the methods by using different ones. These 'boosters' can be used when students are learning independently or in the classroom. Many virtual learning environments (VLEs) have facilities to enable these methods.

Some useful boosters for teaching without talking include:

- **pair check:** mutually checking and correcting their partners' draft work, followed by dialogue

- **snowballing:** where students work individually first, then work in pairs and then the pairs combine into fours, to gradually arrive through discussion at an agreed best piece of work

- **self-assessment or peer assessment:** these can be done against answers, worked solutions, checklists or assessment criteria provided by you

- **discussion forums:** there can be class discussion of model ideas/solutions, or of ideas/solutions suggested by students

- **formative quiz:** understanding of vital content is checked and corrected (see Chapter 11). Students can prepare for this quiz in small groups and the groups compete against each other if you like, or better, compete against a target to get, say, 8/10 in the quiz. Crucially, the groups and teacher then help fix any misunderstandings found

- **spoof assessment:** models like those above can be imperfect, in which case students can assess, improve, complete or comment on those models (see Chapter 11).

Teaching without talking methods

Underlining to create key points and questions

> ### 🙋 Try this in the classroom
>
> **1** Students are given resources and asked to read them for the gist.
>
> **2** They then read again and underline the key points. They may print out the material and underline with a pencil, or copy it into a word-processing program that allows highlighting and underlining. It helps if they can remove any underlining they did earlier if they change their mind, which makes coloured pen highlighters problematical.
>
> **3** Students adapt the underlining/highlighting until only about 10% of the text is underlined.
>
> **4** Students identify the key points made, and formulate questions that the resources don't seem to answer.
>
> **5** Students share their key points. If students are out of class, they could upload their key points onto your institution's VLE or intranet, for example.
>
> **6** You make your own key points available and students improve their own.
>
> **7** Students also share their questions which you, or the class answers.

After this activity, explain that it models good study and independent learning habits and teach for transfer by 'bridging', as described in Chapter 13, which looks at this vital method in detail.

Inserting headings, and writing under headings

Students are given a handout with no headings or subheadings, but with spaces for these. Students read the handout and create headings that summarise what follows in that section of text in the form of a statement.

This produces headings such as 'The heart is a blood pump', 'The heart has four chambers', 'Arteries take blood from the heart', etc.

You can of course adapt an existing handout by removing existing headings, and maybe leaving space for more.

You can do this activity the other way around, that is, provide the headings and ask students to find out about each heading and then write a short section on this. This is a good way of structuring independent learning. For example, students studying the heart could be given the headings and asked to study and then write short notes under each heading.

Summarising a topic with a graphic organiser such as a mind map

This activity is known to be exceptionally powerful (see Chapter 3). Students are given resources on an unfamiliar topic, for example the quality system in a manufacturing company. They are asked to study the resources by underlining and deciding upon key points, as described above. Then they produce a 'graphic organiser', such as a mind map, flow diagram, Venn diagram, comparison table, or same-and-different diagram. The organiser must summarise the topic. You could stipulate which type of organiser should be produced; however, when students are more experienced with organisers, you could teach them to choose the most appropriate one for themselves.

If students create an organiser on a computer, this can be uploaded or emailed for peer assessment. If organisers are created on paper, they can be photographed and again uploaded or emailed. Organisers can be displayed on the intranet, Internet or VLE, either for peer assessment, teacher assessment, or just for display and revision purposes. Students are motivated if there is an audience for their work, especially if it can be shown to family or friends.

Graphic organiser ping-pong

Any digital work can be ping-ponged like this, not just a graphic organiser (see Figure 3.20: Graphic organiser ping-pong).

Here, students make a graphic organiser that 'ping-pongs' between them and you:

1 Students create a graphic organiser from resources as described above.

2 Students create their graphic organiser using a word-processing application.

3 Students email their graphic organiser to you.

4 Then you send them *your* graphic organiser, asking the student to self-assess their graphic organiser using yours as a model. Alternatively, send key points asking *'Are these on your organiser?'*

5 Students improve their organiser in red, without copying yours.

6 They email their improved organiser to you. You check the red additions.

7 Optionally, they could take an online quiz to confirm their understanding a day or two later.

You can of course stop at step 4. The quiz could be added to any of the methods in this section. You can also ask students to peer assess by emailing organisers to each other. This is described below. They can all upload their organisers onto a common VLE or website page and compare their work with that of others. They can also present their organisers using a slideshow presentation, on shared webpages, or on interactive whiteboards, for example.

Complete the organiser

You give students a graphic organiser such as a table or mind map that is nowhere near complete. In effect this is an advance organiser, which outlines the most important subtopics that they are about to learn. Students complete this after studying resources. This might be a useful activity to get students used to graphic organisers.

> **Also see**
>
> Students can use a word-processing or slideshow program or similar to create their graphic organiser. However, you might like to consider dedicated software such as Mindgenius: see www.mindgenius.com.

Transforming graphic organisers

Suppose you made use of a flow diagram to describe stocktaking. You could ask students to use this organiser to create another, say, a holistic mind map looking at stocktaking from the points of view of the customer, retail manager, and retail worker.

Answering a ladder of questions

This is the familiar 'worksheet', with a 'ladder' of questions. The ladder first requires students to reproduce facts given in the resources, then there are questions that require simple reasoning that are not answered directly by the resources, then later questions are open and challenging, as described in Chapter 1.

There is a danger that students just search through the resources for answers to your questions without first trying to understand the topic as a whole. Consequently, try as a first task asking students to summarise the resources or topic with one of the methods mentioned earlier in this section.

Formulating questions

Students study appropriate resources using one of the methods above. Then they formulate questions on this content, along with model answers. These questions are used as a quiz for a second student to answer. Once the quiz is completed, students are given the model answers to mark their own work.

Alternatively, students work in groups to formulate questions and answers. Then they take a quiz devised by another group, and they mark their own work using that group's model answers. These quizzes can address different subtopics, or can all address the topic as a whole.

Student presentation

After studying a topic, preferably using one of the methods above, students prepare a presentation on the topic or a subtopic, alone or in groups. They video their presentation. If presentations are to be done live, divide the topic up, and ask each group to present a different subtopic. Don't tell students which subtopic they will present until *after* they have studied the topic as a whole, to ensure that they do not overspecialise. Students could study the material using one of the other strategies described above.

The videoed presentations can be uploaded for peer assessment, or for a 'ping-pong', as described above for graphic organisers.

Peer explaining of subtopics

Students in pairs are given two sets of resources on related topics that have not been explained to them, for example one about measles and another about mumps. They each use the resources to study one of these topics alone for, say, five minutes. Alternatively, they could use the same text/video, but look at different aspects of it. For example, students could watch a video or read a text on the marketing policy of a small company, and one student could look out for strengths in the policy and another for weaknesses.

Each student explains their subtopic to their partner; this can be done in a video call or similar, but might be better in person. The student receiving the explanation asks questions until they understand.

Integrative task: The pair then works together at a task that requires them to work *together* on *both* subtopics. A useful question for this is to ask students to 'State what is the same, and what is different about measles and mumps' or 'Considering both strengths and weaknesses, what do you think of the marketing policy? How could strengths be built upon, and weaknesses addressed?' This method is, in effect, a mini 'jigsaw', and could finish with students preparing for, and then taking a short test.

Jigsaw

Try peer explaining before using jigsaw: students will need this skill to succeed with jigsaw. Do a small topic for your first jigsaw, so you and especially your students get the hang of the method.

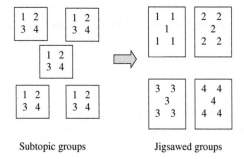

Subtopic groups   Jigsawed groups

Figure 8.4: Jigsaw

In the diagram above, each number is a student and each rectangle a table. I imagine in the diagram, and below, a class of 20 students being taught a topic with five subtopics. For example, a teacher might teach childhood diseases, and split this into the five subtopics of measles, mumps, meningitis, chickenpox, and whooping cough. However, the jigsaw method does not need a specific number of students or subtopics (download my 'jigsaw arithmetic'). Try the following in the classroom:

 Divide a topic up into, say, five subtopics.

 Divide students into five groups, each of which studies one subtopic for about ten minutes from resources, writing key points that are then checked by you. These resources can obviously include digital resources such as video, for example.

The students in each group now number themselves '1', '2', '3', and so on. All the '1s' go to one table, and all the '2s' to another, and so on. The new groups now form a jigsaw of random social composition, which contains one student 'expert' on each of the five subtopics.

3 In these jigsaw groups, students:

    a. Teach each other their subtopic, covering all the key points.

    b. Complete a 'combined task' together that requires knowledge of all the subtopics. For example, *'Find three characteristics all the childhood diseases share, and two that are unique for each. Then place the diseases in order of severity, and prepare a justification for your ranking.'*

    c. The groups present their ideas for the combined task and the teacher debriefs the whole class on this.

    d. Students, still in jigsaw groups, prepare for a short quiz on the key points, led by a member of their group. They should know this is coming. They are given the challenge to ensure each member of their group gets a minimum of, say, 7/10 in a quiz they must take as individuals.

    e. Students complete the short quiz individually and mark their own papers. Great cheers all round if their group all get 7/10 in the test. (A challenge is more motivating than a competition as all groups can win against a challenge.)

4 Then each group asks themselves these questions about how they operated as a group:

    a. In what two ways did our group work well together?

    b. In what way could we do better next time?

5 You debrief the class on the group goals above and remind them of these before the next jigsaw.

You may need to split the activity between two lessons if you use jigsaw on a large topic. The obvious place to 'break' the activity is between steps 2 and 3 above. Jigsaw can work with classes of almost any size – download my 'jigsaw arithmetic' to see how.

Independent learning

You can try the following:

1 Any easy section of the syllabus is identified and this is not taught.

2 Instead, students are given an assignment that describes in detail what they must learn. More experienced independent learners might need less direction.

3 Students work on this task in pairs or small groups, usually outside of class contact time. The assignment activities require students to work in pairs or groups, are thought-provoking, and are not entirely 'book and biro'. Visual representations and other methods above make good tasks. At least one task requires students to go beyond the simple reproduction of the ideas in the materials and to apply their learning. This is to encourage deep learning, otherwise students may simply collect information and write it down without really thinking about it or understanding it.

4 Students' work is monitored by a designated 'leader' in their group or by the teacher.

5 The students' notes are *not* marked (except perhaps in the first use of this method in order to check their ability to make effective notes). Instead, their learning is assessed by a short test. One assignment task is to prepare for this. Optionally, students can be required to retake tests or do other remedial work if their test result is unsatisfactory.

6 After completing this independent learning assignment, or indeed before, students use an independent learning competences questionnaire to identify their weaknesses as an independent learner, and to set themselves targets for their next independent learning assignment.

This is not an easy teaching method to use, but it is greatly enjoyed by students if it is managed well. See Chapter 31 of Petty's *Teaching Today* (2014) for a fuller description.

Spectacles

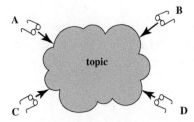

Figure 8.5: Spectacles

This method is best explained by examples. Suppose a teacher wants to teach the topic of 'saving'. Students need to know about building society accounts, bank accounts, shares, and other ways of saving money. She asks her students to study materials on this topic, which describe all the relevant methods of saving, and asks them to consider each method of saving from a number of points of view, such as: *rate of interest, ease of withdrawal, can the value go down as well as up?* She asks them to make notes on an A3-sized table as shown. Alternatively they could produce an holistic mind map

How can we save?				
	Rate of interest Why high or low?	Ease of withdrawal Why?	Can the value go down as well as up? Why?	
Building society account				
Bank account				
Shares				

Figure 8.6: A comparison table using different 'spectacles'

If the evaluation criteria are well chosen, the students must study and understand the different methods of saving very well in order to make their judgements. The judgements students make are a measure of how well they have understood the method of saving. Groups can compare their judgements by placing them on a class grid provided on a flip-chart or board. They enjoy this, and the controversy this creates can help clarify misunderstandings.

Like the other methods described in this chapter, the aim is to get students to learn content (in this case, methods of saving) without direct explanation from the teacher. However, if the learning points are brought out with 'bridging' (as described in Chapter 13), this method will also develop analysis and evaluation skills. Using a table in which to present ideas is not essential.

Other examples of the use of 'spectacles' include:

- learning about childhood diseases by using criteria such as 'method of immunisation', 'ease of immunisation' or 'likelihood of permanent effects'

- learning about computer printers with criteria such as print method, cost or speed, for example.

If the criteria are right, the analysis can lead to a realistic evaluation. This method is greatly enjoyed, and is best done in groups. It can be used to develop analytical thinking skills and evaluation skills.

Co-operative learning – learning teams do questions on resource material

This is similar to teaching by asking with resources above, but more complex and structured. It is a useful preparation for 'learning together' and other co-operative learning methods. For example, you could try the following:

1. Students are given a range of resources on a topic and they are asked to use them to answer a range of questions from simple reproduction questions to ones requiring simple and then more complex reasoning. They are told in advance that they must complete the quiz, test or exam-style question mentioned below.

2. Students are given questions that relate to the key points in the resources and to the key lesson objectives. Questions should be thought-provoking. For example, *'Who supported Cromwell and why?'*

3. The answer to the question(s) should *not* appear baldly and simply stated in one place in the resources. Students should need to construct their own understanding in order to answer the question, not just repeat the resources back to you.

4. Consider having a range of materials of differing difficulty shared by the group. Or give each student in the group different resources that may not be read by or to others, but can be explained to them by that student.

5. It may help to give students individual roles in their group such as scribe, vocabulary checker, etc., as described at the end of this chapter.

Students work in groups, and when they have finished, feedback can be elicited from the groups one idea at a time, in assertive questioning style (see Chapter 5).

Finally, learning is tested with a quick quiz or test or with an exam-style question on the subject on which students work individually. This method is very similar to 'learning together', a co-operative learning method that has been found to be most effective. If you like it, do read up on co-operative learning.

Summary diagram: learning from resources

If students are learning from resources, it is not enough to point to resources and then assess them with an assignment.

Orientation

- There is a check and correct of relevant prior learning.
- An advance organiser outlines the topic to be learned.
- A goal is given in advance preferably with success criteria.
- Warning is given of any assessment procedure.

Resources explain the new content

These could include text, video, podcasts, simulations, animations and other online resources.

A task is set that *requires* the learner to create a meaning from the resource

The student:

- underlines key points and then summarises the topic
- creates a graphic organiser to summarise the topic
- puts explanatory headings into the text
- answers questions on the text.

This may be enough for students to develop an adequate 'surface' understanding. If not, a ladder of tasks of increasing difficulty can be set.

Support while student does the task (boosters)

Students:

- work in pairs or small groups for example with discussion groups; Facebook groups; by email, Twitter, phone, etc.
- peer check and correct: face-to-face, by email, etc.
- snowball
- undertake co-operative learning for example, or learning teams.

Student's work and their construct is checked and corrected

The student's work and construct is improved by check and correct:

- self- and or peer assessment against answers, model, worked example, success criteria, etc.
- formative improvement, for example of any written work
- formative test
- Quality Learning boosters.

Extension tasks to deepen understanding

Students attempt another task to deepen understanding using the ladder of tasks (Chapters 1 and 9).

Figure 8.7: Learning from resources

Effective management of active learning strategies to maximise participation

The methods we have considered in this chapter work well for e-learning or other forms of independent learning. However, they can also be used in the classroom along with the methods in Chapter 9. This diagram summarises how; there is much more detail in Petty (2009).

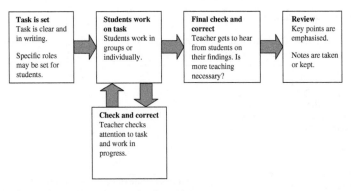

Figure 8.8: Managing active learning

You may need to agree ground rules for student activities with your class, persuade them of the power and purpose of active learning; and ensure that seating arrangements are conducive to group work. Sitting round tables is better than sitting in auditorium-style or at computers, for example. As ever, it helps to 'orientate' students, as described in Chapter 6, and in particular to confirm any prior learning required for success at the task. The process below could then be followed.

 Try this in the classroom

Task is set

- The task is clear and in writing. There may be different tasks for each group.

- It often helps for a 'scribe' to be identified by the group or the teacher. There may be a task sheet to fill in.

- Time allowed for the task and subtasks is given in advance. Require *all* learners to be prepared to feed back for their group and justify their answer, as in assertive questioning (see Chapter 5).

- Ensure that at least some of the tasks involve reasoning rather than just reproduction of material or skills given to the student. For example, make use of analysis ('why' questions), synthesis ('how' questions) and evaluation ('which' or 'how good is this' questions).

- As well as scribe, consider giving some students roles such as teacher, checker, vocabulary checker, questioner, summariser or leader, as described below.

- Challenging time constraints are given, i.e. the task doesn't go on too long.

Students work on task

- Groups are formed, preferably at random, for example by numbering round the room.

- A group scribe is appointed (by the group or teacher) to record ideas in progress. Avoid giving this role to slow writers or students with dyslexia unless they can work verbally. Rotate such roles from lesson to lesson.

Check and correct

- This teacher's role is particularly important in active learning.

- **Check** attention to task: are all students contributing?

- **Look** at the scribe's notes: are they on the right track?

- **Ask and listen.** Ask them to explain their ideas and listen carefully asking *'Why do you think that?'* and other clarifying questions. Try to get your students' trust; you must not appear threatening, which is difficult if students lack confidence. Do not over-help. If they are having trouble, leave them with a clarifying question and say you will come back in a couple of minutes or so. Try to diagnose any misconceptions and to correct them with questioning.

- Also use questioning to move them on. For example, after each visit try to leave the group with a question or a task such as: *'Look at this bit of the materials. Why do you think a sole trader would need to do this?'* or *'What about the data? Does it fit your hypothesis?'*

- Encourage and cajole. Feedback is 'medal and mission' at least some of the time: a 'medal' for progress made to date, effort or ideas, and a 'mission' challenging them to go further.

- Challenge with support.

Final check and correct

- Every group is asked for their findings and no single group provides all the answers (for example, each group is asked to make one point only, one group at a time).

- Consider appointing a 'checker' and then picking anyone in a group at random to explain their findings.

- Key learning points are emphasised and written up on the board.

- 'Assertive questioning' style is used to get the class to summarise key points.

Review

- Students are asked to state their key learning points; these are then improved by discussion.

- There is a tangible outcome, for example notes, mind map or summarising handouts given out.

- Key points are reviewed by quiz, test or by Q and A at some later time.

Using roles to maximise participation

It helps to give students in groups specific roles such as those below. It is unlikely that you would use all of these roles at the same time. Useful combinations of roles are given later.

Role descriptors are given in a manner suitable for level 3 or adult learners. Please change these descriptors to suit your students. Students enjoy these roles and soon get used to them. However, don't expect students to use them effectively without practice. Just after the first time your class uses a role, ask students to reflect on how to make them work well, and then ask them for their ideas. Record any learning points for the next time you use such roles. If you give unmotivated students a role, it prevents them becoming 'passengers'. Consider rotating the roles.

Try this in the classroom

Role-card descriptors: usually only one or two of these roles are used at once

Teacher: Your role is to study an aspect or section of the materials that I give you, and to explain this to the other students in your group/pair.

You will be the only student in your group/pair to study your particular aspect of the topic, so make sure you understand it well and think about how to explain it. You can ask me for help if you get stuck. You are not allowed to show any *written* materials to your group, but you can show any *diagrams*.

Checker: I will choose students at random from your group to report back on what your group has learned and decided. I may ask questions of more than one student from your group. I may also set a quiz or test on the material. Your role is to check that *all* the students in your group understand what your group has decided and why, and can report it to the rest of the class clearly. Do this by preparing and asking questions of your group. You are allowed a full (five) minutes to do this. If one of your group can't answer my questions, guess whose responsibility this will be!

Scribe: Your role is to summarise the key points that your group are making, check that the whole group agrees with them, and then write them down. There is much more to being a scribe than just writing!

Questioner: Your role is to 'skim' the resources and then decide on important questions that the resources should answer. For example *'Who supported Cromwell and why?'* The aim is to focus the group's attention on the key points. You then give your questions to the group for them (including you!) to answer. I might check your questions are okay.

You can add to or change your questions as you get more familiar with the materials. You may also ask supportive and clarifying questions to help the group complete their task(s).

Vocabulary chief: There is some technical vocabulary in this material. Your role is to research and explain the meaning of all the technical terms. You could devise a glossary for your group if you think this would help. You will need to run a quiz with your group to check *everyone* can explain each technical term.

> **Leader:** Your role is to lead and manage your group in a democratic way, to ensure that the group completes all their tasks in the time available, and that every student participates, because each role is important. You can give other students in your group specific roles if you think this helps. You will need to share out the resources in a way that helps the group to work with maximum effectiveness.

These roles work best if you make sure that you will test *every* student's learning after the activity. This can be done during feedback or with a quiz or test warned of in advance. If students know that any member of their group might be asked questions on the material, they will work with their checker to ensure that all members understand all the points.

The roles of questioner and checker help to show students good practice in reading text. Do point this out to students. For example, good readers formulate important questions that the text might answer; they ask themselves *'Do I understand this?'* and *'Is this important?'* as they read. They also check they know the vocabulary and summarise key points, etc. Hence the roles are not arbitrary or purely managerial, but model good study practice.

Students can be given 'role cards' with all the roles described until they get used to it. Roles can rotate from lesson to lesson.

Checking and correcting learning during the 'receive' phase

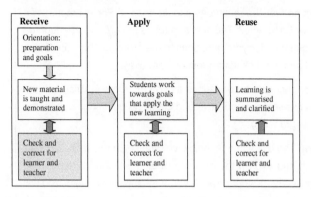

Figure 8.9: Checking and correcting is a key part of the receive phase

You have just thrown some mud at the wall, but how much has stuck? We must now use check and correct methods to inform each student, and you, of the quality of the student's present understanding. These methods must also require that any weaknesses in the constructs are corrected by the student, or by you, or both. We saw in Chapter 5 how some questioning methods can provide this check and correct. In Chapter 11 there are more check-and-correct methods that work for this receive phase as well as for the 'apply' phase.

Evidence for Chapter 8 on the 'receive' phase: presenting new content to students

Chapter 14 establishes that the most reliable sources of evidence are summary evidence, and we should triangulate three sources.

Evidence from summaries of qualitative research: Teaching can hardly take place without students receiving new content. Active attention is clearly needed for students to create an understanding.

Evidence from summaries of quantitative research: Marzano and Hattie find the following to be very effective: note-taking (students making their own notes); mnemonics; concept mapping (students creating graphic organisers); students summarising; feedback (e.g. embedding 'boosters' to check and correct learning); jigsaw; seeking help from peers; and co-operative learning. Underlining is only moderately effective if it does not include summarising. Computer-assisted instruction is only moderately effective in my view because it rarely follows the RAR structure and the other advice in this book. Teaching by asking is more contentious, but Ayres finds that exceptional teachers make extensive use of it.

Evidence from research on the most effective teachers: The most effective teachers break down content delivery into bite-sized pieces and deliver it in a very engaging way that requires participation from students, for example by peppering the delivery with questioning.

At least two sources have good evidence that at least some of the tasks in this chapter are worth trying in your classroom.

Further reading

See also the principal references in Chapter 15 Further reading and references.

Free online resources

Search for 'peer instruction', 'whole-class interactive teaching', 'co-operative learning' and 'the arithmetic of jigsaw'.

J. Chizmar and A. Ostrosky, 'The one-minute paper: some empirical findings' (Research in Economic Education, 1998).

A. Savinainen, 'An evaluation of interactive teaching methods in mechanics: using the Force Concept Inventory to monitor student learning, (IOP Science, 2001).

Books and papers

W.M. Carroll, 'Using worked examples as an instructional support in the algebra classroom' (*Journal of Educational Psychology* 83, pages 360–367, 1994).

P. Ginnis, *The Teacher's Toolkit* (Carmarthen: Crown House Publishing, 2002).

R. Marzano, *The Art and Science of Teaching: A Comprehensive Framework for Effective Instruction* (Alexandria, VA: ASCD, 2007). A free pdf 'Learning Map' of the Teacher Evaluation Model based on this book is also available.

E. Mazur, *Peer Instruction: A User's Manual* (London: Pearson, 1996).

B. Moss and V. Loh-Hagan, *40 Strategies for Guiding Readers Through Informational Texts* (New York: The Guildford Press, 2016).

Chapter 9

Getting students to apply their learning

There are hundreds of thousands of experiments in real classrooms that have required the teacher to make time for a student activity and, consequently, spend less time giving detailed explanations. Certain student activities requiring students to apply their learning have repeatedly created huge gains in student achievement. But almost any student can learn effectively if you embed 'boosters', as we will see.

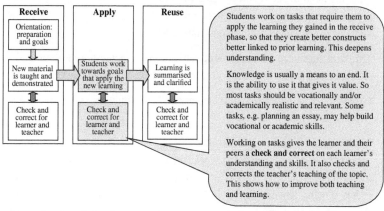

Figure 9.1: Applying learning deepens a student's understanding

The diagram above shows where we are in the RAR structure. Students have been 'orientated', so they have been persuaded of the purpose and value of what they are about to learn, had it summarised, had goals set, and recalled useful prior learning. They have received this new material, by teacher explanation or some other means, and skills have been modelled if necessary; so basic concepts have been developed, checked and corrected. However, this has created a construct (understanding in memory) that is incomplete, contains errors, and is surface level rather than deep. That is, constructs are not sufficiently integrated and related within themselves or with other learning and experience. Consequently, learning is not 'functional', as described in Chapter 1, so the learner will not yet be able to use it reliably to complete real tasks.

Applying learning is crucial and not well understood, so I will try to explain it carefully.

Students will almost always need to think more and harder about the content they have received if they are to achieve deep learning (see Chapter 1). This is for the following reasons.

- Students need to familiarise themselves more with the content. Encountering it once or twice is not enough; they need to experience helpful repetition of the new content.

- Students need to link the new material well with their prior learning; this requires thought-provoking tasks that require the learner to use these links. This deepens their learning. They also need to create links within the construct.

- Students need to see the new material in different contexts, from different perspectives, and have it represented in different ways, for example visually as well as verbally (see Chapter 2).

- Thinking about the new topic will help correct errors and omissions in the student's self-made construct that they made in the receive phase.

- Students may know the 'what' of the topic – but they also need the 'why', 'when', and 'how'.

- If learning is to be functional, that is, if the student is to be able to make use of the learning in realistic ways, then just presenting new material to them in some way, even very effectively, is not sufficient. Students need practice using the new material in realistic, varied, and important ways. For example, they might need to complete typical exam-style questions, or carry out typical vocationally relevant tasks that make use of the knowledge. Being able to do this may be the point of the content being on the syllabus in the first place.

In short, we need deep learning, not just surface learning. But what sort of tasks should we set? Tasks that require learners to *think with the important aspects of the content they have just learned*. These tasks need to gradually move from easy to challenging, to transfer gradually deepening learning. Let's look at a few types of task that you might like to try.

Build a 'ladder' of tasks

In the diagram below, 'task' includes:

- verbal or written questions

- lesson activities

- assignments

- worksheets

- homework, etc.

Tasks aiming for transfer of learning

More challenging reasoning tasks, the later ones being open

Simple reasoning tasks that are mainly closed

Simple reproduction tasks

Figure 9.2: A ladder of tasks is needed to teach a topic

How do we make sure all students learn a topic well, despite their differences in ability, prior learning, motivation, and so on? Often the best approach is to provide a ladder of tasks, starting with simple reproduction tasks that all students can succeed with and ending with open, reasoning tasks that challenge even the best students. Some students will get to the top of the ladder, some may not, but all students should do at least some simple reasoning tasks. In this way, every student achieves some success and every student is challenged. As explained in Chapter 1, deep learning and functional learning require that students reason with the new content. This enables recall and understanding, so is necessary even if your students' assessments just require recall.

Consider

Open and closed tasks

A **closed** question or task has one answer, for example:

'What is the capital of France?'

'Solve 4 + x = 9'

An **open** question or task can never be entirely completed, for example:

'What are the leisure opportunities in Paris?'

'Write some interesting quadratic equations, providing your answers.'

Near the top of the ladder we need open tasks such as:

'What are the main similarities and differences between power and energy?'

'Write some algebraic equations that describe real-life situations, such as the amount of paint required to redecorate a room. Draw a diagram to explain your equation. Simplify your equation if you can.'

'Write a story describing a difficult journey using many metaphors.'

'What would happen if district nurses were abolished and the care they provide was given by others in the health service?'

Open tasks like these can stretch the most-able student almost indefinitely, as long as the task requires reasoning. The last example above could be a book! But a weaker student who has spent most of their time on the lower rungs on the ladder of tasks would still be able to write a sentence or two in response to such open tasks. In this way, open tasks either 'stretch' or 'contract' to accommodate students of different ability or who have less or more time for the task. Consequently, open tasks suit a much wider range of student ability than a closed reproduction task such as *'State the three main roles of a hospital porter'*, so these open tasks 'differentiate' (accommodate differences in students). They provide what is called 'differentiation by outcome' where all students have the same tasks, but the teacher accepts that the students' responses to these open tasks will be different in quality and quantity. The tasks are the same, but the outcome different.

In the past, teachers have often been advised to group students and to set different tasks for the different groups. This is a lot of work for the teacher, and is called 'differentiation by task'. However, grouping students often doesn't work well, see Hattie (2009). Differentiation by task is much better and it is recommended by Wiliam (2016) and in an influential paper by Hattie and Yates (2016). There is an added advantage that the ladder of tasks approach makes lesson planning much easier.

It's important to realise that open tasks can never be completed, so even the most-able student will not finish and so will always have productive and challenging work to do. There is a danger that if you provide only reproduction tasks, your more-able students will never be challenged and may well get to the end of these easy tasks, so have nothing to do while weaker students are still struggling on the lower rungs of the ladder. But as is described in more detail below, an open task will keep such students engaged in challenging and productive learning right to the end of your lesson.

Other advantages of open tasks that require reasoning are many:

- They are often more interesting than closed tasks, especially those that just require recall.

- They often prepare students for tasks that they will encounter in exams, on courses they might progress to, or at work

- Because they are quite challenging, they tend to discover weaknesses in students' constructs, enabling these to be improved. They provide a better check and correct than tasks that do not require reasoning.

- They require the student to make sense of the topic, linking it to their prior learning and stressing the relations between different aspects of the topic. They deepen learning.

Some open tasks can help students to transfer their learning, as I show at the end of this chapter.

Types of task for your ladder

Here are some types of task to consider when you are building a ladder of tasks to teach your topic, starting at the bottom rung.

Simple recall of important points made in the receive phase, for example in your presentation

'What unit do we use to measure power?'

'Who is likely to be the district nurse's line manager?'

'What is a metaphor?'

'What would you do first to solve $2x + 4x = 24$?'

These are of course reproduction tasks, but they are important as they ensure students have learned the basic background or 'surface' knowledge and they prepare students for tasks higher on the ladder. For example, it makes sense to ask students *'What is a metaphor?'* before asking them to identify metaphors in a piece of text. You might think such simple questions are a waste of time, but they take little time to answer, and much more time is wasted by weak students trying to identify metaphors when they haven't clarified what one is.

So this lower rung on the ladder is similar to the check on prerequisite prior learning we saw in Chapter 6: 'relevant recall questions'.

Simple reasoning questions

'Why is power called a rate? What other rates do you know of? Give some examples.'

'Is "The moon was a ghostly galleon" a metaphor or not? Explain your answer.'

'Why can't you add together 3a and 4x?'

'Why do district nurses have a large proportion of elderly patients?'

Simple reasoning questions like these often seem unnecessary to teachers, but they are very helpful for learners, especially the weaker ones. They help to establish understanding at an elementary level, preparing students for more challenging tasks. They can help students to link the new learning to their prior learning and generally help learners to make sense of the topic. Also, if well designed, they check learning required for later questions.

Tasks required by the learning objective

You might have objectives such as the following for your lesson. If so, they must appear on your learning ladder:

'Students should be able to:

- *distinguish between power and energy*

- *identify metaphors used in a piece of writing*

- *solve simple linear algebraic equations such as $2x + 4 = 12$*

- *explain the role of the district nurse.'*

Clearly, if your objective is to get students to be able to explain the role of the district nurse, then you must ask them to do so.

But is this the only task you should set? No, students need simpler tasks lower down the ladder to prepare them for such tasks.

Will such a task create a deep understanding? Not necessarily; you might need to ask other questions that probe understanding more deeply to create links with other concepts and show the logic of the topic.

It's not hard to imagine a student being able to solve equations such as *2x + 4 = 12* without really understanding what they're doing or why. Students learn from concrete to abstract. Consider a task such as *'An interior decorator has asked you for an algebraic formula that would calculate the area of the four walls in a room of length L, width W, and height H.'* This task goes beyond the objective but, if going beyond the objective creates deeper, more meaningful learning, it is worth trying.

Similarly, simply identifying metaphors may satisfy the examiner, but what if you want your students to use metaphors in their own writing? What if some students will 'get' how to identify metaphors very quickly and then be bored while their classmates try to catch up? An open, challenging task such as *'Describe a dance video or sports event you have seen, making use of many metaphors'* might be useful here, even though it goes beyond the objectives that you have been set by an examining body or your department's shared scheme of work.

In summary, do attend to your objectives, but don't limit your teaching to them, even if they are provided by an authoritative source such as an examining body or a senior manager. Students need interesting tasks that challenge and stretch them and give a purpose to their learning, and these are usually open tasks. There is strong evidence that expert teachers take control of their curriculum, refusing to let others set a ceiling on learning in their classes (Ayers, 2004).

Types of reasoning task

The best reasoning tasks require students to think hard about the important aspects of the topic that you have explained to them or asked them to study. It's very important to set the task to focus on this vital content. For example, suppose a teacher considers it very important that her students learn that a district nurse must carefully liaise with other health professionals such as doctors and surgeons. In that case, a vague task such as *'Would you enjoy being a district nurse?'* would be unlikely to focus students' thinking on this liaison. If students are to learn how a district nurse liaises, then a better task might be *'Is the district nurse a solo performer, or is she one part of a team effort? Explain your answer with some examples.'*

The aim of reasoning tasks is to get students to *think hard about what you want them to learn*. Not all reasoning tasks are focused on vital content. In Chapter 13 we will see that reasoning tasks can also be used to deliberately teach the reasoning skills and study skills that are vital for your subject, for student attainment, and also in your students' life outside education.

What we hope to achieve with reasoning tasks

While you read through the example teaching methods below, bear in mind what we are trying to achieve with them. As explained in Chapter 1, we want:

- students to focus with some intensity on at least the vital content of the topic you are teaching

- a high participation rate – every student, not just some of them, thinking hard

- a check and correct for students: spontaneous or planned self-checks, peer checks, and opportunities for dialogue between students so they can correct any errors or omissions in learning

- a check and correct for you – opportunities for you to discover the strengths and weaknesses in students' learning so you can fix any problems and gauge progress

- an enjoyable learning experience

- an insight into the way your subject works, if possible.

Quality Learning boosters

How can you make sure every learner is going around the Quality Learning Cycle while they complete your task? One way is to make good use of what I call 'Quality Learning boosters' during the task.

Suppose some teachers decide on the following tasks for students to do in their classes:

'*Critically appraise an experiment to measure the power of a small electric motor.*'

'*Give the strengths and weaknesses of this job description for a district nurse.*'

'*Write a critical appreciation of the use of metaphor in this poem.*'

'*Tania, Safa, Antonio and Mabel tried to solve the equation $3x = 7x + 24$ in the four different ways shown. Which, if any, of these approaches are valid, and why? Why are the other methods mistaken?*'

Many teachers would simply set such evaluative tasks for students to do alone, after preparing students appropriately. But these tasks are hard and many students will need constant help and checks and corrects to succeed. How can we deliberately drive students around the Quality Learning Cycle while doing the above tasks? Luckily, research on teaching methods has identified generic methods that work exceptionally well and can easily be integrated into the delivery of tasks such as those above. They are also greatly enjoyed by students.

 Try this in the classroom

Models: For example, a teacher can model how to evaluate an experiment before asking students to do so. Students are shown 'models', that is, model solutions, exemplar work, worked examples, videos of expert performance, etc. The aim is to show how. Students can then study, annotate, and/or peer explain these models in pairs, as described in Chapter 7.

Spoof assessment: Models like those above can be imperfect, in which case students can assess, improve, complete or comment on these. See Chapters 7 and 11.

Pair check: Students mutually check and correct their partners' work, followed by dialogue.

Snowballing: Students work individually first, then work in pairs and then the pairs combine into fours, to gradually arrive through discussion at an agreed best piece of work.

Self or peer assessment: Students can assess against worked solutions, the answers, checklists, or assessment/success criteria, provided by you.

Assertive questioning: There can be class discussion of model ideas/ solutions, or of ideas/solutions suggested by students.

Teacher check: For example, *'When you have completed questions 1 to 4, tell me and I'll mark them.'*

Formative quiz: A quiz that checks but also corrects recall and understanding of vital content (see Chapter 11). Students can prepare for this quiz in small groups and the groups compete against each other if you like. The groups and teacher then help fix any misunderstandings found.

You can combine the above elements to drive students around the Quality Learning Cycle while they work on the task you have set, as shown in the case studies just below. This ensures that students do a good deal of self-correcting, which makes your marking less laborious as well as improving learning.

Case studies of boosters embedded into teaching

Here are a few examples that offer increasing amounts of support to students. In all of these cases, students would need to be suitably prepared before they start on these sequences of tasks. They would need suitable teacher explanation and modelling. But these sequences would be likely to work much better for many classrooms than simply giving the tasks for students to work on alone without the boosters, which I show in italics.

Students punctuating text given by the teacher

 **Case study**

Following suitable preparation including the modelling of good punctuation:

1 Students complete a task to punctuate a short paragraph alone.

2 When the teacher judges the class is ready, *students compare their work with a peer and discuss*.

3 The teacher provides a *model answer*, and students *self-assess* against it, with *peer discussion*.

4 The teacher explains any difficult points (*assertive questioning* is used to uncover misconceptions here).

5 The above sequence repeats with a more difficult paragraph of text to punctuate.

Students learning how to justify a design for a spreadsheet

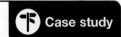 **Case study**

- The teacher provides *two model spreadsheet designs*, each with its own justification. In pairs, each student studies a different one of these, then *peer explains* the justification to their partner.

- *Assertive questioning* develops some criteria to justify a spreadsheet design.

- Working alone, students prepare a justification for a design they completed last lesson, *checking it against the criteria* developed in 'step 2' above.

- Students *peer assess* each other's justification, using the criteria in 'step 2', and suggest improvements.

- Students improve their justification and hand it in for a *teacher check*.

The mind map lesson described in Chapter 1 is another example of a teaching sequence that makes use of these boosters. Clearly, a lot of professional judgement needs to be used to decide which boosters are necessary and what sequences of them will best provide support for your students. As ever, the design of the lesson must meet the needs of the students in front of you. This is an art, not a science!

The basic idea is to embed highly-effective teaching strategies (boosters) into the task you are setting students. This supports learners on the task and forces them around the Quality Learning Cycle.

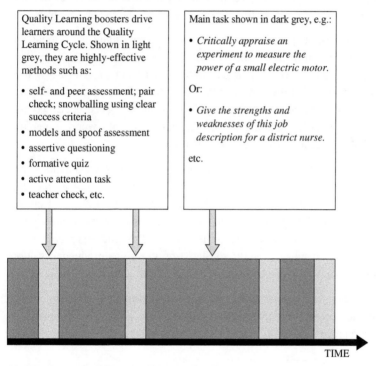

Figure 9.3: Embedding Quality Learning boosters

Boosters can be added to the high-performance methods mentioned in Chapter 8. This should make them even more effective. However, they can also be used on more routine tasks or teaching methods such as teacher-talk or reading or watching a video; this has the potential to make these more effective than they would otherwise be. It may not be necessary to stick to a diet of highly-effective teaching methods if other methods can be rendered highly effective by embedding boosters.

The delights and dangers of setting reasoning tasks

Researchers in the USA were dismayed to find that, despite using the enjoyable active reasoning task of designing a rocket, US students were not learning Newton's first law of motion as well as some students in poorer Eastern European countries. The European students were not designing a rocket, they were set tasks to reason directly about the consequences of Newton's first law, and so learned the first law better. Designing and making rockets is fun, but it might not get students to think about and learn what the teacher wants.

We want reasoning tasks that ensure your students think hard about the content you want them to learn. Not all reasoning tasks do that. By content, I mean the basic facts and understandings you want them to learn. It is important then, that the reasoning task itself does not distract students from this content, and is not too difficult or too time-consuming in itself. Otherwise, the reasoning task will dominate, swamping the students' working memory and distracting the learner from what you want them to learn.

Let's take as examples students videoing each other's explanations and discussions about health and safety in the kitchen, or about a character in Dickens's *Hard Times*. How much time and effort will be spent on the vital surface and deep learning you want them to acquire? How much effort will they spend on learning to use the video editor and arguments about the background music? Even if you insist on low video production values, students may be too distracted from essential content learning.

On the other hand, reasoning tasks can be much more interesting and motivating than routine tasks, tests and quizzes. So, if the reasoning task is simple enough it can improve the learning – if it is too hard, it will prevent learning.

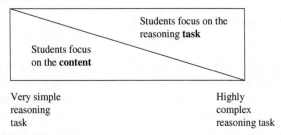

Figure 9.4: Will students focus on the task or content?

However, reasoning tasks of some kind are vital. Daniel Willingham, a most respected cognitive psychologist, has made the often quoted remark: 'Memory is the residue of thought.' He means that we learn what we think about: the harder and more often we think about facts, the better we learn them. There is more to learning than recall practice. The ideal reasoning task is one that is relevant to your subject, then both the content and the reasoning task itself provide vital learning in a 'double-decker' lesson (see Chapter 13).

Reasoning tasks force the learner to form relations within their constructs, and relations between the construct and prior learning. They deepen learning, as described in Chapter 1.

Suppose two teachers of horticulture were teaching students about the use of compost.

Teacher A *thinks, there is a lot to know about compost. I will lecture them about its production, characteristics, benefits and uses, and then set a worksheet that tests their recall.*

Teacher B *thinks, I will spend less time lecturing than teacher A, but will set a reasoning task, where students in groups will have to decide which plants in a garden get compost, which won't, and why, when there is a limited supply.*

In class B, students have been set a real-life task that will prepare them for the world of work and for academic progression. The vocational relevance and persuasive purpose of the task will motivate students in class B more than those in class A. The reasoning and arguing with peers in class B will create engagement. Also, as they argue students will focus on the characteristics, benefits and uses of compost. They may also reuse prior learning, such as the care of roses. All of this will help fix important content in the students' minds, as long as the task is well designed and managed by the teacher.

There is a more subtle and more important gain for class B: reasoning creates and strengthens the links between constructs and within them. This fixes the learning more firmly in memory, but it also makes the learning deeper and more functional, as we saw in Chapter 1.

Biggs and Collis developed the SOLO taxonomy (see Petty, 2009), which shows that knowledge acquisition transfers from surface learning to deeper learning (as shown in Figure 9.5).

Surface learning

Students add more detail.
They see the content in different contexts,
and from different perspectives.
They see logical and other relations **within**
the content.
They see logical and other relations **between**
the content and **other** content they have learned.
They see **general principles** that apply to both
this content and to other content that is not
otherwise related.

Deeper learning

Figure 9.5: We need both surface and deep learning

By 'see' in Figure 9.5, I mean 'come to understand'.

◉ Reflection

SOLO stands for Structure of the Observed Learning Outcome. Biggs and Collis found that as students deepened their understanding they created work that showed the progression described in Figure 9.5 above, comparing surface with deep learning. SOLO is used to grade students in some establishments: students' work is analysed to see where it falls on the continuum shown (see Petty, 2009).

Only reasoning tasks require students to create these logical and other relations; only reasoning tasks enable them to 'see' and fully understand the general principles that structure your subject. Telling is not enough. Mager reminds us that 'if telling were the same as teaching, we'd all be so smart we could hardly stand it'.

These relations and general principles that link different aspects of your subject must be created by the students in their own heads. They must create them in their own constructs. These manifest physically as neural links between brain cells.

The more relational links the student has within and between constructs:

- the firmer the construct will be embedded in memory both physically and cognitively

- the better able students will be at using their learning in real life and in unfamiliar contexts.

In short, reasoning tasks improve memory and understanding. I am sympathetic with teacher A; he is anxious to convey everything he knows. But he knows too much. The task for the teacher is not to maximise delivery, but to maximise the arrival of learning.

In Chapter 1, I described a girl, Jo, learning division. See the diagram on page 12. I pointed out that relational links between 'division', 'cutting up' and 'sharing out' helped Jo create a meaning for division. Thanks to her interlinked constructs, Jo might say: *'Divide means to, sort of, share it out.'* Simple as that statement seems, many primary students could not make that explanation. Their learning isn't deep enough yet. Quality learning requires very careful teaching.

We noticed that these relational links made her learning functional, enabling her to argue: *'This problem is about sharing out bulbs into different flower beds, so I need to divide.'*

Some widely applicable reasoning tasks that assist deep learning

The following tasks are hard, so students will need help. The boosters described on page 167 will often assist. In the same chapter we saw that matching, grouping, and sequencing cards or text boxes are most useful tasks.

Some widely applicable evaluative tasks

Evaluative tasks require students to assess the *value* of something. This usually requires them to think hard about what they are evaluating. So, if you want students to understand care plans, why not ask them to evaluate some good care plans? You can teach almost anything with an evaluative task. They are excellent for near the top of your ladder of tasks. Some typical evaluation tasks follow – in each case it is worth asking students specifically for a justification. For example: *'What are the best ways to heat a small home? Give your reasoning.'*

What are the arguments in favour (or against, or both)...

'What are the main reasons for using traditional slates rather than alternatives?'

'Why did the use of conventional timber for kitchen worktops fall out of favour?'

'How well does Wikipedia explain antibiotic resistance?'

'Is there bias in this manufacturer's website account of nutritional supplements?'

'What are the strengths and weaknesses of this plan?'

'What is the evidence for X?'

Compare and contrast (same-and-different diagrams help enormously here; see Chapter 3)

'What are the similarities and differences between viral and bacterial infections?'

'Compare and contrast Hughes' and Larkin's use of metaphor in the poems we've studied.'

What would happen if...

'What would happen if rivers dried up before reaching the sea?'

'What would happen if the government banned the production of diesel cars?'

'What would happen if you tried to use a graph to solve this exponential problem?'

How could you improve...

'How could you improve the employment prospects of newly-trained plumbers?'

'How could you improve this essay on Charles I?'

'How could the foreign policy of Atlee's government have been improved?'

'Can you improve on this solution?' (to a mathematics problem)

Review/evaluate/rate/assess... (the tasks above may help prepare for this)

'Evaluate the customer services procedure in the case study.'

'Review the various methods of image generation we have seen on this course.'

'Review the equations we have seen in this mechanics unit, stating their uses and limitations.'

Which are the best...

'Which are the best ways to motivate senior employees in media companies?'

'What is the best way to include depreciation in interim accounts?'

'What is the safest way to store music files, and why?'

'Does X give good value for money?'

'Does X give good value for effort?'

'Is X fit for purpose?'

'What are the alternatives to X?'

Which of these is the best...

'Which of these care plans most suits Mrs Gregory in the case study, and why?'

'Which city provides the best public transport?'

'Which of these knives is best for slicing apples?'

Evaluate using specific criteria

'Comment on the reliability and validity of this experimental design.'

Reflect on your experience

'Reflect on how you created your design and what you would do differently had you more time.'

'Does your management style encourage intrinsic or extrinsic motivation in your staff?'

'How did your shopping trip go? What would have helped you?' (Students with learning difficulties)

Search for counterexamples

'Are there circumstances where extrinsic motivation works better than intrinsic?'

'"The USA abhors totalitarianism, that's why it got involved with wars in Central America." What counterexamples are there to this claim?'

If you want students to evaluate in a particular way, you will need to model this, as described in Chapter 7. For example, if they are to evaluate a biology experiment using the concepts of validity and reliability, and so on, you will need to evaluate a few experiments yourself in this way, thinking aloud while you do so. Obviously, the concepts of validity and reliability would also need teaching.

Evaluative tasks can prepare students for writing, as can the ideas in Chapter 10.

 Just so you know

Students assessing work is an evaluative task

Evaluating work in order to learn is sometimes called 'spoof assessment' (see Chapter 11). For example: 'Here is Ahmed's account of the use of metaphor in this poem. What are the strengths and weaknesses of Ahmed's account?'

Students need to be prepared for evaluative tasks in two ways. First, they need to be familiar with – and understand – they are about to evaluate, so evaluative tasks should nearly always be at the end of a ladder of tasks designed to familiarise students with what they will evaluate. For example, to compare and contrast the roles of a district nurse with a practice nurse, students must be familiar with the roles of both.

Second, students need to understand exactly what you want them to do when you ask them to, for example 'evaluate' or 'give arguments for and against' or 'compare and contrast'. You will need to model the evaluative processes that you want your students to use, thinking aloud, as explained in Chapter 7. Double–decker lessons can then develop these evaluative skills, as described in Chapter 13.

Although students need to understand the content in order to evaluate it, the process of doing an evaluation will deepen their understanding of the content further. So even if an exam does not require students to evaluate but just to recall content, it is often worth setting evaluative tasks. They deepen understanding, are often more interesting than lower order tasks, and they prepare students for progression onto more demanding courses.

As ever, it helps to embed boosters when students work on these tasks. The following methods both require evaluative thinking, and both do exceptionally well in rigorous trials. They embed boosters and it's worth noting how.

Off–the–peg evaluative tasks with embedded boosters

Hypothesis testing

This method requires students to think hard about the content you have taught or are teaching. The teacher gives students a 'hypothesis', that is, a statement about what they have just learned, which is partly true and partly false.

A history teacher gives the students the statement: 'Cromwell's motivation was religious.'

A building construction teacher shows students a design for shuttering a trench with the statement: 'This is the best design for shuttering a trench.'

A business studies lecturer gives students a marketing plan along with the statement: 'This is an ideal care/marketing plan for our Red Lion Hotel.'

A mathematics teacher gives students a problem and its solution, but the solution is in some senses incorrectly worked: 'Here is a proposed solution to that problem: what do you think of it?'

An English literature teacher gives students the hypothesis: 'Hamlet hates his mother.'

The method opposite is then followed.

🐢 Try this in the classroom

1 Students work alone to decide arguments both for and against the hypothesis. This might require students to give evidence for their views or justify them in some other way. For example, finding supporting evidence in a text or handout.

2 These ideas are then snowballed: students get together in pairs to combine and improve their arguments for and against. Then the pairs could get together into fours, to again combine and improve their arguments.

3 You now use assertive questioning, as described in Chapter 5. You ask the groups, one by one, to give one argument in favour of the hypothesis. You don't evaluate arguments at this stage, you just thank students for their ideas. Once an argument is given by a group, you ask the class if they agree with it or if they would like to amend it. If the class agrees, you write it on the board (even if *you* disagree with it!).

4 Having collected all the 'agree' statements from the groups, you do the same for 'disagree' statements, again writing those 'disagree' statements that the class approves of on the board.

5 Only now do you evaluate the statements made by the class. This method gives you a very rich and detailed account of your students' understanding and its weaknesses. You can now correct misconceptions and errors in your class's reasoning.

This method is a very useful task to prepare students for writing an essay, for example in history, economics or English literature, or for preparing students for a task on a vocational assignment that involves extended writing. If you use the task in this way it is worth pointing out to students that they could go through a similar process to prepare for writing tasks that require them to evaluate.

Academic controversy

This method is similar to 'hypothesis testing' above, but is more active. It requires two or more conflicting points of view, one of them not obviously much better than the other. For example:

'Do prisons work?'

'Is this marketing policy effective for a small country hotel?'

'Is this mathematical procedure sound?'

'Is this account of Harold Wilson's premiership biased?'

You can make almost any topic into a controversy by presenting an argument or policy and asking whether it is right or wrong, effective or ineffective, etc.

The method requires some emotional maturity in your learners. You may need to stress that they will need to listen without getting angry.

My description below assumes that there are just two points of view, but it is easily adapted for more.

 Try this in the classroom

1 Students are allocated a position to support or contest the statement, given materials that explain the topic, and, if really necessary, some hints about their point of view. They research and prepare their point of view and its justification, preparing a persuasive 'best case possible' for their position. They could pair up with someone else who is preparing the same point of view to do this. They could also work in groups.

2 Students are randomly assigned to a peer with the opposing point of view to theirs (or into groups of four with two students for each point of view). Sides take turns to present their position in as persuasive a manner as possible. No interruption from the other side is allowed at this stage.

3 Once both views have been expressed, students engage in an open discussion in which they argue forcefully against the other side, and rebut any points made by their opponents in step 2 above.

4 Integration: students drop their advocacy roles. They try to reach a consensus on the issue by considering both of the two positions.

Optionally, between steps 3 and 4 above, students can swap positions and present the other position as accurately, completely, persuasively and forcefully as they can. If you feel mischievous, you can spring this on students and make a teaching point about how badly they listened earlier on! Students can check each other's arguments for the swapped positions.

Again, this method can be an excellent way to prepare students for an extended writing task

The top of the ladder: open tasks that attempt transfer

As a schoolkid, I could do fractions but couldn't do percentages. Then my teacher pointed out that percentages *were* fractions (45/100 is 45%) and this helped me enormously. Suddenly percentages made sense – they were even calculated in the same way as fractions. Teaching topics in silos is unhelpful.

This is a very simple example, but I hope that it makes the point that transferring learning creates more cognitive efficiency. It is known, for example, that experts structure their knowledge around general principles rather than around topics – this enables transfer.

So, mixed in with your other open tasks, or towards the end of them, you should try to get transfer of learning by asking students to look for links between the topic they are studying and other topics they have studied. This can be done in a number of ways.

Looking for similarities or links

'What other uses of ratios can you think of, including practical uses?'

'Where else have we seen hormones coordinating processes in the body?'

'Power is a "rate". What other rates have we come across in science studies and elsewhere?'

'What uses are made of the concept of power in our everyday lives?'

'How could you go about making more use of metaphor in your own writing?'

Looking for similarities and differences between related topics

'What are the similarities and differences between ratios and fractions?'

'Create a same-and-different diagram for Hitler and Mussolini.'

'How do you rate metaphor as a poetic device, compared with other poetic devices?'

Looking for general principles

'Where else have we seen this?' is a useful generic question that requires students to look for transfer. Other generic tasks that aid transfer are to ask students to:

Use general principles to explain the current topic, for example:

- *'Where else have you come across ratios in your mathematics or elsewhere?'*

- *'How is the principle that we must satisfy customer needs, related to stocktaking?'*

- *'What conservation principle could be used to explain the acceleration of a falling object?'*

- *'Where else have we seen the precautionary principle inform our studies?'*

- *'Where else have we seen the church battle the state?'*

And more difficult:

Ask students which general principles are in evidence in the current topic, for example:

- *'Which general principles did we use to derive the formulae?'*

- *'Which general management principles are evident in this staff complaint process?'*

Some students may see your subject as an esoteric game, played only in education. But transfer shows your subject to be a coherent whole, making it much more intellectually interesting, and it can also show it applying in the real world. Transfer creates links to other learning, which makes learning deeper and more easily remembered, and more functional, as we saw in Chapter 1.

Evidence for Chapter 9 on getting students to apply their learning

Chapter 14 establishes that the most reliable sources of evidence are summary evidence, and we should triangulate three sources.

Evidence from summaries of qualitative research: The references starting on page 284 all stress that students must apply their learning, and most mention that they should strive for deep learning. 'The best barometer for every lesson plan is "Of what will it make the students think?"' (Willingham, 2009). There seems to be a common acceptance in the references starting on page 284 that learning needs to go from easy to challenging, from known to unknown, and from concrete to abstract. This suggests a ladder of tasks. Transfer of learning is mentioned explicitly in the first three references, but they all make the case that this does not happen automatically, but must be facilitated.

Evidence from summaries of quantitative research: Hattie and Donoghue (2016) state explicitly that you should set different tasks and ask different questions as learners move through surface learning to deep learning and then onto the transfer of their learning.

Evidence from research on the most effective teachers: Both Ayres (2004) and Hattie (2003) find that the most effective teachers set challenging tasks, and Hattie finds that the tasks probe for deep learning. Lemov's book (2015) shows very high expectations throughout.

There is strong evidence for sustained student activity, and good evidence for a ladder of tasks for each topic, so these should be worth a try in your classroom.

Further reading

See also the principal references in Chapter 15 Further reading and references.

Free online resources

Search for 'active learning', 'problem-based learning', 'co-operative learning', 'transfer of learning' and 'Bloom's taxonomy'.

K. Ericsson et al., 'The role of deliberate practice in the acquisition of expert performance' (*Psychological Review*, Vol. 100, No. 3. 363–406, 1993). We learn from practising in a particular way, then checking and correcting that practice; the antidote to the 'intelligence is inherited' view. There is a summary of this most important paper on my website and you can download the original paper for free – search for title and author.

J.A.C. Hattie and G.M. Donoghue, 'Learning strategies: a synthesis and conceptual model' (*NPJ Science of Learning*, 2016). This explains the need for a ladder of tasks to teach students a topic, including transfer of learning.

R. Marzano, 'A theory-based meta-analysis of research on instruction' (1998). This can be downloaded free online. Search for title and author. Note: the paper is large and complex.

Books and papers

S. Allison and A. Tharby, *Making Every Lesson Count* (Carmarthen: Crown House Publishing, 2015). Brilliant and highly readable book with lots of detail on strategy.

P. Ayres et al., 'Effective teaching in the context of a Grade 12 high-stakes external examination in New South Wales, Australia'; (*British Educational Research Journal*, Vol. 30, No. 1, February 2004). Teachers in the top one per cent nationally for six years running – how do they teach? Fascinating!

P. Ginnis, *The Teacher's Toolkit* (Carmarthen: Crown House Publishing, 2002). Lots of teaching methods to try, lots of detail on these. Well worth a look.

D. Lemov, *Teach Like a Champion 2.0* (San Francisco: Jossey-Bass, 2015). This is an important book as it gives detail about strategies used by excellent teachers.

R. Marzano, 'The Marzano Compendium of Instructional Strategies' (Online resource by subscription published by www.marzanoresearch.com, 2016).

R. Marzano et al., *Classroom Instruction that Works* (Alexandria, VA: ASCD, 2001).

Chapter 10

Helping students to write essays, reports and assignments

I'm imagining students aged 14–16 here, but you can adapt the strategy for almost any learners.

I assume that the teacher has explained the topic the students will write about, or the content has been delivered in some other way. It will help greatly if students have access to a handout summarising the topic as they plan and write. The process of planning the writing will help students to understand the content, whether or not they write up what they have planned. So planning an essay is a great in-lesson activity.

I will call the piece of writing an 'essay' below, but the strategy works with any extended writing, a report, assignment, or dissertation, etc.

I assume the teacher has set a title for the piece of writing, which is open, challenging, and that makes the student think about the most important aspects of the content. (Not just a simple description task, where the student is expected to reproduce explanations already given by the teacher.) There is something to be said for giving this title *before* you teach the content, rather than after as most teachers do. Students then have a reason and a focus for listening to you.

In some forms of writing, for example certain 'reports', there is a set structure and the content must fit into this. In essays and some other forms, there is usually no prescribed structure, so the student must create the structure as well as deciding on what content goes where. Some cognitive scientists claim teachers should not teach students how to structure, plan and write essays, but I show how to teach academic skills (see also Chapter 9).

Staged strategy to plan and write

The aim of the nine stages below is to ensure students:

- **clarify and respond directly to the writing brief**, attempting to learn from and improve upon their past practice (stages 1, 2 and 3)

- **choose all the vital content** and arguments relevant to the brief (stage 4)

- **structure and sequence this content** in a logical way in a plan (stage 5)

- **deepen their understanding of the content**, rather than just reproduce content (stages 6, 7 and 8). This may be more relevant for older and more able students

- **understand the above process**, so they can use it appropriately without help (stage 8 and particularly stage 9).

If you want to adapt the process below, and miss out stages, try to do this in a way that still achieves the above bullet points.

1. Orientation

Students remind themselves of targets from previous writing tasks and set themselves targets. See learning loops in Chapter 11.

These targets can be process targets: *'I need to reread the essay title from time to time to make sure I don't digress.'*

Or product targets: *'I must remember to break my writing into paragraphs.'*

2. Preparation

Students study the essay title, underline key words, looking them up if necessary.

There may need to be class discussion to check understanding of what is, and what is not, meant by the essay title.

3. Studying exemplars

(This may not always be necessary.) If students are attempting a style of writing for the first time, for example a reflective journal or an unusual essay type such as a 'to what extent' essay, they may benefit from looking at an example, or a plan for such an essay. See Chapter 7.

4. The students brainstorm content for the essay

The teacher may improve these suggestions; this includes atomistic and holistic analysis, as described in Chapter 3 (see Figures 3.1 and 3.2 on page 43).

Atomistic analysis is where the content is cut up into parts and each part is considered one by one.

Holistic analysis is where all the content is looked at from different points of view or perspectives, or with different questions in mind. These 'spectacles' are best given by you when students are new to this form of analysis. Later they can decide on their own spectacles and you can check them before they use them if necessary.

This brainstorm for content could be done as a snowballing session where students work alone to begin with for a few minutes, then share ideas in pairs, then pairs combine into fours. Each grouping shares ideas and improves upon them. You then hear the ideas from each of the foursomes in turn, asking others whether they agree with those points and why. See 'assertive questioning' on page 81.

You comment on the brainstorm and the atomistic/holistic analysis done by the groups, then explain the strengths, and any improvements that could be made, to individual groups and/or to the class as a whole. You deliver any criticism of the students' ideas in a forward-looking and positive way: *'It would be better if...'* Students note these suggestions.

5. The brainstormed content is sorted

First this is sorted into conceptual groups and then into a logical order. The major themes in the content, including teacher suggestions, are put onto cards and students manipulate these to create a structure for the writing. Which cards go together? What causes what? Which goes first, second, etc.? Students in effect create a graphic organiser with their cards here. As mentioned in Chapter 3, different graphic organisers suit different types of essay question.

For a descriptive question such as *'What are the main functions of a marketing manager?'* a **mind map** or a **description table** is often best.

For a process, or for a cause and effect question, a **flow diagram** can be very useful. For example:

'Explain how a bill passes through parliament' (a process question).

'*What were the main reasons for Margaret Thatcher winning the 1987 election?*' (a cause and effect question).

For a comparison question, such as:

- '*What are the strengths and weaknesses of oil and gas central heating?*'

- '*Compare and contrast viral and bacterial infections.*'

- '*Distinguish between the forestry methods used in conifer and deciduous forests.*'

use a **comparison table** and/or a **same-and-different Venn diagram**.

'**To what extent...**' questions are comparison questions in disguise, as I explain below.

So the choice of graphic organiser reflects the structure required by the type of essay question.

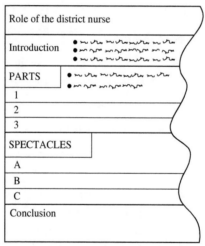

Figure 10.1: A description table for planning an assignment on 'The role of the district nurse'

Labelling categories: Each group of cards, or each section in the graphic organiser, is given a conceptual heading. For example, an essay on the causes of the Industrial Revolution might have 'developments in technology' as a heading for one of the causes. This cause may cluster a number of cards reading 'invention of steam engine' and 'invention of Spinning Jenny', etc.

Other causes of the Industrial Revolution might be *capital investment* and *the agricultural revolution*; each of these will have a cluster of cards giving the detail in outline.

Students do the card sort in groups so there can be discussion. You comment on the structure created by each group, and again suggest possible improvements to this structure, and to the content.

Students can now use the structure they have created as a plan for their writing. They need only decide on an order for the cards they have arranged, and then expand the points on each card into a paragraph or more. The writing that results should then be logically ordered. Even if students find it hard and so need your help, try to consider stages 6 and 7 below, but even if you pass on 6 and 7, please consider stages 8 and 9.

6. Relational thinking

Looking at the parts of the topic 'Causes of the Industrial Revolution', and the different spectacles used to look at it, are there any *relationships* between them? For example, students might notice that 'capital investment' would have helped fund 'developments in technology'. There is a relationship between these two causes.

7. Extended abstract thinking

Students ask: 'How does this topic/content or essay question relate to other topics/content or essay questions we have experienced?' For example, they ask:

'Have we seen something like this before?'

'If so, how is it similar, and how is it different?'

'Is there a general principle here, relating to both what I study now, and what I studied before?'

Extended abstract thinking is very holistic: for example look at the topic 'Causes of the Industrial Revolution' as a whole and try to relate it to distant topics. Students may realise the Industrial Revolution is just one example of where technological developments have changed human life and work. In this respect it is similar to the development of stone tools or the invention of agriculture, for example.

It often helps to plan a couple of essays before students actually write one, as planning is a difficult skill. It is worth practising planning by itself by missing out stage 8 below, but don't miss out stage 9. Once planning is done well, writing becomes easier. The plan itself is a useful note. The staged planning process is based on Biggs' SOLO taxonomy, which I have described in Petty (2009). Biggs and Collis (1982) noticed that students got higher grades when they used relational and extended abstract thinking.

It's important that students plan the content of their essay before they start writing the introduction. It's not possible to introduce your essay if you don't know what it is going to say. Introductions can set out the argument the essay will make in an holistic 'big picture' outline, or it can raise the questions that the essay will attempt to answer. The latter is easier for students as they can change their thinking more easily during the writing process.

8. Students begin to write, perhaps using a writing frame

This process can take place outside the classroom using the above preparation. You can download examples of writing frames (choose 'Approaches to generic skills teaching') here: http://geoffpetty.com/for-teachers/skills/

Writing frames can help students by suggesting vocabulary, structures for paragraphs or sections.

Students will need to draft and redraft work and then present it. During this process, students could peer assess, or peer edit each other's work.

9. Meta-cognition and bridging

This is vital if students are to develop the skill of writing independently. In the previous stages above, students will be concentrating on the essay question and on the content, but they also need to learn the skills and processes involved in planning writing.

To ensure this you say:

'*You have just planned and/or written an essay, (or report, etc.).*'

'***How did you do that?***'

'*Why did you do it that way?*'

'*What was the first step? What was the second?... Why?*'

'*What would have happened if you missed out that step?*'

Then:

'***Where else could you use that process?***'

'*Does it only work for the Industrial Revolution/history/economics, etc.?*'

'*Does it only work for essays/reports/assignments, etc.?*'

Students make a note of the process they adopted and the reason for each phase. Then they set themselves targets for the next time they do an extended piece of writing (see learning loops in Chapter 11). Students are reminded of their targets just before the next piece of extended writing and put their target at the top of the piece of work for you to see, so you can respond to any improvement or difficulties.

The above activities such as card-sorting and the creation of mind maps is called 'scaffolding'.

The dangers of scaffolding

The above process guides students in their planning and writing. We want students to be able to use something like this process independently, of course. So ideally this 'scaffolding' is gradually removed, though students still use the process or something like it without you prompting.

Coda: planning 'To what extent...' questions using Venn diagrams

Only some teachers need this. Venn diagrams are helpful in testing hypotheses or planning responses to *'To what extent...'* questions such as:

'To what extent did the Treaty of Versailles cause the Second World War?'

'To what extent was the use of force responsible for Hitler's rise to power?'

'To what extent do prisons work?'

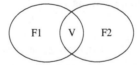

Figure 10.2: Same-and-different diagrams assist 'to what extent' writing

For the first essay title above, the circle on the left could be the Treaty of Versailles, the circle on the right the causes of the Second World War. The overlap, V, is causes of the war due to the treaty. F1 is aspects of the treaty that did **not** cause the war. F2 is causes of the war **not** due to the treaty.

With *'To what extent do prisons work?'*, the circle on the left describes the nature of prisons, and the right-hand circle describes what it means to 'work'. The extent to which prisons work is shown by the overlap. Aspects of prisons that **don't** work is F1. Aspects of 'working' **not** provided by prisons is F2. It's rare for students to manage a *'To what extent...'* question well without some sort of scaffolding like this.

Structuring writing with organisers

 **Case study**

Here's a good way to show students how to structure writing with organisers. A teacher introduces a description table by asking students to use one to write a note for his lesson on the impact of Internet shopping on retail in the UK.

- After studying the topic, students work in threes to complete an A3 description table, first deciding on parts such as Internet shopping sites, methods of payment, etc. Then they choose 'spectacles' such as customer and retailer perspectives, and the impact on high streets (see Holistic analysis, or analysis by spectacles, page 44).

- Students write conclusion and introduction notes in that order.

- The teacher visits groups as they work, and each presents an aspect of their table at the end of the lesson.

- The teacher then 'bridges' by saying *'You have just planned an essay – how did you do that and why? Where else could we use a description table?'*

The table constituted a good activity for the lesson, and provides a great note as well. But this was a 'double-decker' lesson, teaching Internet retail *and* essay writing in the same lesson. (Chapter 13 has detail on double-decker lessons.)

Evidence for Chapter 10

 **Evidence**

See the evidence box for Chapter 13 Teaching study skills and academic skills: strategy training on page 253, which applies equally to Chapter 10.

Further reading

See also the principal references in Chapter 15 Further reading and references.

Free online resources

Search for 'meta-cognition', 'essay writing' and 'planning essays'.

Books and papers

S. Allison and A. Tharby, *Making Every Lesson Count* (Carmarthen: Crown House Publishing, 2015). Brilliant and highly readable book with lots of detail on strategy.

J.B. Biggs and K.F. Collis, *Evaluating the Quality of Learning: The SOLO Taxonomy (Structure of the Observed Learning Outcome)* (Academic Press, 1982). One of the greatest contributions to our understanding of what understanding means – highly influential. I summarised it in Petty (2009).

J.A.C. Hattie, 'The role of learning strategies in today's classrooms' (The 34th Vernon-Wall Lecture, British Psychological Society, 2014). This goes into more detail on the Hattie Donoghue model. You can download it for a small fee.

J.A.C. Hattie, J. Biggs and N. Purdie, 'Effects of learning skills interventions on student learning: A meta-analysis' (*Review of Educational Research* 66, pages 99–136, 1996). A seminal paper showing that academic skills, study skills, thinking skills and the like are teachable – if you do it the right way. There is a summary of this paper on my website.

J.C. Nesbit and O. Adesope, 'Learning with concept and knowledge maps: A meta-analysis. (*Review of Educational Research* 76, page 413, 2006). More readable than most meta-analyses.

G. Petty, *Evidence-Based Teaching* (Oxford: Oxford University Press, 2009). See also www.geoffpetty.com

Chapter 11

Methods to check and correct learning

If you think back to the Quality Learning Cycle and the idea of co-constructivism in Chapter 1, it is easy to see why checking and correcting is so important. We saw that students don't usually construct meanings fully or accurately – at least at first – and so need to know their errors and omissions in order to improve their constructs and understanding. *You* also need a check on students' understandings to help improve these, and your teaching.

We have seen embedded 'check and correct' in nearly all the methods suggested in earlier chapters. For example, in Chapter 1 we saw a way of checking and correcting students as they worked towards creating a mind map.

I use the term 'check and correct' because the terms 'feedback', 'Assessment for Learning', and even 'formative assessment' are often misunderstood to mean:

a. what the teacher writes on students' written work (not what a student *does* as a consequence of these teacher comments)

b. a formal process such as a test or piece of written work

c. assigning marks or grades to students' work

d. keeping data on students' marks to assesses their progress.

But you can't fatten a pig by weighing it. So none of a–d above will impact learning as much as checking a student's learning and then correcting both their work and their understanding, as is done in the strategies that follow. Indeed, assigning grades has been shown to actually reduce attainment for at least half of learners, as I explain below.

The main purpose of the methods in this chapter is to get students to improve their own performance by making it increasingly clear what the goals and success criteria are, how these can be achieved, what students have done well and what they haven't, and how they could do it better. Why monitor students' marks when you could be improving them?

Check and correct should give priority to students:

a. developing a deep understanding of the task, the goals, and the success criteria for the tasks they have been set

b. examining good work to determine success criteria

c. developing a repertoire of ways to meet success criteria

d. checking and correcting their own and each other's work so that they learn how to improve their own work independently

e. talking in pairs or small groups about their work and ideas, especially in order to make progress on a–d above.

And!...

f. Check and correct should also be focused on your teaching of the topic, so you can adapt it to make good any weaknesses in learning.

The aim of check and correct is not for the teacher to fill in their mark book. The aim is for the students to improve their understanding and their work in progress. A related aim is for you to improve your teaching.

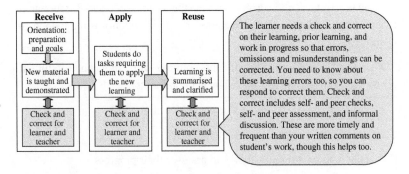

Figure 11.1: Students' constructs need checking and correcting

Common and best practice compared

Let's compare two imaginary case studies to see why a good-quality check and correct for the students and teacher is so important. In the first case study 'Janet' describes *common* practice, and in the second 'Tina' describes *good* practice. We will imagine that these two teachers have similar experience, and have parallel groups of students of the same ability. To begin with we will eavesdrop on the teachers' first lessons on drawing a graph.

> **Janet**  **Case study**
>
> **1** Janet first explains how to draw a graph, showing how on the board.
>
> **2** She asks some questions to check understanding and the questions are answered well by volunteers.
>
> **3** Then she sets a task to complete some graphs in class.
>
> **4** Students complete the graphs while she circulates, giving help where necessary: for example, *'You need to make sure you have a unit as part of your label.'*
>
> **5** She collects the work in and takes it home for marking.
>
> **6** She marks the work by giving it a mark out of ten, and by writing comments on the work such as 'label axes', 'good' or 'neat work'. She records the marks in her mark book.
>
> **7** She gives the marked work back to her students in the next lesson and discusses weaknesses in the work with her class.

Janet's approach is so common many teachers would be at a loss to know what was wrong with it, but compare it with Tina taking a similar class. There are several differences: see if you can spot them and their purposes:

> **Tina**  **Case study**
>
> **1** Tina asks her students what they already know about how to draw graphs. She writes up salient points they make on the board.
>
> **2** She discovers they know a surprising amount already, but little about how to choose a scale, which she then describes. She shows some examples where the scales were badly chosen and asks what's wrong and how to fix it.
>
> **3** She asks students to devise criteria for a good graph. Students work in pairs, and make suggestions such as *'All axes labelled with a unit'*. She writes agreed criteria on the board.
>
> **4** She sets students some graphs to draw and tells them that they will be peer assessed.

5 Students complete their graphs while she circulates to give help where necessary. If she spots a weakness, she says: *'Look at the criteria for axes. How have you done?'* She uses the answer to diagnose any student difficulty and to help them.

6 While they work she reminds students to check their own work against the criteria before the peer assessment.

7 She collects the first graph from each student and gives these out for peers to mark.

8 Students mark their peer's work against the criteria agreed in step 3 above, writing comments in pencil. She circulates to help this process.

9 The work goes back to the rightful owner and she leaves a little time for them to read the comments on their work, to check the marking, and to improve the work. She asks two students whose work she was not happy with to redo it and to submit it to her at the start of the next class.

10 She asks what issues came up in the marking and clarifies a few points.

There are more steps in Tina's approach but some won't take long, for example 6, 7, and 10. Step 1 might actually save time. Black et al. (2003) describe how teachers who made use of Tina's steps 1 and 2 found that on average these steps saved more time than they took.

Even if Janet does teach it quicker, her students will learn it slower. They will be less clear of the goals and will make more mistakes, and some will practise these mistakes many times before Janet discovers and corrects them. Lots of class practice and homework will be required to correct misunderstandings; even so, the weaker students may never become competent.

What is the difference in their two approaches, and what beliefs about learning cause them?

Janet's approach: is to teach, test the learning, grade it, and then move on. She does give students some comments on how to improve, but her main aim when marking is to grade the work as accurately as possible.

A common assumption behind this approach is that learning quality and quantity depend on talent or ability, and that the role of assessment is to measure this ability. Poor learning is usually attributed to a lack of ability, flair or intelligence.

Tina's approach: Tina is a co-constructivist teacher, and believes that ability is not innate, but learned. She finds out what students already know, corrects any misconceptions, and then builds onto this. She wants students to understand the goals well enough to be able to give *themselves* good, continuous, informative feedback on their progress towards the goals.

Her approach to assessment is to make the goals clear, to diagnose errors and omissions in learning and then to correct these. In short, she sees the purpose of assessment as improvement, not measurement. Weaknesses in learning are attributed to a misunderstanding of the goals, or more likely, lack of practice. I hope you noted her use of boosters such as self- and peer assessment. With a weaker class she may have used others such as modelling.

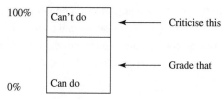

Figure 11.2: Common practice: teach, test, grade, and move on

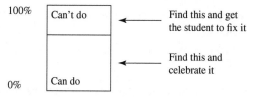

Figure 11.3: Best practice: 'Find faults and fix'

Medals, missions and goals

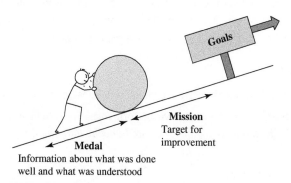

Figure 11.4: Mind the gap!

In a highly influential journal article, Sadler (1989) showed that when completing a learning task students need feedback that gives them *information* about the quality of their work, not just generalised praise and encouragement.

He argued that whether you were teaching yourself or being taught by another, there were just three things that you needed to know. I call these the goal, a medal, and a mission.

The goal

This is what students are aiming for, and is the nature of good work: the objectives, the proper interpretation of the tasks they have been set and of the success criteria or assessment criteria. The goals express the nature of excellence for this task. It is not easy to make these clear to students especially, as not all expectations are explicit, for example *'Slang should not be used in essays'* or *'Don't use American spellings.'*

A medal

This is where the student is now in relation to the goal(s).

- Task-centred information on what they did/did not do well, in terms of the goals. This needs to be in the form of informative comments, not grades or marks, as we will see. For example, *'Your axes are correctly labelled'*, not *'Good graph'* or *'9/10'*.

- These 'medals' can be for process (*how* they did it), for example *'Your essay plan is logically structured.'* Medals can also be for the product (*what* they did), for example *'The opening paragraph summarised the issue well.'*

- Overall grades and marks are not medals as they don't give detailed enough information about *what* aspects of the task were done well, and they distract students from the task, making students focus on their egotistical response to the grade. This is explained later.

A mission

This is how to close the gap between where the student is now and the goal(s).

This is a specific target to improve performance. You might have process targets: *'Check your work against the criteria before handing it in'* or product targets: *'Make sure your axes are labelled.'*

Missions could include:

- corrective work or other improvements on work: *'Please rewrite the last paragraph, adding a justification.'*

- very short-term targets that are forward-looking and positive for future work. It is common for 'missions' to be backward-looking and negative, for example *'There are too many spelling mistakes'*, when they should be forward-looking and positive, for example *'Next time, check your spelling.'*

 Consider

Turn backward-looking and negative comments into forward-looking positive comments.

Process mission:

'Your rough notes were not structured well enough before you started writing' is backward-looking and negative.

'Next time, get your notes logically structured before you start writing' is forward-looking and positive.

Product mission:

'Your paragraphs are far too long' is backward-looking and negative.

'Break your paragraphs more often – whenever you change subject' is forward-looking and positive.

Missions should be challenging but achievable, and if possible for process as well as product. Forward-looking and positive comments sound like advice, and are more easily accepted emotionally than backward-looking negative comments, which sound like criticism.

I have shown medals, missions and goals diagrammatically in Figure 11.4, imagining learning as like rolling a rock up a slope. Hopefully, the rock is not quite as heavy as it looks! The idea of medal and mission is explored in more detail in Chapters 6 and 43 of Petty (2014).

Students can get this informative check and correct from themselves (self-assessment) and from others (peer assessment), as well as from the teacher; but eventually they must learn to provide it for themselves.

 Also see

The importance of 'mission'

A big meta-study by Kluger and DeNisi (1996) found that feedback only leads to learning gains when it includes guidance on how to improve (a mission). See the methods below, which provide medals, missions, and goals.

Students need to give themselves checks and corrects to improve work in progress

Sadler explains that students need to be able to give *themselves* feedback *while they are working*. Otherwise they will be unable to succeed with tasks, or to improve. To do this they need to understand the goals and to be able to evaluate their work in progress against these. See Figure 11.5 below.

In the Janet and Tina examples above, Janet wrote *'neat work'* on some students' work and praised them for finishing. So a weak student may think the main goal is to work neatly and finish quickly, and they may believe they have drawn a good graph when they haven't. Until they understand the real goals and success criteria, can evaluate their methods and their work in progress against these, and until they know how to fix any deficiency they find, then they cannot improve. *'I know the scales are wrong on this graph, but how do I fix it?'* In short, self-assessment skills are a prerequisite for learning. The cycle in Figure 11.5 shows why.

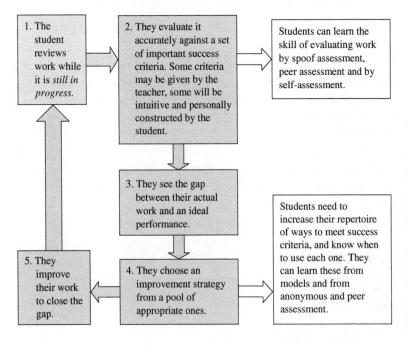

Figure 11.5: Students need to be able to improve work in progress

Students find it difficult to clarify goals

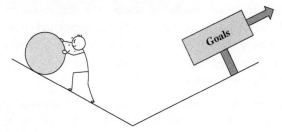

Figure 11.6: Failure of intent

Many students suffer from 'failure of intent'; that is, they are trying to do the wrong thing because they have misinterpreted the tasks and assessment or success criteria. Consequently, they are striving in the wrong direction. They fail not because they are *unable* to produce good work, but because they don't know what it is. Learning what good work looks like is best done by modelling, as we saw in Chapter 7.

Understanding how to justify an argument or what is meant by a 'viable marketing plan' is what Sadler calls 'guild knowledge', and we need to bring students 'into the know' about this. Students are not likely to score until they know where the goalposts are. Chapter 7 shows how to do this.

Grading degrades learning

What sort of feedback maintains students' interest and improves learning most? In a seminal experiment, Ruth Butler gave students a series of three tasks, each followed by feedback. Her experiment included both the most-able 25% of students and the least-able 25%.

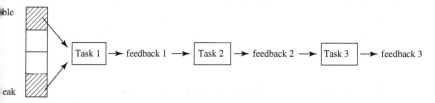

Figure 11.7: Butler (1988)

Butler gave her students one of three types of feedback:

- A third received comment only.
- A third received grades only.
- A third received both comments and grades.

Each third was a mix of the most-able and least-able students.

Butler found that the students' performance improved by 33% if they received comments-only feedback, which was like medal and mission feedback. However, if they received a grade, or a grade and comments, their performance declined. Why? When graded, weak students despaired: *'I can't do this';* and the more-able students became complacent: *'I got a B, so why should I read the comments, let alone act on them?'*

The interest of low achievers in the tasks was undermined by grading, but the interest of the more able was sustained at a high level throughout, though they were not interested in reading the teacher's helpful comments. Are you surprised!?

As students climb the attainment slope, the 'better' students tend to stay in front and the 'weaker' ones behind. Black et al. (2003) argue that for this reason summative grading carries an unintended hidden message that ability is innate rather than learned: *'I always get good/bad grades so I must be good/bad at this subject.'* This is a very disempowering message for at least half the learners, as Butler and others have shown.

This is a serious problem, as students' work must often be graded to meet the needs of examining bodies. In any case, students need to know how they are doing so they can plan for progression or careers. But how *often* do they need this graded summative information that measures their learning, rather than formative information such as medals and missions?

This depends on the course, but on many full-time courses summative information once or twice a term may well be sufficient, in some cases less often. An exception might be if a student is failing. Other strategies for coping with the grading problem are given at the end of this chapter.

Do your students crave grades? Black et al. (2003) found that students prefer marking to be in pencil rather than red pen, and to be legible and understandable, but found they were very happy not to be graded. Their teachers were very surprised by this!

Medal and mission feedback is non-judgemental about attainment

To avoid the problem that grading can lead to despair or complacency, medal and mission feedback should *accept* the student's present position on the rock-rolling diagram in Figure 11.4 without judgement. Whether the learner's attainment is high or low, they need to know what they did well and what they need to do to improve. This creates a 'task focus', in contrast to an 'ego focus'.

Consider

Carl Rogers stressed the importance of 'unconditional positive regard' in supporting learning over 60 years ago.

Black et al.'s review included a close look at research on the feedback actually given to students by their teachers. They found that, even when giving formative feedback, teachers tended to respond (consciously or not) to the learner's class position.

- Able students tended to get medals but no mission – they weren't stretched.

- Weaker students tended to get a mission but no medal – their effort and learning was not acknowledged.

However, there was a disturbing exception. Students of very low attainment tended to get 'empty praise'; that is, praise with no information about what was done well: *'Well done, Jo'* or *'You've worked well today, Peter. I'm proud of you.'* So they didn't get 'missions'.

The weakest learners got the least helpful check and correct information. These are the very learners who will find it difficult to work out for themselves what they have done well or what they need to improve. In effect, they were being prevented from learning by poor-quality feedback.

The psychological effects of judgemental and informative feedback is summarised in Figure 11.12 at the end of this chapter.

Checking and correcting in the lesson

How can we make sure all learners get clear goals and high-quality medal- and mission-style feedback? Don't forget that *you* need a check and correct on your teaching of the topic too, so that you can adjust your teaching. Here are some methods to try in the lesson; later I look at methods than can be used between or after lessons.

We saw above that students need to be able to check and correct their own work, while they work. This is a difficult skill, but can be established if students climb a staircase of experiences, as described below and in Figure 11.8.

Self-assessment, peer assessment and anonymous assessment

Below is a sequence of activities designed to develop students' abilities to make accurate assessment decisions independently. Students can never improve their work in progress unless they can make such assessment decisions while they work, so this is a vital activity. Essentially, you are teaching students to give themselves medals and missions and to understand the goals.

When a student hands in rubbish it is usually because they couldn't self-assess. It's a vital skill indeed, and in many cases it saves you more time than it takes.

The staircase to self-improvement

If the topic you are teaching is challenging, it makes sense to use at least one method from each of the sections a, b, c, d and e in Figure 11.8. This is because each of these sections prepares students for the section above. The sections eventually lead to good self-assessment: your main aim. Your student can now improve independently in the topic.

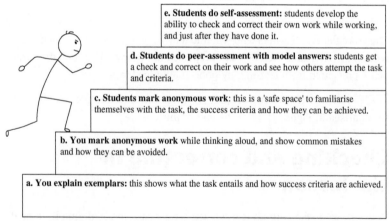

e. Students do self-assessment: students develop the ability to check and correct their own work while working, and just after they have done it.

d. Students do peer-assessment with model answers: students get a check and correct on their work and see how others attempt the task and criteria.

c. Students mark anonymous work: this is a 'safe space' to familiarise themselves with the task, the success criteria and how they can be achieved.

b. You mark anonymous work while thinking aloud, and show common mistakes and how they can be avoided.

a. You explain exemplars: this shows what the task entails and how success criteria are achieved.

Figure 11.8: The staircase to self-improvement in a topic

If the topic is straightforward, you can probably do without steps a, b, and even c. Just try peer and self-assessment. However, if you find students can't cope with one of the steps, prepare them for it with an earlier step.

The methods can be used during digital learning, e-learning and the like, and as homework if digital media is used to communicate between students for peer assessment. Most Virtual Learning Environments (VLEs) such as Moodle or Blackboard can do this for you. Of course, the methods can also be used in class, and below I describe the methods as they would be used in the classroom or similar environment.

For all the methods below, students can make their assessment decisions using one or more of the following as guides: worked examples, model answers, mark schemes, success criteria, assessment criteria and/or grade descriptors.

For simplicity, in the descriptions below I assume that you are using success criteria.

Can peers really help each other assess?

The evidence shows that peer assessment is exceptionally effective. However, some teachers think that peers will mislead each other, but this is only rarely the case if there is a model or mark scheme for them to refer to. It's worth noting the gains from peer assessment.

- The student knows others will see their work, so they attend to the task carefully (if they know peers will assess them in advance). They also attend to the marking as this will be scrutinised by the peer.

- The student studies the mark scheme with care in order to mark their peer's work fairly as their judgement will be held to account. They will carefully refer to any varied exemplars you have shown them to help their judgement in difficult cases.

- Students see other ways to approach the task – : the peer's and that described in the mark scheme, and perhaps in your exemplars. These may be better than their own approach, providing a 'mission'.

- Then they get their work back, marked by someone they don't trust, so they look hard at their work, the peer's comments, and at the success criteria or marking scheme to verify the marking. *'Why did Fabien think my answer to question 2 was unsatisfactory? The mark scheme says...'* Discussion follows. Consequently, students become clear about what they should have done, what they did in fact do, and how to close the gap between these. That is, they provide themselves with a medal and a mission, as well as more deeply understanding the goals.

- They study the task and its answers at least three times. They discuss the meaning of the task and the success criteria with a passion, as they are committed to their own work and to their marking of the peer.

- Their discussions go beyond the success criteria: *'You can't use slang words like "lousy" in a history essay...'* *'Why not?'* So students develop 'guild knowledge' as Sadler calls it.

These gains are prodigious. Compare them with students' work being marked by a 'Janet': the student picks up his paper, sees he has 7/10 and thinks 'good enough' and so doesn't read the teacher's comments. It is not surprising that some experiments have found that peer assessment with model answers doubles students' attainment. See Biggs (2011).

There are similar gains if students work in groups to help each other to peer or self-assess, as described below.

It does not matter if students do not make perfect judgements, and you need not correct them all. They will sort out most differences by looking at the mark scheme with care and most others they will ask you to adjudicate. As in all other areas of human endeavour, students learn to make good decisions by discovering when they have made bad ones. Your expert marking is needed too, of course!

Let's now look at each step in the staircase to self-improvement in detail. Please imagine that you are teaching students how to complete work that is very demanding, and where students have trouble understanding the success criteria and how to achieve them. An example might be a task to write a reflective learning journal in a specific way. The following methods climb the staircase that leads to the skill of self-assessment and self-improvement from the bottom up.

a. You explain exemplars

Having explained the task that you are about to set your students, you show students the success criteria and some 'exemplars', that is, examples of good work. This is described in detail in Chapter 7. You could show three pieces of example work: one adequate, one good, one excellent. You explain carefully how the exemplar work meets, or does not meet, the success criteria.

An alternative is to get students to peer explain examples as described in Chapter 7.

b. You mark anonymous work

Having established the task and success criteria, you show students an anonymous piece of work that is imperfect. You ask students to determine where it falls down and how it could be improved. Now you mark this imperfect work using the success criteria, thinking aloud, while the class watches. (This could be on the board or in the form of a video.)

The above sequence gives students corrective feedback on their understanding of the task and success criteria, and so how to make assessment decisions. Students should be thinking for example, *'What? I thought that work met the criteria, but the teacher says even more detail is required.'*

This is an example of 'cognitive conflict' being used to improve understanding. Any conflict between a student's assessment of the example work and your own assessment causes the student to change their understanding of the requirements of the task or the success criteria. This is a very powerful way to learn – it's showing how, and goes from concrete to abstract.

c. Students mark anonymous work

You give all students the same piece of imperfect work, which they mark using the success criteria.

Then you show the same work marked by you. We saw this in the modelling chapter.

(It's usually best if students mark work in pencil so they can change their decisions; this is probably the case for all self-, peer, and anonymous assessment.)

The advantage of anonymous work is that there are no egos involved, and the whole class is looking at the same piece of work, which enables class discussion. With self-assessment and peer assessment, everyone is looking at a different piece of work, and discussion is much harder. For example, if you are using anonymous work you can ask questions like: *'On the third line, should there be a comma after "Mr Smith"?'*

You can display anonymous work using handouts, electronic files or, if the work is short, with presentation software.

Students can mark anonymous work in pairs, in groups, or using snowballing, as described below. Remember that the aim is for students to establish a deep understanding of the requirements of the task and the meaning of the success criteria, and the various means of meeting the success criteria. It will usually help students to work in pairs or groups, as the discussion created effectively checks and corrects understanding.

Some teachers object to showing students work with errors in it. Sadly, students will see work with errors in it all the time – their own. They cannot be protected from error-ridden work. What they need is the capacity to detect errors and to put them right. This is precisely what this staircase to self-assessment achieves.

In pairs

Students can take turns to mark two different pieces of anonymous work, thinking aloud, while a pair checks.

'He's got a comma here but it should be a full stop.'

'Really? I don't think so.'

Alternatively, they mark different pieces of anonymous work at the same time, swap their work and then discuss any differences or points of confusion.

In groups

Each student has a different piece of anonymous work to mark Students take turns to mark their piece of work, thinking aloud, while the other students in their group watch and listen

'Well, she should have said she's using Pythagoras, otherwise it's fine.'

'No! She's forgotten to square root the answer...'

Assessment decisions can be agreed, or challenged and then discussed.

When groups have finished, you ask if there have been any difficult decisions and adjudicate where necessary. Then you can show the class your own marking of the same pieces of work

An alternative approach is for students to mark their two different pieces of work at the same time, then swap work to check each other's marking. Differences are then discussed.

Groups can be used in the same way for anonymous, peer and for self-assessment.

Snowballing

Snowballing is described on page 91. Students all mark the same anonymous piece of work alone, then they pair up to compare and improve their assessment decisions. Then two pairs combine into a group of four, which again checks the assessment decisions. Disagreements are discussed.

Finally, you show the same piece of work marked by you and ask if there were any decisions that students found hard so you can clarify their difficulties. Snowballing can be used to check anonymous, peer or self-assessment.

Looking at other people's work will show other ways to approach the task, and peer discussion will give different perspectives on the success criteria, and on how to improve deficient work Consequently, anonymous work is a great way to clarify the nature of tasks and success criteria

d. Students mark each other's work – peer assessment

Once students are successful at assessing anonymous work they should have the skills to evaluate and improve their own and each other's work However, they may still benefit from discussion in pairs or in groups to develop their understanding further.

How to

Throughout the next few pages I assume that students assess each other's or their own work using pencil. During e-learning students can write in green text or use comment bubbles. However, they could 'edit' the work instead, writing comments about how the work could be improved.

Peer assessment can be done in pairs, in groups, and with snowballing, as described above for marking anonymous pieces of work.

Many teachers alternate between students working on tasks and peer assessing those tasks. For example, a mathematics teacher sets students 12 problems to do of gradually increasing difficulty. Once both students in a pair have completed four questions, the students are asked to peer assess each other's work. Then they complete the next four questions, and so on. This approach makes students work with care. While my students at least seemed remarkably sanguine about handing in poor-quality work to me, they were more fearful of handing over rubbish to a peer. Of course, it is vital that ground rules are persuasively established, as described in Chapter 5, or you will find your students getting cross with each other.

If your students do not have the maturity to keep to ground rules, you might need to avoid peer assessment. Instead, spend more time on anonymous assessment to establish a good understanding of the task, the success criteria and how to meet them, then skip straight to self-assessment. They might manage self-assessment in groups or pairs though; this gives the benefit of a check and correct through discussion.

Peer assessment in effect provides a check and correct on each student's understandings and assessment skills. So peer assessment prepares students for self-assessment. Once students are able to self-assess well, they can improve their own work as they do it. This was the point of the whole exercise. Self-assessment is a prerequisite for self-improvement, so it's worth the effort of using the methods above.

e. Self-assessment – the only means of self-improvement

Self-assessment does not need to be done alone. If the self-assessment is done in pairs, in a group, or as snowballing, this can check and correct the self-assessment. We saw something very similar on page 206.

Self-assessment alone

All the student needs is the success criteria or the model answers. However, the student does not then get the benefit of having another student's perspective on their work.

It helps develop a student's self-assessment skills if other students are watching them self-assess as they mark their work and think aloud: *'Perhaps my answer would have been clearer if I'd drawn a diagram.'*

So self-assessment can be done in pairs, in groups, or with snowballing for marking anonymous work. This provides a check and correct of self-assessment skills.

One of the most powerful ways to prepare students for an exam is for them to mark their own attempts at old exam questions using your model answers. This vividly portrays a medal, a mission and the goals.

Independence

Once students have gone through the a, b, c, d, and e steps that they need, missing out some, or even most of the steps for less demanding work, they now have the capacity to improve work as they do it. They understand the requirements of the task, the success criteria, and different ways to meet these criteria. They are an independent self-improver and you can put your feet up. Well, perhaps that is an exaggeration, but they should need less help from you! Your marking will be much easier too.

What should I do if my students are bad at self- or peer assessment?

Don't give up. Teach them to do it better. They cannot produce good work until they know what it is, know different ways to create it, and know how to check and correct work in progress – that is, know how to self-assess. It's a vital skill, not just a trendy teaching method. If you hold class discussions on any difficulties or issues that arise, and if they practise, they will get better slowly.

More check and correct methods while students are learning

The next three methods are adapted from Dylan Wiliam (2011).

'See three before me' (C3B4Me)

While students are working in class they are asked to consult three peers before asking the teacher for help.

Traffic-light cups

Each student is given three cardboard cups: red, amber, and green. As the lesson progresses, each student shows the level of their understanding by displaying the appropriate coloured cup on top of the desk in front of them.

Red: I don't understand what is going on.

Amber: I sort of get it, but I am not confident.

Green: I understand it well and could explain it to others.

The teacher can say to a student displaying an amber cup, *'What don't you understand?'*, and then ask a student displaying a green cup to answer the student's question.

When the teacher judges it necessary, because there are some amber or red cups being displayed, he says: *'Okay, red cups over here with me. Those with an amber cup find a student with a green cup and ask them for help.'*

Check and correct at the end of a topic or subtopic

Diagnostic questions to improve understanding

This method is best explained by example.

Which statements below are true?

   A. Area is length x height for a rectangle.

   B. 2 metres squared = 2 metres x 2 metres.

   C. For a square, area is twice the length of one side.

   D. Area is measured in the units of length, such as centimetres or metres.

   E. For a rectangle, the area is always a bigger number than that for its perimeter.

   F. Area is the two dimensional space occupied by a shape, in square units.

Above are six statements on the topic of 'area', which students have just been learning. Students are asked to evaluate which statements are true and which are false. They end up with a list such as A true; B false; C false; D false; E false; F true. But as there are six statements, one can show that there are 64 possible lists of true or false. If there are four statements to choose from, there are 16 possible lists. Students are less likely to get their list right by chance or by guessing, than for a multiple-choice question.

To use diagnostic questions, you devise a number of summarising statements on the topic like those on area above, with some true and others false. Try to make the false statements express common misconceptions of past students. Display the five or six statements and ask students to work alone to consider which are true and which are false. Then students pair up with a neighbour to find and discuss any disagreements.

When they are ready, you ask students to display their answers for each statement one at a time. They do this by putting their thumbs up if they consider the statement true, and giving a thumbs down if they consider it false. You can scan the thumbs to see whether most of the class have 'got it' or not and who hasn't. Ask some students to give their reasons. Then you can confirm whether the statement is true or false with an explanation. If a lot of students have evaluated the statement incorrectly, you might need to reteach the point.

You can use assertive questioning to probe the misconceptions:

'Andy, why do you think C is false?'

Andy: 'Because area is measured in square metres, not just metres.'

'Anyone agree with that?'

Eric Mazur uses a similar technique, which he calls 'peer instruction', to teach physics at Harvard. It has doubled the rate at which students learn and is now quite widely used in higher education all over the world. He presents new information for about 15 minutes, then shows the diagnostic question or statement for what he has just taught, and goes through a similar process to that described above to get and discuss answers. However, he gives students electronic 'clickers', which wirelessly send answers to Mazur's laptop, enabling him to display the number of students who think an answer is true or false. Then he teaches for another 15 minutes, sets another set of diagnostic questions, and so on.

An alternative to using true/false statements is to set a short task that is carefully designed to diagnose the quality of student learning on the subtopic just taught. You could use a series of multiple-choice questions, for example.

The one-minute summary

This is a useful variation of the previous method.

 Students write a one- or two-minute summary of what has just been presented. They include their 'muddiest' point.

2 You give a model, for example your own key points.

3 Students improve their own or each other's summaries using these key points.

4 (Optional) You collect in the papers and address the 'muddy' points in the next class.

Reflective journals and personal targets

This method is widely used in developing professionals, for example in nursing, management, and of course teaching. It can also be used for younger learners, as described below.

Students write a few lines at the end of each lesson or week, describing what they have learned and what they are unclear about, along with personal observations. You might give them some questions to ensure that they focus on important factors:

* Did you bring everything you needed for this lesson?

* Did you follow the class ground rules?

* What have you learned?

* What did you find most difficult or unclear?

* How are you getting on with your latest personal target?

* Have you set yourself another personal target?

Whether or not you use questions like those above, make sure that your students complete their journal entry by setting themselves a personal target for the next class meeting or the next week or so. This encourages students to act on what they have learned from completing the journal.

A research study employing a similar method to the one above doubled attainment in numeracy. See Black and Wiliam (1998).

Find faults and fix methods

The following methods require that the learners directly address the weaknesses discovered by teacher, self- or peer assessment. They don't just provide a 'check', they also require a rigorous 'correct'.

Learning loops

Assessment proformas like the one below are often used for formal assessments, but you can devise your own and use them for any activity. They are best presented before the task is started so the success criteria are clear to students. The example below is for an essay, but the strategy could be used for any task, practical or academic. It is especially useful for tasks students must often repeat, such as writing an essay or refereeing a football match.

Essay writing assessment proforma Title: Name:		
Success criteria	**Self-assessment**	**Teacher assessment**
Did you relate each of your arguments to the essay question?		
Did you give arguments both 'for' **and** 'against': • the proposition in the essay question • any major points or conclusions you made?		
Did you give enough evidence, examples, and illustrations for each of your arguments?		
Did you prioritise the arguments for and against, and evaluate them?		
Did you draw a justified conclusion related directly to the essay title?		
Improvements needed for this essay		
Targets for the next essay		

To use learning loops with such an assessment proforma, you need a double box at the beginning of your assignment sheet or whatever you use to describe the new task. The student then writes the target from the *previous* task or assignment in a target box at the beginning of the next similar piece of work – see Figure 11.9. Students complete the new task, trying to meet their target. Then you assess the extent to which the student has met their target.

There are many more informal ways to use learning loops, for example you can remind students before completing a task that they have done this before and ask: *'What did you learn about doing this last time? What do you need to look out for?'*

When you hand work back, leave time for students to read feedback, correct work, and set themselves targets.

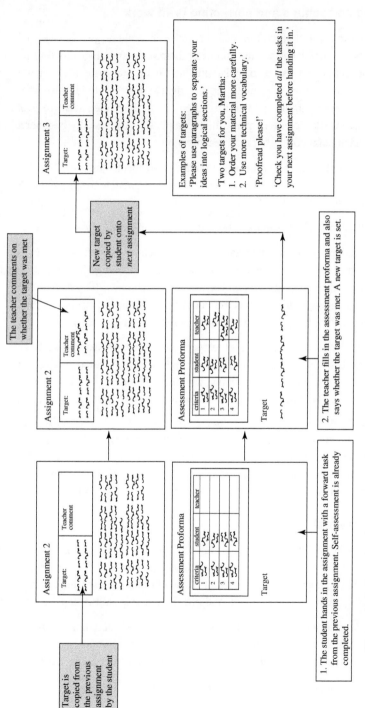

Figure 11.9: Learning loops: targets or 'forward tasks' for assignments

Doing corrections and correcting draft work

This doesn't sound much fun, does it? However, students getting tasks right that they initially got wrong improves their understanding and unlearns misconceptions. It can also make students feel more positive about their performance if they eventually 'get it right'. These methods also make students more careful in their first attempts as they often wish to avoid corrective work. However, errors due to simple slips can usually be ignored; it's fundamental errors that require correction.

1 Students complete an essay, exercise, worksheet, quiz, test, etc. This method can also sometimes be used on a summative assignment or for coursework in draft form.

2 Students' work is marked by you or with self- or peer assessment.

3 Students work in small groups to help each other with what they got wrong. You can help with this, of course. Encourage learners to use any errors to diagnose and correct misconceptions. *'Why do you think you/he got that wrong?'* (You could try choosing the groups yourself, arranging for one relatively strong student in each group.)

4 Students correct or improve their work. One way of checking this is to give students the exercise or quiz again the next lesson and ask them to do only those questions they got wrong last time. Another is to ask students to explain the right answer to a question they got wrong last time to a peer.

This strategy, like most teaching strategies, can be overused. Students may find it too dispiriting if you ask them to correct all their work, and they may well not be able to keep up! However, the method can also be underused. Students sometimes need to have another go at something if they are really to understand how to do it properly. If groups are supportive, this can be greatly enjoyed.

Mastery test

This method is suitable for checking the learning of vital knowledge and skills; it can be used in resource-based learning to assess whether a student is ready to progress to the next unit. It should only be used for low-order, simple reproduction learning or well-practised simple skills.

1 After teaching a topic and after class practice and homework, you confirm learning with a simple three- to five-minute quiz or test, requiring the reproduction of vital key points and skills such as:

- recall questions on key facts

- a number of simple calculations to do

- a practical activity that has been previously well practised

- some simple past paper questions, etc.

2 Students mark their own papers against model answers or mark schemes you give them.

3 Students note the questions they got wrong, and why. In mathematics it may help if they do these questions again, covering the answers while they do so.

4 There is a minimum acceptable mark of, say, 70–80% (it was an easy test on the reproduction of vital material). Students who get less than this take a retest when they are ready, perhaps a few days later; however, they only do the questions like those they got wrong the first time. Students also mark this retest themselves and the cycle repeats.

Lai and Biggs (1994) found that this method tended to encourage exclusively surface learning, so other tasks and assessments are required to foster a deep approach. It might also help if questions ask 'why', not just 'what'. Watch out for rote learning without understanding, even so.

Some teachers and writers, often called 'neo-traditionalists' or 'neo-trads', argue that repeated 'practice testing' is the best means of improving achievement. For example, Christodoulou (2016) has a chapter on improving formative assessments. Her prescription is to use short-answer and multiple-choice tests, apparently without any strategy to fix misunderstandings discovered in these tests.

Students assess each other by writing their own questions

1 Students work in small groups to write questions with answers, perhaps with a mark scheme. Each group could be given their own subtopic to write questions for.

2 You check these and get groups to swap or circulate their questions and answers.

3 Each group passes its questions for another group to answer, working as individuals. They may then swap papers or put their heads together to agree the best answers after doing the questions individually.

4 The work is handed back to the question writers to mark, and they point out how the work could be improved.

Rosenshine et al. (2016) found that students devising questions greatly improves comprehension.

Student questioning and 'mountain climbing'

This is less rigorous than mastery testing, but much more fun. I will describe a version of this game for typical 15-year-old learners, but it can easily be adapted for more advanced learners.

You appoint teams and give each team a subtopic from the last few weeks of teaching. For its subtopic, each team writes three or four reproduction questions on vital material, with answers. You check these questions and answers. Groups make enough copies of their cards for what follows.

 Consider

Wiliam and Leahy (2015) highlight that research on asking students to generate questions and answers for each other has shown that the approach produces very marked improvements in achievement.

The questions can be typed into a table in a word-processing application. (If you set 'autofit' to 'distribute rows and columns evenly', all the cards become the same size.) You can then print on thin card, with a different colour for each subtopic if necessary, and then cut them into question cards. Alternatively, they can be handwritten or an electronic version can be made.

Question:	Question:
Give two key characteristics that make a question suitable for a mastery test.	Give two key differences between a mastery test and a conventional test.
Answer: accept two from:	**Answer:** accept two from:
It should test vital knowledge.	The students must do remedial work.
It should be low on Bloom's taxonomy.	Everyone passes eventually.
The material must have been practised.	There is no mark, just pass, or not yet passed.
	Questions are low on Bloom's taxonomy.

Figure 11.10: Mountain climbing

Students work in pairs, preferably with question cards on every subtopic. Alternatively, card sets can be shared. In their pairs, students take it in turn to ask each other a question from the cards. If the other student gets it right, this student moves their counter up one square on a game board with a mountain drawn on it. There are almost as many squares up the mountain as there are question cards. If students do not get their question right, they keep their 'wrong card' and can study the correct answer during the game. One square before the summit of the mountain is a 'base camp' where students must take a second attempt at all their 'wrong cards'. The object of the game is not to get to the summit first, but for the team of two 'climbers' to both get to the top of the mountain.

This is about twice as much fun as it sounds, yet it has a very serious purpose. Mastery games can be used by themselves, or can of course be used to prepare for mastery tests.

Comparing notes: checking notes, mind maps or graphic organisers

Chapter 3 explained that students creating graphic organisers has been shown to be a very powerful way to learn. However, this method can work with written notes instead.

1 Students create their own notes, concept map or other graphic organiser.

2 Students compare their notes or graphic in groups of about three. They suggest improvements to their own work, and then to each other's.

3 The teacher shows a model note or graphic, or perhaps two. (You could save some from this activity last year.)

4 The groups notice differences between their work and the model, discuss these, and then suggest improvements to their own work, and then to each other's.

5 These improvements are made.

The next two methods are adapted from D. Wiliam's excellent *Embedded Formative Assessment* (2011).

Japanese catch-up

This method is often used in Japanese schools. Say you have 14 lessons to teach a unit of a course:

1 12 lessons are used to teach the unit.

2 At the end of the 12th lesson you give students a short diagnostic test or quiz.

3 The test/quiz papers are not marked by the teacher, who looks them over to discover what students find difficult.

4 Lessons 13 and 14 are used for remedial activity on the difficulties noticed in 3, above.

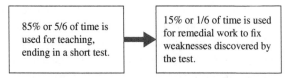

| 85% or 5/6 of time is used for teaching, ending in a short test. | 15% or 1/6 of time is used for remedial work to fix weaknesses discovered by the test. |

Figure 11.11: Japanese catch-up

Co-operative learning to increase student accountability

Many learning tasks are assessed with an individual mark for each student, or a mark for a group product. There is another method that works four times better that is hardly used.

1 You group students so they are not in friendship groups. One way to achieve this simply is to use random groups. Number round the classroom 1, 2, 3, 4, 1, 2, 3, 4... to create four random groups, then all the 1s get together to form one group, all the 2s to form another, and so on.

2 Set a task or tasks for these groups to help them learn something. Explain that this learning will be tested by a *short* test, and that students will take this individually and alone. The mark achieved by the group will then be one of the following (teacher chooses in advance):

- The same as the lowest mark achieved by any individual in that group.

- The same as the average mark of the individuals in that group.

- The same as the average of the two lowest marks in that group.

3 Students do the learning task, then prepare for the *short* quiz or test.

4 Students take the quiz or test as individuals and it is marked.

5 Groups get their group mark.

This method strongly encourages peer helping. It needs to be done in a spirit of fun – not too competitively. If one student gets a poor mark, you can blame the rest of the group for not explaining/helping well enough!

You marking students work

Comments-only marking is best: if you give marks, grades, or percentages, there is a danger that students will become less interested in improving their work or understanding, and more interested in how well they have done compared to others. You want them to focus on the task, not their ego.

Could you use a marking key?

This method is commonly used by teachers of languages, but can be adapted to any subject. You mark written work by writing codes in the margin to show that an error has been made on that line somewhere. However, the exact point where the error occurred and the detail of the error are not shown.

A typical code might be:

S for a spelling mistake

T for a mistake with tenses

SVA for a subject-verb agreement issue

P for a punctuation error

/ for a word that is not needed.

The student looks at your codes, identifies their mistakes, and then corrects them.

Why is the student not told the detail of their error and where it took place? Because the teacher hopes to develop in the student an *understanding* of what they did wrong and how to correct it, along with proofreading skills. This is best achieved by making the student hunt carefully for their mistakes and work out how to correct them. This approach may have a better chance of correcting the construct that 'made the mistake', than you simply correcting the work.

The backwards test

Why should the marking come last?

1. Students are given questions for a test they are about to take.

2. They work in groups to devise a mark scheme for each question in the test.

3. They compare their mark schemes and agree a class mark scheme.

4. Students take the test.

5. Peers mark each other's papers against the agreed mark scheme, then return them.

6. Students discuss disagreements and improve their answers.

If generalised criteria are devised, for example *'Label the axes of your graph: 3 marks'*, or *'Use quotes from the text to give evidence for, and examples of your points of view'*, then the questions in the test they actually take can be different from those they used to devise the criteria. This method is excellent for developing understanding of the success criteria.

Comparing judgemental feedback with medal, mission and goal feedback

Figure 11.12 summarises some key ideas in the Black and Wiliam review from 1998, 'Assessment and classroom learning', in the journal *Assessment in Education*.

Judgemental feedback 'Here is my measurement'	**Informative feedback** 'These are your goals, this is what you do well, and this is how to get better'
Characteristics of this feedback	
The feedback compares students with each other and encourages them to compete. It is 'norm referenced'. The teacher gives grades, marks, and comments that make conscious or unconscious comparisons with others.	There are clear assessment criteria and goals. Feedback consists of information about the extent to which these have been met. There are: medals: for what they have done well missions: showing how to improve.
Effect on self-esteem	
Judgement makes students nervous and protective of their self-esteem. So students avoid risks and challenges. The self-esteem of high-achieving students rises.	The student feels accepted, and that their efforts are being recognised and valued. **Self-esteem and commitment tend to rise and there is increased emotional involvement in tasks.**
Consequent learning strategies	
Maladaptive learning strategies *Surface learning* is likely. Their eye is on the grade, not understanding, learning or the task. The student memorises, seeks shortcuts, copies, etc. 'Right answer' syndrome.	**Effective learning strategies** *Deep learning.* Their eyes are on the goals, assessment criteria, tasks, and their 'missions'. High-quality learning aimed at understanding and improvement. As esteem comes from effort, not comparative attainment, students are prepared to take risks and accept challenges.
Students' learning theory	
Maladaptive and blaming learning theory 'Mistakes are shameful.' 'Effort shows you must be stupid.' 'Ability is the key and it is inborn.' Extrinsic motivation: It's only worth working if you get something out of it.	**Adaptive and blame-free learning theory** 'Effort is the key and it's up to me.' Mistakes are informative feedback. Intrinsic motivation: Learning is an end in itself.
Effect on low achievers	
There is reduced interest, effort, persistence, self-esteem and self-belief, and less emotional investment in learning. In some cases 'learned helplessness': 'No matter what I do I'm bound to fail.' The student withdraws and retires hurt, rejecting the teachers, college, etc. Hostility towards learning. Learning is seen as something for others.	There is increased interest, effort, persistence, self-esteem and self-belief. In time 'learned resourcefulness': 'There must be a way around my difficulties and if I find it, I will succeed.' 'Learning depends on time, effort, corrected practice, and using the right strategies.' Identification with the aims of the course. Learning is seen as an end in itself.

Figure 11.12: Judgemental and informative feedback compared

Evidence for Chapter 11 on checking and correcting learning

 **Evidence**

Chapter 14 establishes that the most reliable sources of evidence are summary evidence, and we should triangulate three sources.

Evidence from summaries of qualitative research: The need to provide students with feedback is universally acknowledged, and is mentioned in all the principal references starting on page 284. Non-judgemental feedback is strongly advocated by humanistic psychologists; cognitive psychology tends to stress informative feedback.

Evidence from summaries of quantitative research: Research reviews by both Hattie and Timperley (2007) and by Black and Wiliam (1998) stress that students need to understand goals, medals, and missions, though they don't use this terminology. With this information student learning is greatly improved, but it need not come from the teacher necessarily. Hattie stresses that the teacher needs feedback on student understanding in order to adapt and improve their teaching. The Education Endowment Foundation (EEF) toolkit gives feedback a pole position in the improvement of learning. Dylan Wiliam, a foremost advocate of formative assessment, has written influential books on embedding formative assessment (check and correct) into teaching.

Evidence from research on the most effective teachers: All the principle references in this area, starting on page 284, stress that excellent teachers give informative feedback. Lemov (2015) shows a multitude of ways in which excellent teachers do this.

Check and correct strategies have remarkable potential, and unless you do this very well already, experimentation with some of the methods in this chapter is likely to be productive.

Further reading

See also the principal references in Chapter 15 Further reading and references.

Free online resources

Search for 'formative assessment' and 'feedback', but remember that the aim is for students to understand the goals and get a medal and a mission – they can often provide this for themselves or each other.

Search online for a video on 'The power of feedback' about John Hattie's research review on this topic.

J. Chizmar and A. Ostrosky, 'The one-minute paper: some empirical findings' (*Research in Economic Education,* Winter 1998). Search for title and author at www.semanticscholar.org.

QCA, 'Assessment for Learning: Using assessment to raise achievement in mathematics: A research report' (2001). Download from: www.qca.org.uk/6311.html.

R. Sadler, 'Formative assessment and the design of instructional systems' (*Instructional Science,* 18, 119–44, 1989). A classic paper, a work of genius, and his insights often ignored.

Books and papers

J. Biggs and C. Tang, *Teaching for Quality Learning at University (4th Edition)* (Maidenhead: McGraw-Hill, 2011).

P.J. Black and D. Wiliam, 'Assessment and classroom learning' (*Assessment in Education: Principles, Policy and Practice,* 5, 1: 7–74, 1998). See also QCA (2001). For a readable summary, search online for 'Inside the Black Box: Black and Wiliam'.

P. Black et al., *Assessment for Learning: Putting it into Practice* (Buckingham: Open University Press, 2003).

R. Butler, 'Enhancing and undermining intrinsic motivation: The effects of task-involving and ego-involving evaluation on interest and performance' (*British Journal of Educational Psychology,* 58(1): 1–14, 1988).

W.M. Carroll, 'Using worked examples as an instructional support in the algebra classroom' (*Journal of Educational Psychology,* 83: 360–367, 1994).

D. Christodoulou, *Making Good Progress?* (Oxford: Oxford University Press, 2016).

A.N. Kluger and N. DeNisi, 'The effects of feedback interventions on performance: A historical review, a meta-analysis, and a preliminary feedback intervention theory' (*Psychological Bulletin,* 119(2): 254–284, 1996).

B. Rosenshine et al., 'Teaching students to generate questions: A review of the intervention studies' (*Review of Educational Research,* Vol. 66, Issue 2, pages 181–221, 2016).

J.A.C. Hattie and H. Timperley, 'The power of feedback' (*Review of Educational Research,* Vol. 77, No. 1 pages 81–112, 2007). Available free online.

P. Lai and J.B. Biggs, 'Who benefits from mastery learning?' (*Contemporary Educational Psychology,* 19: 13–23, 1994).

E. Mazur, *Peer Instruction: A User's Manual* (Prentice Hall, 1997).

G. Petty, *Teaching Today: A Practical Guide* (Oxford: Oxford University Press, 2014). See also www.geoffpetty.com.

D. Wiliam and S. Leahy, *Embedding Formative Assessment* (West Palm Beach: The Learning Sciences, 2015). Very practical ideas on check and correct, and a strong argument for using ladders of tasks in order to differentiate).

D. Wiliam, *Embedded Formative Assessment* (Solution tree, 2011).

Chapter 12

Reusing and reviewing the learning of a topic

At the end of a topic students are often confused about what is vital and what is detail. They can't see the wood for the trees. We need to ensure that their understanding is structured, as unstructured information is extremely difficult to remember. Also, learning needs to move towards deeper learning, making it more structured, stressing relations and other links within the topic, and between it and other topics. This will help us strive for transfer of this learning, even if this might be limited.

It has been chilling for me in researching and writing this book to discover that in my 25 years of teaching I did so many things wrong. Most teachers don't adopt the practice in this chapter, and nor did I. But adopting it improves learning greatly.

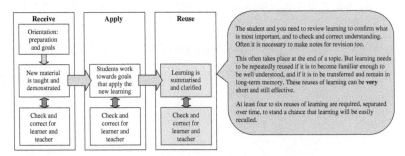

Figure 12.1: Reusing and reviewing will improve learning

Help! They forget faster than I teach

Do you ever get the feeling that teaching is like running a bath with the plug out? A colleague once told me, *'While I'm teaching them Edward II, they're forgetting about Edward I.'* Well there is a solution to this problem, it has been known for centuries, and it creates better learning in less time, but hardly anyone does it.

Suppose you were teaching the mathematical concept of 'ratio', as in *'The ratio of flour to butter in my shortbread recipe is 3:2.'* Imagine you have to teach this topic to two mathematics groups of near identical ability. You teach the two groups in the same way, taking two hours with each, except:

Group 1 has **massed practice**: you teach ratios in a single two-hour class.

Group 2 has **spaced practice**: you teach ratios for half an hour in four separate lessons. The rest of the time in those lessons you teach some other topic.

Otherwise your teaching to the two groups is pretty much identical.

Which group would do best? Most teachers, and most students, believe that the massed practice group will learn best; it's less confusing to do it all in one go, they say. But in trials, spaced practice wins hands down.

There have been many experiments on spaced practice, and a summary of the findings can be found in Hattie (2009) page 185. On average, the spaced practice class does more than a grade better. Given the strength of these findings it is surprising that so little attention is paid to how the teaching of a topic is distributed. Nearly all schemes of work trudge through the curriculum using a massed practice approach, yet we've known about the power of spaced practice for decades.

Students are less likely to forget if teaching is 'spaced' or 'distributed', but there is also a good chance that the learning is deeper. It works for any topic or type of learning. In one experiment students were taught to identify different painters and their characteristics. One group had massed practice, studying one painter at a time, the other had spaced practice, learning about each painter many times, on different days. Then students were shown paintings they had not seen before. The spaced practice group was much better at identifying which artist had painted which paintings. This looks like deep, transferred learning.

Why does spaced practice work so well? Partly it is because the brain has a brilliant system to ensure it is not overloaded with useless memories. It works perfectly and automatically, and it's called forgetting. Forgetting is the brain's default option: teach something today and most of it will be forgotten tomorrow. But if the brain comes across the same material again on another day, it forgets it again, *but more slowly*. After about six encounters, separated in time, the material is forgotten very slowly indeed, and, in effect, it is in the long-term memory.

The time it takes to recall or reuse older learning can be very short indeed, and still be effective. Relearning is a very efficient process.

Learning and forgetting curves

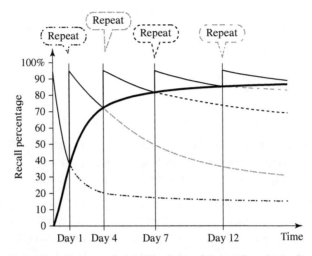

Figure 12.2: Note the irregular timescale on this graph, which shows how we forget over time

How can we make use of this well-known and well-tested strategy?

- We can devise our schemes of work to teach topics in sections spaced by days or months, rather than all at once. (Search online for Bruner's 'spiral curriculum'.)

- We can set activities that require reuse of prior learning. One of my favourites is to compare the similarities and differences of concepts taught today with similar topics taught much earlier, for example: *'What are the similarities and differences between the reigns of Henry I and Henry II?'*; this also helps transfer.

- We can use repeated homework tasks to perfect recall of key points from material taught earlier (see the box below).

- Don't be afraid to set homework or assignments some time after you taught the topic.

- Contrary to popular opinion, delaying your feedback on student work can be better than immediate feedback This is because delayed feedback often makes the student review their work (in order for them to understand your feedback). If your feedback requires an improvement task, the student is bound to review and reuse the learning.

- Go through worksheets used for homework and put a last question on each from an earlier topic.

Try this in the classroom

Most students think revision means reading your notes just before the exam. A better process, below, checks and corrects recall of vital material. If this is done with spaces between the practice sessions, learning is maximised and learning time and effort minimised. Also, you and your students are saved the boredom of massed revision on surface learning.

'Study, cover, recall, check, repeat'

You identify key facts and simple skills your students must know for a topic – really vital stuff. You make it clear what this vital material is, for example by summarising it on a handout. Then you tell students to:

- **study:** look at these vital materials, and read your notes/book, etc., endeavouring to understand it

- **cover:** close the book or cover the handout, then, after a short break...

- **recall:** write down everything you can remember about this vital material, then...

- **check:** look at what you recalled and compare it to the book or handout. What did you get right? What did you forget or get wrong?

- **repeat:** some time later, preferably on another day, until the learning is sound.

You set this work as a homework, which you don't even need to mark – you just give a three-minute test or quiz on *some* of this material at the beginning of the next class, preferably a mastery quiz (see Chapter 11). Make sure you warn students of this quiz in advance.

It is no great surprise then that everything is reviewed six times in the RAR process, or in whole-class interactive teaching, a highly-effective method (Petty, 2009). The details are not vital, but typically learning is reused at the end of the lesson, at the beginning of the next lesson, after about five hours' tuition, after about 20 hours' tuition. (The obvious place for these later reviews is at the end of topics or subtopics.) The learning is reused by a couple of homework tasks: one while the topic is current, and another about a term or more later where a current homework or classwork question is contrived to review material learned very much earlier. These reuse phases should involve students doing it again, not you saying it again.

The aim of the methods in this chapter is to ring the changes during these five reviews and to ensure:

- **structure:** to require students to identify the key points and key principles, and so structure their understanding around these. That is, to 'see the wood for the trees' and see relations within the content. Only structured understanding has a chance of getting into long-term memory.

- **understanding:** to encourage students to express their understanding in their own words, and so require them to create a personal meaning. The reuse of learning should begin to stress relations, similarities and differences between concepts, and the 'why' as well as the 'what' of the topic. This aim is to deepen learning, as described in Chapter 1 – spaced reminders and checking recall are not enough.

- **transfer:** if learning remains in the silo of its own topic, it cannot link with or illuminate learning elsewhere. We need to teach for transfer. This is not easy and will not be completed, but it greatly strengthens learning, as we saw in Chapter 9. Tasks like similarities and differences and 'have we seen something like this before' help transfer, but also make your subject seem like a coherent story rather than a hotchpotch of disconnected facts.

- **repetition:** long-term memory usually requires at least six separate encounters with a topic. Familiarity with the material and over-practising are also required for deep learning.

- **check and correct:** your students' learning and your teaching both need a check and correct. So might the quality of any notes students have made; this last is helped if students leave space for improvements between paragraphs and in margins.

The importance of students' note-making

In these digital days students writing their own notes may seem quaintly old-fashioned, but experiments have repeatedly found that note-making greatly improves learning. I don't mean students copying notes from the board, I mean them expressing their understanding by writing in their own words.

Note-making requires the learner to make sense of the topic and to structure it; it is especially effective if there is a check-and-correct on the note. Yet teachers rarely leave time for note-making in class; instead they often use the following less-effective review methods.

- **You summarise.** This is useful as it shows the key points and structure of the topic, but it is not sufficient in itself. As the bullets on the previous page show, it is the students who must review their understanding, not you!

- **You give notes or handouts.** Both these are usually effortless for students so we should expect them not to work well, and they don't. A 'good set of notes' can create an entirely illusory sense of security in both teacher and student. It is note-*making* not note-*taking* that works. (Your handouts have great value if you set an activity requiring students to read them though, see Chapter 8. We saw a co-constructivist way to give notes in Chapter 7 and more follow.)

If students have a good textbook, or you have some good handouts, use the 'teaching without talking' methods we saw in Chapter 8 for class activities or homework These are co-constructivist, fun, and require little effort from you. Highlighting or underlining key points and then writing a summary is an excellent activity.

Many teachers complain that their students write bad notes. However, the solution to this problem is not dictation, or students filing handouts they never read. Instead you need to teach note-making by modelling, as described in Chapter 7.

So leave time for note-making; it is central to understanding, to learning and to work, and while they are doing it, look over their shoulders to get feedback for yourself. Don't be put off by the bad notes you will certainly see; just get students to improve them with feedback methods, as described below. Students only get to make good notes by first creating bad ones; co-constructivism tells us so.

A week or more after students have written their notes, you can provide your own notes for this lesson, and as a homework students can underline key points in your notes, and self-assess and improve their own notes using yours. It's best not to promise to provide this service in advance, or to provide it for all lessons, as it can make some students lazy: '*I won't write my own notes, I'll just wait for the teacher's.*'

The methods that follow can be used for any of the five reviews mentioned on page 228, and can be especially useful in lessons.

The purpose of the reuse phase is not just to encounter the topic again, but to check and correct the student's understanding of it. Consequently, all the methods in the previous check and correct chapter are ideal 'reuse' activities, but I add some more below.

Mathematics teachers can ask students to write at least some notes in the form of worked examples with the students' own line-by-line annotations. These can explain how the example was done and why or when the method is mathematically valid. Most teachers require more than this, though; mathematics is more than a set of calculation tricks.

Reviewing and making notes in class time

Question-based note-making and other structured note-making methods

Ask a key question or two at the beginning of the lesson or topic, as described in 'Setting goals, at the start of the topic in Chapter 6. Focus your teaching on these questions, discuss them in class, and ensure that useful ideas are written on the board as they occur, by you or by your students. You can now discuss the board notes, ask what's missing and what could improve them, perhaps in an assertive questioning style, then students can use your board notes to write their own notes. Remember, it is not the notes that are effective so much as the process of making them, so it is worth leaving class time for this. You can always cover the detail you had to miss out with 'Reading review as a homework: adding the detail', which is described below.

Rather than use questions, you can structure notes around key points, advance organisers or graphic organisers, if you prefer. However, it often helps to give students a structure of some kind to avoid omissions. You can use snowballing, as described below, with any of these structured note-making methods.

Teacher makes notes with class participation

This works well after snowballing, and was explained on page 90 of Chapter 7.

Creating graphic organisers and other visual notes

Graphic organisers (see Chapter 3) are a powerful note-making device, and may suffice for many topics, or students can add a bit of text to explain them. You can provide an outline graphic as an advance organiser for students to complete; you can ask them to turn the lesson into a specific graphic such as a flow diagram or a decision tree. See page 15 for a rigorous way to do this with embedded learning boosters.

Students can also be asked to create posters, leaflets and graphics for slideshow presentations or websites, the advantage of which is that they can be shared online and peer assessed.

Snowballing

1. You ask individuals to write key points with explanatory notes for each one, leaving plenty of space for improvement between paragraphs and in margins. If students find this difficult, give them key points or key questions and ask them to write a note for each.

2. Students get together in pairs to compare their notes and to improve them.

3. Pairs get into fours and again notes are compared and improved.

4. You ask the groups of four for their key points one point at a time, and for their explanation of each one. Nominate group members rather than ask for volunteers. You can then comment on what was missed, leave time for the class to improve their notes on this point, then move to the next point, and so on.

Snowballing can also be used during the production of graphic organisers. It provides students with support while giving a great insight into what students are noting, and what not.

Reading review in class

You provide students with a handout that summarises the lesson, students highlight or underline the key points, you check what they have highlighted and then discuss. See the 'teaching without talking' methods described in Chapter 8. This could be snowballed as above.

Reviewing with a graphic organiser

You give students an advance organiser in graphic form (see Chapter 6), and at the end of the lesson you go back to this and ask students what they can recall about each part. After discussion, you leave students a few minutes to write about it in their own words, or to add detail to their version of the organiser. You then do the same with the next part of the organiser, and so on.

Students then improve their notes by one of the following methods.

Reviews of practical lessons

I expect you use this already. After the practical activity, students gather round one student's piece of work. The class uses this to go over what they did and why. Students learning practical skills will benefit from making notes after such a discussion, and recalling the lesson in a question and answer session at the beginning of the next.

Completing glossary sheets and principle sheets

You give students a handout that lists the main technical terms and the main principles you will be teaching, with a space for an explanation for each term. This is for the whole course or unit, not just the topic that you are teaching. Students explain the meanings of the terms they have studied in pencil so they can be improved later. After teaching a class, you set students the task of completing explanations for the key ideas and principles that you have covered in that class; as ever, this works best if students are warned that this task will come.

Then you have occasional tests or quizzes where students must recall the vocabulary and principles and give examples, their work then being checked and corrected, as described in the previous chapter.

Reusing surface learning from previous lessons

Reviewing and note-making out of class

The methods that follow are additional to reviewing and note-making in class, rather than a substitute for it. They are great ways to help achieve six separate encounters with the material.

Marzano et al. (2001), reviewing research on homework, explain that homework should have a clear purpose, be meaningful, be related to course aims, and should not involve parents! Marzano found it was much more effective if there were teacher comments on homework, though self- and peer assessment might work as well.

Reading review as a homework: adding the detail

You give students a handout that includes the detail you *didn't* have time to cover in class. Students are asked to read and highlight the most important points in the text; these should have come out in the lesson. However, they will *also* learn the detail, and how this relates to these key points. I know this method is used on many courses that get some of the best results in their subject nationally.

Back-page summary

I use a variant of this in my own reading. Ask students to print out a specific file or webpage from the Internet or your intranet, read it, and highlight/ underline it. Then ask them to write a summary of the key points in their own words on the back.

You ask the class what they have highlighted at the beginning of the next lesson and check and correct it. You can put your own highlighted/ annotated handout version online, and they can compare this with their own. They can also print out your version and use it as an authoritative note for revision.

If you have too much content and too little time (like most of us), this approach solves many problems and makes time for active learning in class time.

Studying worked examples

In mathematics or similar subjects, ask students to study and annotate a few worked examples on learning in earlier lessons, explaining each step, and to prepare to peer-explain them at the beginning of the next class. They could annotate a textbook example if the book is their own or if they use sticky notes.

Teaching without talking methods as homework

You can't talk to students when they are at home, so many of the teaching without talking methods we considered in Chapter 8 make excellent homework tasks.

The dangers of over-emphasis on surface learning

Checking recall of surface learning is necessary but not sufficient, and the methods for it are often boring. One may not have time for quizzes and competitions in class, and it is not easy to create engaging activities for out-of-class work that check recall. Often it is better to strive for deeper learning and transfer, as this involves more interesting tasks, and involves reuse and recall in any case. There may even be mental health issues regarding over-testing for some students.

Methods to deepen and transfer learning

Similarities and differences

This method has shown exceptionally high effectiveness in rigorous studies in classrooms. You might like to guess why. It can, of course, be used to compare two concepts being taught at the same time. However, in the context of this chapter it works best if students compare something being learned currently, with a related topic that was taught some time ago. For example, while studying the reign of one king, students could compare him with a monarch studied earlier. Or students studying pie and bar charts could look at the similarities and differences between these and tables of data.

It is links between topics that help create deep learning. They also help to create transfer. Perhaps the issues in the First and Second World Wars have more similarities than the student had realised, maybe there are some general historical principles at work. Perhaps the methods used to manipulate fractions could be used on percentages.

Similarities and differences plug into the way the brain works. When a baby learns about oranges and then learns about lemons, they do not create a new file in their brain for lemons. They notice the similarities and differences between oranges and lemons, and the brain creates a file that says lemons are like oranges except in the following respects: lemons taste sharp while oranges taste sweet, and so on. In terms of cognitive complexity, this is a much more efficient way of creating concepts than learning them separately in silos because it prevents unnecessary repetition. The fact that oranges have pithy skin does not need to be relearned for the lemons, the lemon concept makes use of the orange concept.

Also, the brain's same-and-different approach encourages transfer. Without being told, I can work out that if I've used the zest of a lemon in my cooking, presumably I could use the zest of an orange. Of course, such reasoning will not always work, but if not, this just updates the similarities and differences files in our brain. A very similar approach is used in computer science to compress large image files in order to save space in computer memory. So the similarities and differences teaching method makes use of the brain's architecture and way of working – this may be why it has such exceptional effectiveness.

Transfer is not easy; you have to teach for it deliberately. But learning is not much use without it, as we can often only use learning in precisely the context in which it was taught, not in unfamiliar contexts, or with unfamiliar problems. This is very limiting indeed. Transfer also makes your subject seem much more interesting, coherent, and easier to understand.

Some examples of similarities and differences tasks

'Draw a same-and-different diagram for:

- osmosis and diffusion
- metaphor and simile
- conservation of energy and conservation of momentum
- the three main types of muscle fibre
- Napoleon and Hitler
- Macbeth and Lady Macbeth.'

'Looking back over the retailers we have studied, in what way do they differ or conform in their approach to customers' needs?'

'How do Auden, Larkin and Shakespeare differ in their use of poetic devices in the pieces we have studied?'

As explained in Chapter 3, it is very powerful to ask students to express similarities and differences in graphical form, such as Venn diagrams, spider diagrams and same/different tables.

As ever, learning boosters will help students while they create these. For example, students could peer check and then self-assess against your diagram in their pairs. Alternatively, you could make use of the graphic organiser ping-pong described in Chapter 3. Learning boosters have the advantage that they reduce or even eliminate the need for you to mark the work

Other transfer tasks

The end of Chapter 9 on applying learning has ideas that can be used to reuse and transfer learning and is well worth revisiting for ideas. We saw there that tasks that assist transfer include:

- looking for similarities or links
- looking for similarities and differences between related topics

- looking for general principles

and more difficult:

- asking students which general principles are in evidence in the current topic.

Mixed tasks

It is often possible to reuse old learning at the same time as developing new learning, for example:

- in foreign language learning, learning new verb constructions while reusing old kitchen vocabulary

- reusing the physics of forces and energy while studying electricity by calculating the efficiency of an electric motor lifting a weight

- reusing knowledge about parliament's workings during new learning about a prime minister

- while studying databases, students designing a website (a process studied last term) to explain how a database works.

These mixed tasks need to be designed into your teaching, and they need creative thinking and planning for, especially in subjects where new learning does not necessarily require old learning. Even in subjects like mathematics and science where new learning is built on old, it is possible for some topics to be used only once and then forgotten unless deliberate reuse is planned.

Preparing for an exam

To get students to be better at answering exam questions, they need to practise answering exam questions. Most teachers mark students' practice exam questions themselves, often as soon as they are completed, but this is a mistake. In Chapter 11 we saw that students need to know for each of their answers:

Goal: what the question required in terms of content, length and detail

Medal: what they got right in their answer

Mission: what they could have done better.

The best way to provide all of this information is for students to attempt an answer and afterwards study your model answer for the same question.

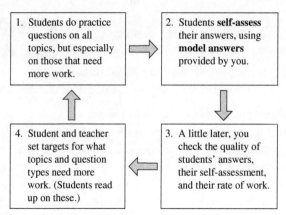

Figure 12.3: Preparing for an exam

Their attempts at exam questions are best checked and corrected in the following way:

The model answers, or perhaps mark scheme, make it clear what each question requires, and if the student compares their own answer with the model, most can easily see what they got right and what they need to improve upon. As you have not marked their work yet, they will be anxious to work out how well they did, and so will study the model answer carefully, as well as the difference between their answer and the model.

In the case of multiple-choice questions, the same strategy works well, but you might need to explain why the right answer is right and the wrong ones wrong.

If you provide model notes or a graphic, your students will want to keep them. So make sure you don't use this method all the time, as students will often make poor notes, knowing yours are coming.

Other feedback review methods

Chapter 11 has many active check and correct methods that can easily be used to reuse or review learning. 'Formative tests and quizzes', 'peer assessment with model answers' and 'student questioning and mountain climbing' are particularly worth considering.

Don't forget homework tasks that require students to use learning done a term or more ago.

Evidence for Chapter 12 on reusing and reviewing the learning of a topic

Chapter 14 establishes that the most reliable sources of evidence are summary evidence, and we should triangulate three sources.

Evidence from summaries of qualitative research: Spaced practice was developed by cognitive scientists and is mentioned positively by most of the principal references starting on page 284. It is almost universally acknowledged that human memory requires repeated reuse of learning to establish it in the long-term memory. Dunolsky (2013) finds that the 'study, cover, recall, check, repeat' strategy explained in this chapter is a highly-effective revision activity but does not stress more challenging tasks to deepen learning.

Evidence from summaries of quantitative research: Hattie finds that the research on spaced practice shows it to be highly effective, and likewise the research on strategies to transfer learning. He finds direct instruction to be a highly-effective method, and this specifically includes reuse of learning.

Marzano et al. (2001) find that students writing their own notes is highly effective, as is students creating their own graphic organisers to summarise. 'Similarities and differences' activities they find to be exceptionally effective.

Evidence from research on the most effective teachers: Lemov (2015) finds that expert teachers find a multitude of engaging ways to reuse former learning. The teachers in Ayres' (2004) research taught 16–19-year-olds, and many were found to use the 'question-based note-making', and 'note-making as homework' described in this chapter.

Three sources of evidence suggest experimentation with some of the methods in this chapter can be productive.

Further reading

See also the principal references in Chapter 15 Further reading and references.

Free online resources

Search for 'spaced practice', 'long-term memory', 'study skills', 'transfer', 'similarities and differences method' and 'revision methods'.

Books and papers

J. Dunlosky et al., 'Strengthening the Student Toolbox' (*American Educator*, Fall 2013). This is focused on revision rather than learning for the first time, a point sometimes missed by those who quote it. Sadly, there is little to nothing on transfer.

J.A.C. Hattie, *Visible Learning: A Synthesis of Over 800 Meta-Analyses Relating to Achievement* (London: Routledge, 2008).

R. Marzano et al., *Classroom Instruction that Works* (Alexandria, VA: ASCD, 2001). See the chapter on homework

G. Petty, *Evidence-Based Teaching* (Oxford: Oxford University Press, 2009). See Chapter 20.

G. Petty, *Teaching Today* (5th Edition), (Oxford: Oxford University Press, 2014). See Chapter 23.

Chapter 13

Teaching study skills and academic skills: strategy training

We began looking at how to teach study skills and other academic skills in Chapter 7 on modelling, and in Chapter 10 where we looked at how to help students with extended writing. This chapter completes the topic and provides an overview.

Depending on your subject and the assessment procedures on your course, students might for example need to do the following in order to get good grades:

- Analyse (as described at the beginning of Chapter 3).

- Evaluate.

- Read and comprehend text that is not easy for them.

- Solve problems unlike those they have seen before.

- Do extended writing such as essays or assignments.

You might think you have enough to do teaching the content required by your syllabus, but teaching the skills required by your subject and its assessment procedures greatly improves students' attainment. Interestingly, it also increases students' understanding of the content (see Hattie, Biggs and Purdie, 1996); this is because these skills require students to think hard about content.

Reflection

'You can't teach skills': Oh yes you can!

The 2000 National Curriculum in England and Wales included an approach to 'generic skills'. This did not work well, and led some teachers and even writers on education to conclude that it was not possible to teach skills, only knowledge. This antagonism to skills teaching was supported by some cognitive psychologists, who argued that the more content knowledge (declarative knowledge) a student has, the more skilfully they will write and evaluate. This is certainly true. But they went onto argue or imply that the *only* way to increase academic skills was to teach more content. That conclusion is emphatically contradicted by the empirical evidence, as we will see at the end of this chapter. But skills teaching is not easy: simply practising skills doesn't necessarily improve them, they have to be taught the right way. The case study below shows how by example.

Study 1: Teaching careful reading

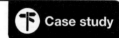 **Case study**

'Careful reading' is the skill of close reading a text or similar for deep understanding.

Start with your students' needs: Alice, the teacher in this case study, has noticed that her students do not read carefully. Also, one of their exams requires students to answer a comprehension question, where they must read a piece of text they have not seen before and answer questions on it. Her students often do badly on such questions.

She also sets reading homework, and finds students have difficulty making sense of the textbook. For these reasons, Alice decides to teach reading comprehension skills. This process of identifying the skills your students need because of the nature of your subject or its assessment, and then teaching these skills systematically throughout the course, is called 'constructive alignment' by John Biggs. You align the teaching with the skills you want to foster. It's a common-sense strategy but few teachers do it, often because their scheme of work is solely focused on covering the *content* the syllabus requires. These teachers tend to attribute weaknesses in skills to low intelligence rather than a deficiency in the skill strategies that the students are using. For example, some students will read a difficult piece of text once, then stop, saying they don't understand it *'... it's too hard... I'm not clever enough.'* A better reading strategy would help them understand the text better.

Assisted by some books on study skills, Alice breaks down the task of careful reading into a sequence that she summarises in the following handout. (This sequence allows the skill of careful reading to be developed, rather than embodying the skill in its entirety.)

Careful reading skill sheet

> **Read for the gist**
> Read the source twice to get the basic idea. Pay special attention to titles, diagrams and the first and last paragraphs.

> **Help, I don't understand this bit!**
> Read the hard bit over a few times. Use a dictionary to check meanings. If you still don't get it, mark the section with a question mark and continue reading. Then go back to the hard bits when you have read the whole text.

> **Underline the main points**
> Try to underline about 10% or less, 20% maximum. Use a pencil so you can rub out underlining.

> **Summarise with key points or a mind map or other suitable graphic**
> Read back over the underlined bits to ensure you have all the really important bits in your summary.

> **Now you will understand the text much better!**

Figure 13.1: A process to help teach careful reading

Alice looks over her scheme of work to find suitable topics for making use of the skill of careful reading. She identifies three different topics, separated by a few weeks in her scheme. She plans to teach these topics in part by asking students to do some careful reading on some text that explains aspects of the topics. The sections of text are short, taking students about five minutes to read, underline, and summarise. This will teach the skill of careful reading, but also some of the content in the topic at the same time. This is called a 'double-decker' lesson, or perhaps less grandly a 'double-decker task'.

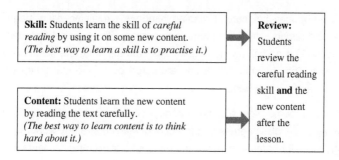

Figure 13.2: A double-decker task or lesson teaches both skill and content by using the skill *on* the content

The best way to learn a skill is to practise it, and the best way to learn content is to think hard about that content. So double-decker lessons provide both these 'best ways' at the same time – a very efficient way to teach. Alice realises that careful reading requires the subskills of underlining and summarising, but this group is able and she thinks that she can teach these skills all at the same time.

Classes vary, and Alice adapts to each. With another group she teaches underlining separately, then summarising separately, then teaches careful reading. She teaches the subskills in the same way described for careful reading, with double-decker tasks. (See the case study on page 248 for a summary of the process.)

As well as the three lessons with their double-decker tasks, Alice plans a series of homework tasks requiring students to read and summarise sections of their textbook. Students will then compare their summaries with her own in a self-assessment exercise, setting themselves targets for improvement for the next time they do careful reading.

Establish the need for the skill: With her more-able group, Alice introduces careful reading by asking her students to read a short piece of text on cell division, less than one side of A4. She has not yet shown them her 'careful reading' handout. Then she asks students questions on it, finding, as she expects, that they don't understand most of it. The students complain that the text is not easy to understand. She asks some questions such as *'How many times did you read the text?'* and *'Did you reread the more difficult passages?'* Most students answer no, but some of the more-able students answer 'yes'. Alice establishes with her class that for many of them, their reading strategy does not cope with more difficult text.

She introduces her careful reading handout, explaining each stage and asking students why each stage is necessary. She now asks students to read the text on cell division again, this time following the careful reading strategy. The students do so, and are surprised to find that they begin to understand it much better.

Alice asks some more questions about cell division and gets much better answers. The class agrees that the careful reading strategy works well, but suggests slight amendments to the handout, for example students want to call the skill 'careful reading' while Alice had originally called it 'close reading for deep understanding'.

Meta-cognition: At the end of the lesson, Alice summarises the main points concerning the topic that students have been reading about – the content for the lesson. Having reviewed the 'lower deck' of her double-decker lesson, she begins reviewing the 'top deck' – the skill.

> *Alice: In this lesson we did some careful reading. How did we do it?*
> *Student 1: We underlined important bits.*
> *Alice: We did later, but what did we do first?*
> *Student 2: We read it, but just roughly, looking at the headings and the beginning and end. And the diagrams and that.*
> *Alice: Why did we skim read it roughly first? Why not start underlining right away?*
> *Student 3: You don't know what's important until you've read it a bit first.*
> *Alice: Exactly. So, what would have happened if we had started underlining right away?*
> *Student 4: We probably would have underlined too much…*
> *Student 5: … and underlined all the wrong bits.*
> *Alice: That's right. So, we skim read it, then read it again a few times to get the basics, to get what's called the 'gist'. What's next in careful reading?*

In this way, Alice gets the students to step through the careful reading process stage by stage, explaining and justifying each stage. This is a check and correct process, of course. Alice stresses what would have happened if that stage were missed out, or done badly.

The process just described is sometimes called 'meta-cognition'. It has a high impact on student learning in itself (Marzano's meta), especially if students do it for themselves, as they will later, and helps the students think about the processes and the thinking they do when they learn or carry out a skill. Meta-cognition is the students thinking about their own thinking and their own ways of working.

Then Alice summarises the stages: *'So we read a few times for the gist, to get a basic understanding of what the text is about, at least roughly. We reread hard bits a few times, going back to them later if necessary. Then we read it again, underlining the important bits. Then we summarised the text in our own words.'*

Bridging – teaching for transfer: The next phase of teaching a skill is called bridging, and assists transfer. Alice asks *'Where else could we use this careful reading process?'* There is class discussion in the assertive questioning style described in Chapter 5.

> **Alice:** *Could you use it to read text you found online?*
> **Student 6:** *No, you can't underline on the Web, can you?*
> **Alice:** *Really?*
> **Student 7:** *You could print it out, then underline.*
> **Alice:** *Yes! Also, if you copied the text into your word-processing software, there is often an underlining feature there.*

Then Alice establishes when the careful reading approach would *not* be used. *'Would you use this approach if the reading was easy and short?'* The students answer, *'No, but it might be useful if the reading was easy and long, so as to easily find the important parts later'*.

Eventually, students add to their 'careful reading' handout the following text:

*'The process below is suitable for reading **handouts**, but also **websites** (print the relevant bits or copy and paste into word-processing software), and **books** including **library books** (photocopy the relevant parts of the library book). If the text is easy and short, it might not help much.'*

Learning loop targets: Students are now asked to reflect on their experience of careful reading and to give themselves advice on how to do it better next time. This is proper meta-cognition as it's personalised. They write this target down on their skill sheet for careful reading, which goes in the back of their folder.

It's important to recognise that the lesson just described involved the learning of new content as well as learning about careful reading. Most of the time in the lesson was focused on this new content. Subsequent lessons using the careful reading skill will need even less time devoted to the skill.

Notice in this case study that Alice was not just concerned in teaching the skill, she was also intent on unteaching the students' present habitual response to reading a difficult text. This old habitual approach will have been very well practised and will tend to predominate especially in times of hurry or stress, such as in an exam. This is why Alice stresses the inadequacies of the 'read-it-once-and-then-wonder-why-you-don't-understand-it' strategy. This should slowly encourage students to use careful reading whenever it is necessary.

Further practice: Skills take some time to develop, so one lesson will never be enough. Alice sets her students a series of reading homework tasks where students must hand in their underlined texts and their bullet-point or mind-map summaries. Before they do these tasks, students are asked to look at the learning loop targets for improving this skill that they set themselves the last time they used the process and wrote on their skills sheet. This is the learning loops strategy from Chapter 11.

Sometimes Alice provides students with a model after they have completed their close reading, that is, the text underlined by herself and her own bullet-point summary. Students use this to self-assess against, to check and correct their underlining and summarising skills.

In subsequent lessons she also uses snowballing. Students are given a short text to read using the careful reading strategy. Students work alone to read and underline key points and prepare a summary. Then they pair up to compare their work: what was underlined and what was not? Who did the best summary? Then pairs get together into groups of four to peruse each other's work again and to produce an agreed summary. Sometimes Alice runs a class discussion on the more difficult points in the content they were reading. Sometimes discussion is about the skill of careful reading.

Alice could also have used modelling by thinking aloud, as described in Chapter 7, to show the skills of careful reading, underlining, and summarising, however she decided against this for careful reading, though uses the approach for other skills. Good teachers adapt strategies to the context.

Each time students practise the skill of careful reading, Alice finishes by going through the meta-cognition and bridging process described above, saying:

> 'You've just done some careful reading:
> **'How did you do that?** Why? What would happen if you missed that step out?'
> **'Where else can you use this careful reading procedure?'**
> **'Please set yourself targets** for improvement for the next time you do some careful reading. What did you find difficult? How could you improve?'

It might seem unnecessary to go over the meta-cognition and bridging process repeatedly like this. But reading new content is demanding for students and they will tend to focus on the meaning of this content. This leaves no room in their working memory for the skill procedure that Alice is trying to teach. So it's vital to change focus from the content to the skill review for a short period. In later practice lessons this skill review only takes two or three minutes, but it ensures the skill is reflected upon, reinforced, and improved by the target setting.

Developing independence: If Alice always reminded students to use the careful reading process whenever it was useful, students would not develop the independence required to use the procedure appropriately and unprompted. So Alice gradually reduces the prompting.

In the early practice of this skill, Alice prompts students to get their skills sheets out of their folders, read their target from the last time they used the skill, then do their careful reading following the procedure without omissions. However, in later practice sessions when the skill is practised in class, she just sets the reading task, stresses it should be done with care, then waits to see how many students follow the careful-reading procedure. After a minute or two of observing the class, she notices some students are not underlining. She stops them and asks: *'How many of you are following the careful-reading procedure?'* Class discussion follows.

Some skills will take many practice sessions to develop. Ideally the 'scaffolding' of the skills sheet and Alice's prompts can be given progressively less time and emphasis, until students use the skill well whenever it is useful.

It's important to notice that there is more to the skill of careful reading than the procedure described in Alice's handout. However, following the procedure helps students to develop the skill of careful reading much more quickly than if they were left to discover it for themselves. Indeed, they may not discover it. Obviously this skill can be transferred to other subjects, but this requires deliberate teaching.

 Reflection

The first time I set an underlining task with able 17-year-olds I found that students underlined almost all the text, often leaving out only the 'ands' and the 'buts'. Yet one of the 'buts' was crucial! I realised the task was asking students to make sense of the whole text, and was more demanding than I had thought.

Study 2: Teaching other skills

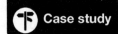 **Case study**

In preparing to teach each of her classes Alice did a skills audit, considering the skills required:

- by the nature of the subject
- by assessments
- because students seemed to struggle with this skill in previous years
- for smooth progression onto the next course, though such skills are only taught in outline.

She decided on the following skills as a minimum set: underlining, summarising, mind mapping, careful reading, analytical thinking, evaluative thinking, extended writing. Alice taught all of these skills in a similar way to careful reading.

1 Teach any subskills separately if they are substantial or if the group is weak.

2 If students are overconfident in their present use of the skill, establish the need to learn the skill Alice's way. This is done by demonstrating that students' present procedures are inadequate and that there is a better way.

3 Model the skill if this is useful and practicable.

4 Summarise the skill on a skills sheet and include on this a box for students to write their learning loops targets (see learning loops in Chapter 11).

5 Develop a series of double-decker lessons or tasks to practise the skill, including meta-cognition and bridging, that is, asking students:

'How did you do that?'
'Where else could you use this procedure?'
'Set yourself a target for improvement and write it on your skills sheet.'

6 Repeat the double-decker lesson practice sessions, using learning loops and occasionally using snowballing. Give students as much practice in the skill as possible, for example using them in homework. Gradually reduce the prompts and help until students become competent independently.

Teaching skills using the product

As well as teaching a *process* or procedure to help teach a skill as described above, you can check and correct the *products* that students create to improve their use of the skill. For example, check and correct an essay to improve essay writing skills.

You can create an assessment proforma that gives success criteria for a good essay and then use this as described in Chapter 11 under 'learning loops' to assist students in their self-assessment, and to give feedback to students yourself. Then students can create or be given targets for improvement.

Examining the product is of course the way most teachers try to improve skills, and it works up to a point, but teaching students a procedure, a *process*, the 'how' of the skill, is one of the best ways to improve the product. Many teachers fail to teach such processes and then attribute their students' poor performance to lack of ability, when it was due to lack of teaching.

A series of skills sheets and assessment proformas to help skills development is available on my website: http://geoffpetty.com/for-teachers/skills/ – these are free downloads.

Here is an example from these downloads for problem-solving in mathematics or applied mathematics:

Problem-solving in mathematics: What to do when you don't know what to do!

Start the process in Figure 13.3 from 'read the question'. If you remain stuck, try working clockwise around the diagram in, at least until you are familiar with all the strategies.

Reflection on problem-solving

Once you have solved a problem ask students, or get them to ask themselves:

- *'How did we crack this one?'* Which of the strategies in the diagram below worked and why?

- *'How (else) could we have cracked this one?'* If you didn't solve the problem, which strategy *would* have worked and why? If you did solve it, which *other* strategy would have helped?

- *'Where else have we seen this strategy work well?'* If you have been using the strategies in Figure 13.3 before, then ask students of other successes or failures in problem-solving using the same strategy.

- *'Under what conditions is this strategy useful?'* For example, spectacles is always useful, but particularly if you have read the question carefully and drawn a diagram.

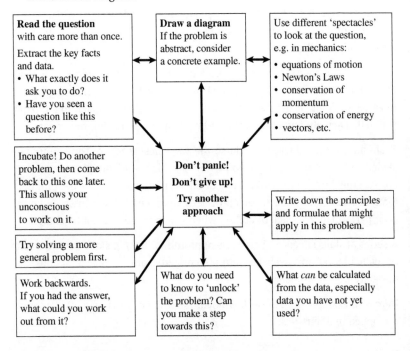

Figure 13.3: Problem-solving in mathematics

Demonstrating problem-solving strategies

It can greatly help students if you demonstrate the skill of problem-solving yourself, referring to the diagram. Think aloud, stepping through the strategies, pretending that you are stuck – see Chapter 7 on modelling.

The evidence on how to teach skills and strategies effectively

The most comprehensive review of research on 'strategy training' or skills teaching considered in this chapter is still Hattie, Biggs and Purdie (1996). There is a summary of this meta-study on my website, see 'Further reading' on page 254.

Here are the key findings of the meta-study:

What strategies/skills most improved students' attainment?

The study skills programmes that had the greatest success included structural aids and 'attribution training'.

Structural aids

Structural aids are ways to show the *structure* and *meaning* of what is being learned. The review found that students need to be taught how to use these aids, along with when and why they are used. Structural aids include skills such as:

- extracting the key points from the content being studied. This includes physically highlighting, underlining, or otherwise annotating text.

- producing 'concept maps' (mind maps, spider diagrams, etc.); that is, the graphic organisers described in Chapter 3

- 'advanced organisers' where students are told in advance what they will learn in a lesson or unit (see Chapter 6)

- note-making skills: the student summarising content (see Chapters 7, 8 and 13).

Many teachers would regard many of these skills as too simple to teach, underlining for example. But the review showed that even academic 16–19-year-olds benefit greatly from having such skills deliberately taught.

Attribution training

'Positive attribution training' is teaching students to attribute their success to effort, time, practice, using the right strategy, asking for help and other factors *in* their control, and not attribute their successes to IQ, ability, luck, or other factors *outside* their control. Carol Dweck is the foremost theorist in this area with her stress on the 'growth mindset'.

How were study skills taught on the most effective programmes?

It is important first to identify the study skills and thinking skills required for success on your course and in your subject and decide to teach these. Having done this, Hattie, Biggs and Purdie found that the most effective strategy for teaching these skills was as follows:

- To embed the teaching of skills with the teaching of content (double-decker lessons or tasks) rather than teach the skills 'up front' in a separate module, which is only moderately successful by comparison.

The tasks you set to teach the skills should be real, embedded, and subject specific. (Alice started her teaching of careful reading with an activity on cell division, which she had to teach anyway. Other practice reading was also on necessary content learning.)

- Students are taught the importance of these skills and how to use them.

- Students self-assess how effectively they use these study skills; teacher assessment may also help. Then they work on the aspect of the study skill they find most difficult. This self-assessment can take place before, during, or after the main instruction on study skills.

- Students learn the skills actively. They actually *do it*, they don't just hear about how it should be done.

- The different skills such as skim reading, note-taking, highlighting or mind mapping are 'orchestrated' to the demands of the particular task and context. They are not just taught and used independently. The skills might need to be taught separately to begin with though.

- The student takes control and chooses which technique to use, when and why, while maintaining a clear sense of purpose. The use of skills is directed towards the subject-specific task(s), for example studying a handout or writing an assignment or essay.

- Students are required to self-monitor, self-assess, and self-regulate their use of these skills, setting themselves targets for experimentation and improvement. This 'meta-cognition' is given a heavy emphasis in this review. The effectiveness of programmes that required meta-cognition were nearly double the effectiveness of those that did not. Meta-cognition on, say, note-making (*how* I take notes) is of course quite different to reflecting on the *content* the student is learning.

- The very best programmes used bridging to encourage transfer of what students have learned to other aspects of their study. For example, a student taught to improve their note-making on amphibians in biology is asked to consider their note-making on other biology topics and in other subjects, and the importance of isolating key points in study generally. (A bridge is built from the current learning to other possible applications, hence 'bridging'.)

- Study skills or strategy training done in the above way produced a very large improvement in students' achievement compared to other learning interventions, so was more than worth the time and effort involved for both teachers and students.

The case studies in this chapter follow this authoritative advice and show how skills teaching can be done in practice. The general approach used by Alice, summarised in the second case study in this chapter, can be adapted to teach pretty much any skill.

Simply giving students practice in academic reading will develop the skill of reading only very slowly, and with some students it will hardly develop at all. Students need to be given guided practice in the skill and in the other skills you want them to learn. As described in this chapter, your skills teaching needs to be embedded into your teaching of content. Critics of skills teaching need to face up to the evidence that skills teaching *can* be highly effective *if* it is done in the right way, and we know how to do it. To fail to teach students academic skills such as reading, essay writing, and evaluative thinking abandons students to the worst form of unguided 'discovery learning', which is known not to work well, and which critics of generic skills teaching often criticise in other contexts.

Evidence for Chapter 13 on teaching study skills and academic skills: strategy training

 **Evidence**

Chapter 14 establishes that the most reliable sources of evidence are summary evidence, and we should triangulate three sources.

Evidence from summaries of qualitative research: The evidence is contentious. Cognitive scientists highly prize the modelling of skills; breaking complex skills down to their component parts and teaching these one by one; meta-cognition (thinking about your own thinking and learning processes and use of skills); and teachers 'scaffolding' difficult tasks with help of some sort. All of these are present in the strategies in this chapter. However, it is important to recognise that a student's skill in any domain is limited by the knowledge they have in that domain. Some teachers interpret this to mean that you can't teach skills (Christodoulou, 2014), and that the only way to develop an intellectual skill is to increase background knowledge of facts. But I can't find a cognitive scientist who makes this claim. For example, Willingham (2009) states: 'The conclusion from this work in cognitive science is straightforward: we must ensure that students acquire background knowledge parallel with practicing critical thinking.' In other words, he advises that skills teaching needs to be embedded into the teaching of content. Many cognitive science summaries avoid the issue of skills altogether.

Evidence from summaries of quantitative research: Hattie, Biggs and Purdie (1996) (a summary of which can be found on my website) make it plain that learning-to-learn skills can be taught, are best taught by using the skills on real content, and the effect of teaching skills is to increase student attainment markedly.

Evidence from research on the most effective teachers: Ayers (2004) finds that highly-effective teachers set challenging tasks that require students to use intellectual skills, to the point of going beyond the syllabus they are teaching.

The jury is out perhaps, but it would be worth identifying skills that are important in your subject and for your students' assessments, then trying to teach these as described in this chapter and see if it works.

Further reading

See also the principal references in Chapter 15 Further reading and references.

Free online resources

Search for 'study skills', 'thinking skills', 'critical thinking' and 'comprehension strategies'.

I have written some blogs on my website (www.geoffpetty.com) on skills teaching that have attracted lively comments.

There is a free download on my website summarising Hattie, Biggs and Purdie (1996), a quantitative research review on teaching study skills, thinking skills and the like, stressing the importance of embedding skills teaching with content teaching.

K. Ericsson, R. Krampe and C. Tesch-Romer, 'The role of deliberate practice in the acquisition of expert performance' (*Psychological Review* 1993, Vol. 100, No. 3. 363–406). A classic paper showing that ability is learned by a particular way of practising with check and correct; it is not just inherited.

J.A.C. Hattie and G.M. Donoghue, 'Learning strategies: a synthesis and conceptual model' (*NPJ Science of Learning,* 2016).

Books and papers

P.C. Abrami et al., 'Instructional interventions affecting critical thinking skills and dispositions: A stage 1 meta-analysis' (*Review of Educational Research,* 78(4), 1102–1134, 2008).

P.C. Abrami et al., 'Strategies for teaching students to think critically: A meta-analysis' (*Review of Educational Research,* 85, 275–314, 2015).

D. Christodoulou, *Seven Myths about Education* (London: Routledge, 2014).

D.F. Halpern, 'Assessing the effectiveness of critical thinking instruction' (*Journal of General Education,* 50, 270–286, 2001).

J.A.C. Hattie, J. Biggs and N. Purdie, 'Effects of learning skills interventions on student learning: A meta-analysis' (*Review of Educational Research,* Vol. 66, No. 2, pages 99–136, 1996).

S. Johnson and H. Siegel, *Teaching Thinking Skills* (London: Continuum, 2010). This gives both sides of the argument about whether thinking skills can be taught, but largely ignores quantitative research.

R.J. Marzano, 'A Theory-based Meta-analysis of Research on Instruction' (Aurora, CO: Mid-continent Research for Education and Learning, 1998). This gives strong evidence for the importance of meta-cognition.

J. Mannion and N. Mercer, 'Learning to learn: improving attainment, closing the gap at Key Stage 3' (*The Curriculum Journal,* 2016).

D. Moseley et al., *Frameworks for Thinking: A Handbook for Teaching and Learning* (Cambridge: Cambridge University Press, 2005).

C. Peltier and K. Vannest, 'A meta-analysis of schema instruction on the problem-solving performance of elementary school students' (*Review of Educational Research,* pages 1–22, July 2017).

R.D. Renaud and H.G. Murray, 'A comparison of a subject-specific and a general measure of critical thinking' (*Thinking Skills and Creativity,* 3, 85–93, 2008).

Part 3: Looking at evidence

Chapter 14

Sifting educational evidence

T he best evidence is flawed, the rest is worse. But there are ways to navigate this uncertainty.

No evidence or advice is perfect, but some sources of evidence are much more trustworthy than others. You can often tell a better source from a worse one, as I will explain. High-quality evidence will suggest many ways to help you improve your practice, and steer you away from approaches that are not likely to work so well. This will save you much time and trouble.

However, if a teaching method works in theory, or in other people's classrooms, that's no guarantee it will work for you. The ultimate authority is your own professional experience: does the method work for you and your students? Don't, though, abandon a method if it doesn't work first time. Because of the great complexity in teaching, it takes about five trials to determine whether a method will work for you, and about 25 to use it with 80% effectiveness, see Joyce and Showers (2002).

Just about any teacher can become an outstanding teacher if they learn well how to use outstanding teaching methods. The last pages in this chapter explain how.

But how do you find the methods most likely to work among literally tonnes of suggestions in research? I argue we should look at *summary* evidence from three different schools of inquiry, looking for where they agree. The three main sources of evidence about how best to teach are qualitative research, quantitative research and field studies on the best teachers from a value-added perspective. More on these later. This approach of looking for agreements between different sources is called 'triangulation'. It is common in journalism, in science, and elsewhere.

Once you know what methods are best to experiment with you can choose those most likely to help your students and you. When you have trialled a new method a few times in your own classrooms you should trust our own professional judgement as to whether you can make the method work for your students.

When I read how to improve teaching, authors hardly ever use triangulation, and bias is common. Let's look in more detail at types of evidence now.

Effect size studies: the quantitative evidence

Quantitative studies, effect size studies, or randomised controlled trials (RCTs) are particularly helpful as they tell us which teaching methods have the *greatest* effect on achievement. Many regard them as the gold standard in educational research. They are a 'suck it and see' research method, based on the question: *'Never mind the theory – does it work in practice?'*

Imagine that an experimenter wants to test out the effectiveness of an instructional activity where students create their own mind maps to summarise topics and subtopics. The researcher finds a school or college and a group of teachers prepared to carry out the experiment. The researcher trains the teachers in mind-mapping techniques, and then assigns a large group of students to control and experimental groups.

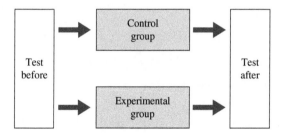

Figure 14.1: Trialling a teaching method

The two groups are given a 'pre-test' to discover what they know about the topic they will be taught before they are taught it. They might know next to nothing of course! Then the control and experimental groups are taught this topic for the same length of time, by the same teachers, or by teachers of the same ability, using the same methods and resources, and so on, except of course that the experimental group uses student-created mind maps to summarise topics and subtopics, while the control group uses a conventional method, for example teacher summaries. Only the experimental group experiences the 'treatment' of student mind mapping – the control group is just for comparison purposes.

Once the topic has been taught, both groups are given another test on the topic called the 'post-test'. For each student, the difference between their pre-test and post-test scores is a measure of how much they have learned.

The test results of the two groups can be shown graphically as in Figure 14.2.

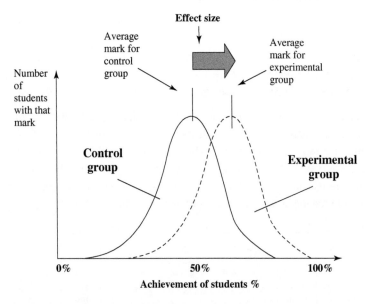

Figure 14.2: Trialling shows the effectiveness of the method

In the better studies (experiments) that get into the research reviews, the group sizes are large. Many have over 100 students and so many classes are needed to form the control and experimental groups. Consequently, if the researchers plot the number of students (N) that get a mark in a certain band (for example, between 55% and 60%), they can create a graph like that shown in Figure 14.2. Many students get a middling mark for their group, and only a few in each group do very well, or very badly compared to the others in their group. This creates the bell-shaped curve you can see in the diagram.

Suppose Figure 14.2 is the graph we get for our mind map experiment. You can see that the average mark for the control group is about 45%, but for the experimental group it is about 65%. If the experiment is well designed, then this improved achievement can only be attributed to mind mapping, as it is the only difference between the two groups.

So the difference between the average marks of the control and experimental groups is a measure of the effectiveness of mind mapping during this experiment. It is called the 'effect size' of the experiment.

What is the effect size measured in?

Now it would be misleading to say that the experimental group had learned 20% more than the control group, even though this is true in this one case. If we did the experiment again with tests that were twice as hard, then students would get half the marks, and so the difference in the average marks would also be half as much, that is, 10% instead of 20%. How is this improvement we call the 'effect size' therefore to be expressed? Statisticians get over this problem of the test difficulty, and other problems, by expressing the effect size in units of 'standard deviation'.

Standard deviation is explained in any good statistics textbook, and can be shown to be a much fairer scale to compare the control and experimental groups. If you are familiar with graded national exam taken by nearly all students, and these are graded say from A to G, or from 1 to 9, then (during the experiment):

A teaching method with an effect size of 0.5 gives roughly a one-grade leap. A teaching method with an effect size of 1.0 gives roughly a two-grade leap.

Imagine that the effect size of students creating mind map summaries of what they have learned is about 1.0 standard deviation in our experiment. This means that if a student in the control group in the experiment described above got a C grade, then she would have got an A grade if she were in the experimental group. An effect size of 1.0 clearly has dramatic consequences.

However, this 'two-grade leap' is a very rough estimate indeed. More accurately, if the effect size of a strategy is 1.0 standard deviation, then an *average* student in the experimental group will do better than 84% of the students in the control group. This is equivalent to a student who was 50th in a class of 100 becoming 16th. If the effect size is 0.5, then the average student in the experimental group will do better than 69% of the control group.

An effect size of 1.0 for our mind map experiment was clearly enormous! But this was just *one* experiment. It might have been a fluke result, however carefully it was carried out. To overcome this problem, an expert statistician and researcher averages the results of *all* the effective experiments on mind maps over the last few decades. It will usually be found that these experiments have been carried out on students working at almost every academic level, in every curriculum area, and in many different countries. The statistician creates an average effect size from hundreds, even thousands of experiments. By combining experiments like this, the statistician is in effect creating one enormous experiment out of many smaller ones. The resulting article might be called a 'research review', 'research synthesis', or a 'meta-study'. 'Meta-study' means a study of studies.

To write this review of research the expert, usually a university professor who has specialised in this area, searches systematically for *all* the effective experiments on mind maps, and other reviews and commentaries on the topic. The review will include an average effect size for student mind mapping as a means of learning a topic. Poor experiments are eliminated from this review, first because poorly designed experiments are unlikely to be published in the first place, and second because the statistician and the mind map expert will look very carefully at the experimental designs of the experiments reviewed, and will abandon those that don't meet stated criteria. For example, if the method of assigning students to the control and experimental groups was not thorough enough, the study will be removed from the review. Academics carrying out such reviews set a very high standard indeed and often reject the vast majority of published research on their chosen topic as not being up to standard.

Nesbit and Adesope (2006) wrote such a research review on learning with concept and knowledge maps (mind mapping). The studies in their review showed that mind mapping if carried out in the best way, *could* create an effect size of about 1.0 which, as we have seen, is very high indeed. Students were then learning at twice the rate of the very similar students in the control group who did something else instead of mapping. Nesbit and Adesope discovered which uses of these maps gives the highest effect sizes, which is really useful. For example, they found it helps students understand and remember central ideas more than it helps them with detail. Good reviews suggest how to use methods effectively in your classroom, at least in outline; most are vague about this practical detail though.

However, there are a number of research reviews on the use of concept maps, and there are thousands of research reviews published every year, so we can't read them all. What are we to do?

Reflection

Hattie (2009) suggests that an effect size of 0.2 is small, 0.4 is medium and 0.6 is large when judging educational outcomes. Remember, these are *average* effect sizes attained by teachers with careful training in the methodology. Wiliam (2009) finds that to get the research average effect size you need two years of work in a community of practice. Effect sizes are very rough measures of relative effectiveness, but they are the only way to compare methods and usually the only way to show cause and effect. The average effect sizes below were kindly provided by John Hattie, in a private communication in September 2017.

Jigsaw method	1.20	Mastery learning	0.57
Strategy to integrate with prior knowledge	0.93	Practice testing	0.54
Transfer strategies	0.86	Peer tutoring	0.53
Seeking help from peers	0.83	Co-operative learning versus competitive	0.53
Classroom discussion	0.82	Underlining and highlighting	0.50
Summarisation	0.79	Students making notes	0.50
Deliberate practice	0.79	Questioning	0.48
Mnemonics	0.76	Small-group learning	0.47
Feedback	0.70	Computer-assisted instruction	0.47
Deep motivation and approach	0.69	Study skills	0.46
Goals	0.68	Inductive teaching	0.44
Problem-solving teaching	0.68	Worked examples	0.37
Outlining and transforming	0.66	Principals and school leaders	0.32
Concept mapping	0.64	Finances	0.21
Setting standards for self-judgement	0.62	Interleaved practice	0.21
Spaced versus massed practice	0.60	Ability grouping	0.12
Meta-cognitive strategies	0.60	Surface motivation and approach	-0.11
Direct instruction	0.60		

Syntheses of effect size study research

Luckily, some academics have read these research reviews or meta-studies for us, and have averaged the findings of the different research reviews. This creates an average of average effect sizes! Combining all the reviews on concept mapping, Hattie finds an average effect size of 0.64. This is high, but includes all the studies, however the concept map was used.

One of the great strengths of effect sizes is that it enables us to *compare* teaching methods, strategies, techniques or other factors that might affect students' attainment, to see what factors have the greatest effect. Indeed, it is the only means of doing so. Also, quantitative studies are the most reliable way of identifying cause and effect.

It is not just quantitative effect size research that can be summarised and reviewed over and over like this; the same can be done with qualitative research. These reviews of reviews are going to be more reliable than individual studies.

> 'Meta-analysis is a summary, or synthesis, of relevant research findings. It looks at all of the individual studies done on a particular topic and summarises them.'
>
> *Robert J. Marzano, www.marzanoresearch.com*

Criticisms of the effect size approach

Wiliam (2016) warns us that effect sizes are problematic and not reliable, and certainly should not be relied upon by themselves. He recommends teachers use 'best evidence reviews of research'. As well as identifying which methods work, these discuss why the methods work. However, there are not many of them.

The main problems with effect size studies are: they are usually short-term, often a matter of a few weeks; the tests, if not standardised, *may* measure only low-level surface learning; and if they are standardised, for technical reasons they will underestimate what students have learned. Effect sizes are calculated in a way that means students under the age of about 10 or 12 get higher effect sizes than older students.

Some critics argue that different studies on, say, 'self-assessment' will do self-assessment in different ways, and to combine these studies is combining apples with oranges. However, if a teaching method, despite being vaguely defined and being done in different ways, on average has a high effect size, this shows us it is a robust and adaptable method that works in many contexts, and it might well be worth trying in our own classrooms. The variability in implementation is a benefit, not a problem. Also, a good meta-study teases out why some implementations are more effective than others, and advises how to get the best from the method.

The main argument against these criticisms is that the relative stability of effect sizes would not occur if there were great differences between studies of the same intervention. Those who review effect size studies usually find that effect sizes are at least reasonably stable from study to study, and only rarely influenced by 'moderators' such as academic level.

Effect size studies have been subjected to three rigorous tests and passed them all. These tests are to compare effect size studies with other ways to discover the better teaching methods. There is a notable agreement that can give us heart.

- Qualitative studies of teaching methods (see Chapter 1) suggest what I call co-constructivist teaching methods, and these turn out to have high effect sizes. For example, 'feedback' and 'relevant recall questions' and summarising.

- The very best teachers use many methods with very high effect sizes, for example challenging tasks and class discussion (see Petty, 2009).

The third test is this. If effect size studies and meta-studies were not reliable, they would tend to produce random results. When throwing dice, the more often you throw, the more likely the average of all your throws will be a middling score rather than six or one. So, if RCTs didn't give meaningful results, the more studies carried out on a given teaching method, the more likely it would be that there would be a moderate effect size for that method. In reality, we find the exact opposite. Many methods subjected to a very large number of studies have very high effect sizes, and other methods very low ones.

While the notion of effect size has weaknesses for some academics, and others in search of shining scientific certainties, *they work well for teachers*. Teachers can make do with a rough sifting of methods to determine which are worth experimenting with and which not. This is confirmed by the finding that methods with high effect sizes do in fact deliver the promised boost in student attainment when a teacher has trialled them in the way described below for a couple of years (see Wiliam, 2009).

However, effect size research might sift out many methods that could work well for you, so don't allow them to do all the critical work; in the end, as described below, the supreme court is what works for you and your students.

Average effect sizes are like a map, showing us the way to teaching methods that *might* work in our classroom. The map is imperfect. But if you throw it away, what are you left with? When it comes to deciding which methods are best, only blind guesswork, bias, exhortations from those who would like you to hop on their ideological bandwagon, and your own limited experience. Better to use the map, but not to trust it blindly. Try the high effect size methods that might fix your, or your students' problems a few times.

Reflect on them and adapt them. If they don't work for you, dump them and try another, as explained below.

The problem of bias

Summary research evidence should help us overcome bias – in ourselves and in others. Bias includes:

Confirmation bias: We tend to look for, choose and remember ideas that confirm our present views and avoid or forget those that contradict them. Lefties might read the *The Guardian*, Righties might read *The Daily Telegraph*. It's just easier to stick with your present views and practices.

Groupthink: If all my colleagues think ability grouping is a good idea, I will feel uncomfortable disagreeing with them. We are tribal animals, and we like to fit in.

Doc shopping: Given the above, there is a strong tendency to look for and quote authorities who agree with us. It is not hard to find **doc**torates (PhDs) and **doc**uments on the Web that reflect your prejudices with persuasive eloquence. But most docs might *disagree* with you! It's not just you who has this problem, everyone you read has it too, to some degree.

Let's look at some other examples of this ocean of self-deluding opinion.

Comparing some sources of evidence

'*Well, it works for me.*' Okay, but could something else work even better? Teaching is impossible to do perfectly and there are lots of alternative approaches.

'*Everybody else does it.*' This is groupthink. Sometimes groups are right, sometimes not. The most commonly used questioning methods in UK classrooms are among the worst available, as we saw in Chapter 5.

What inspectors recommend: Inspectorates exist in some countries, but they are not as prescriptive as teachers often believe. In the UK there is Ofsted, but it does not dictate *how* you should teach, thankfully, as their inspection handbook makes clear.

Ofsted wants outcomes, not particular methods, so you are on your own. Be grateful! However, many people claim to know what methods Ofsted inspectors are 'really' looking for – ask them how they know. I've never heard a credible answer.

Ofsted publishes advice on 'best practice', but it's only based on their own experience and so doesn't pass the bias test. Christodoulou (2014) criticises their advice on best practice and makes a strong case.

Read published research studies. An advantage of anything published in a recognised journal is that it will normally be 'peer reviewed', meaning some anonymous experts will have vetted the study. If the study was not published, it probably hasn't been vetted.

Individual studies can often provide the very information you are after, though you need good searching skills to find the study you want: ask a librarian to help you.

A problem with reading individual studies is that for every study that says one thing, there may be others that say the opposite. And you are unlikely to have the time to read *all* the studies on any given issue or method. Luckily, someone else may have done that work for you and more to create a 'research review', as explained above.

Read published quantitative research studies. The only way of finding out whether something works is to try it out with real teachers and real students in a rigorous trial, as described above. But summary evidence, for example meta-studies or research reviews, is more reliable than an individual study.

Read cognitive psychology research studies. These give the theory of how to teach based on experiments that have mainly been done in psychology labs, although increasingly cognitive psychologists are doing classroom-based experiments. Research reviews of cognitive psychology findings are more useful than reading individual studies usually, as they consider all the evidence dispassionately. One major review of research in cognitive psychology is Bransford (2000). The general principles of cognitive psychology give us many useful ideas on how to teach. The co-constructivist approach used in this book comes from this source.

Read books by experts. Experts are subject to bias unless they make fair use of the best evidence available. Books are edited, but they are rarely peer reviewed before publication. If a book is recommended, you might think it will be a more reliable or useful guide. But does the recommender pass the bias test, or do they like the book because it confirms their preferred practice and prejudices?

Use advice backed up by references. People often give references to back up their opinions. But if all their references are just individual studies, then they may well be omitting the evidence *against* their point of view.

If they reference research *reviews*, this is much more reliable. Look for terms like this in their references: 'meta-study', 'meta-analysis', 'best evidence syntheses (BES)' or 'systematic review'.

Read blogs, websites, social media, newspaper articles, etc. Are the ideas based on evidence in research reviews, or just individual studies, or on opinion only? A favourite trick to defend a bias is to find a poor piece of research, or an extreme view, and correctly criticise this, leaving gullible readers believing the author has disproved that position, and so proved their own, when neither was the case. Misrepresenting an opponent's view and then arguing against it is called a 'straw man argument'.

Many social media and newspaper articles are thought-provoking, informative, up-to-the-minute, and useful, but systematic reviews are far more trustworthy.

Unfortunately, the best way to get attention on social media is to be controversial, angry, and a critic of received wisdom. Writing a tweet or a blog that summarises faithfully research review evidence will only rarely get attention on social media, especially if the findings are unsurprising. However, if you write a blog or tweet arguing that commonly-held views are bunk, you often will get attention. Consequently, there is a strong (though sometimes unconscious) bias on social media towards misleading you. Be careful who you follow!

Using more than one source of evidence: 'triangulation'

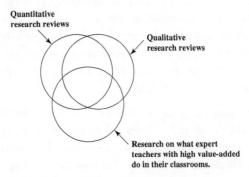

Figure 14.3: Triangulating sources of evidence

So the most reliable sources of information are quantitative research reviews, or reviews of these reviews, and qualitative research reviews. I will add a very much smaller type of research, 'field research', on what the very best teachers do in terms of their value-added (*improvement* in students' learning), or academic studies on 'expert teachers'. I explain these more below. Many quantitative reviews include qualitative findings and vice versa, so the sources of evidence are not as separate as Figure 14.3 suggests.

	Some advantages	Some disadvantages
Quantitative research reviews	Allow us to compare effect sizes and so prioritise what to experiment with. Real classrooms and students. Can show cause and effect.	Effect size measures are not entirely reliable. Only achievement is considered usually.
Qualitative research reviews	Give us theoretical understanding of the learning process. Help explain why methods work.	Research is often done in a laboratory context, not in classrooms. Can't compare methods.
Research on what expert teachers with high value-added do in their classrooms: field research	The teachers have exceptional achievement over many years rather than just during a study. Real classrooms and students.	There is very little of this research. Can every teacher adopt the strategies of exceptional teachers? Hard to identify what aspects of their teaching is the cause of their excellence.

Figure 14.4: Schools of educational research compared

Figure 14.4 greatly simplifies a very complex situation on the best forms of evidence. Notice that no source of evidence gets unqualified approval; they all make a useful contribution and they all have weaknesses. Educationalists sometimes critique one of these schools of evidence, ignoring its strengths while ignoring the weaknesses of the alternatives they advocate. This selective perfectionism is unfair, but quite common.

I suggest we do what journalists are taught to do: use multiple sources of evidence. If a method, strategy or other variable is recommended by qualitative research, has a high effect size, and is used by teachers who get exceptional value-added, then it is worth a try in our own classrooms, especially if it might fix a problem we, or our learners, are having. If a method gets the thumbs up from two out of three of these schools, it is also worth consideration.

I have used this 'triangulation' approach in *Evidence-Based Teaching* (2009) and in this book, but it is certainly not unique to me. Triangulation is a widely accepted approach used in many disciplines, for example the Intergovernmental Panel on Climate Change uses something like it, though much more nuanced. In education, something like triangulation (though more nuanced) is used by organisations such as the Education Endowment

Fund (EEF) and the EPPI-Centre to give very carefully considered advice, see pages 278 and 279.

However, some organisations that claim to use evidence or research are much more casual and cavalier in their use of such sources. I believe triangulation, or something very like it, is a minimum expectation if we want reliable conclusions from research.

Comparing sources of evidence

The following table needs to be taken with a pinch of salt. It only works for average examples of the sources of evidence. Real examples will often be better or worse than this average. It would be better to use the criteria at the top of the table to evaluate the source of evidence you are considering; that would be much fairer.

Note: The more stars the better, a blank means no stars at all!

Comparing different sources of evidence. Warning: it works for typical evidence, but not for all cases					
	Is it checked with others, preferably peer reviewed?	Does it try systematically to include all good evidence?	Are the findings based on classrooms (preferably) like my own?	Is there a control group?	Is there an effect size to compare a method with others?
What works for me			★ ★ ★ ★		
What everybody else does	★ ★		★ ★ ★		
What Ofsted recommends	★ ★ ★		★ ★ ★		
Published quantitative research study	★ ★ ★		★ ★ ★	Usually, not always, up to: ★ ★ ★	★ ★ ★
Quantitative research reviews: These include meta-studies, meta-analyses, best evidence syntheses and systematic reviews	★ ★ ★ ★	★ ★ ★	★ ★ ★	★ ★ ★	★ ★ ★ ★

(continued)

Qualitative research reviews, e.g. systematic reviews	★ ★ ★ ★	★ ★ ★	★ ★	★	
Cognitive psychology research studies	★ ★		★	Not always	
Books by experts	★ ★	Usually not	Sometimes		Usually not
Advice backed up by references	★		Sometimes	Usually not	Usually not
Blogs, websites, social media, etc.	There are often comments by others on blogs		Many blogs are		Usually not
Read research on what the best value-added teachers do	★ ★	In effect it usually includes all teachers, but certainly not all the evidence	★ ★ ★	★ ★ ★ The control is those teachers with lower value-added	No, but these teachers were compared to others
The bodies in this chapter such as the EEF and the EPPI-Centre	★ ★ ★ ★	★ ★ ★ ★	★ ★ ★ ★	★ ★ ★ ★	Sometimes

More reliable sources of evidence in education

Some organisations, documents, and individuals systematically sift reliable evidence to find the teaching methods and other factors that affect student achievement. As they take care to avoid bias and to find all relevant evidence, they are the most reliable sources of advice for teachers and their managers. They use triangulation along with more sophisticated approaches. They are all worth your time and study; however they tend to give general principles and general strategies and methods, and often do not include as much procedural detail as in this book. What follows is not a complete list, but will get you started.

Sources of information on cognitive science – qualitative research

Chapter 1, indeed this whole book, draws on insights from cognitive science. While there are many books that summarise how cognitive science can help teachers, Willingham (2009) is deservedly popular, but the most authoritative is Bransford (2000). The latter was a two-year project where more than 25 scholars collaborated to summarise the science of learning at the request of the USA's National Academies of Sciences and Engineering, the Institute of Medicine, and the National Research Council. It is well worth reading. Among many other factors it stressed meaning-making and the importance of both surface and deep learning (though these terms were not used), and transfer of learning. The review also stresses the importance of students learning for its own sake, rather than just to satisfy external pressures.

Marzarno and Hattie below make careful use of cognitive science. Baker (2015) finds that over half of psychology studies fail the reproducibility test, so individual studies are less reliable than careful reviews of research.

Research on the teaching of the very best teachers

What do really exceptional teachers do that good teachers don't? This is a very under-researched question but we are beginning to get some answers. What makes brilliant teachers brilliant is not who they are, but what they do in the classroom, and some of the techniques they use anyone could adopt.

Doug Lemov works in the USA, and he went to some of the highest achieving schools in the worst areas of social and economic deprivation. Then he asked these schools if he could watch their two very best teachers, and 'camped out in their classrooms'. He found these exceptional teachers often used similar strategies, which were key to their success, but often under the radar of most educational research.

One such teacher achieved the top mathematics results in his county, but 80% of his students claimed free school meals, almost all were from minority ethnic backgrounds, and 90% counted as poor. Yet his students achieved a 100% pass rate, surpassing the results of others from privileged areas.

Lemov studied about 100 such teachers and found that they used a great deal of 'explicit teaching' (similar to the RAR model in this book) with very high expectations and very high participation rates. There was a great deal of immediate check and correct. They were strict but caring, and saw these qualities as two sides of the same coin: 'tough love'. A questioning method at the end of Chapter 5 in this book, 'Right is Right', comes directly from Lemov's excellent book *Teach like a Champion*. However, the insights from his work are peppered throughout this book.

Paul Ayres et al. (2004) made a rigorous study of teachers who were in the top 1% nationally in terms of value-added for six years running. He found that the lessons of these exceptional teachers were highly structured and teacher-led, with high focus and energy. There was no 'spoon-feeding' and students had to write their own notes. They taught topics from surface to deep with a ladder of tasks, beginning with closed tasks but requiring full explanations for students' answers. Then they moved onto individual or group work on challenging tasks to develop deep learning. They monitored learning carefully and provided a constant check and correct, stressing student interest, and making use of high-quality classroom discussion where they did not give the answer away (assertive questioning). This confirms much quantitative and qualitative research.

John Hattie (2003) empirically determined the criteria that best distinguished expert teachers from less-effective teachers with the same amount of experience. He found expert teachers set their students challenging goals that focused on deep learning. He also found that 74% of work produced by students in the classes of expert teachers was relational or abstract, that is, deep. But only 29% of learning was deep in the classes of non-expert but equally experienced teachers. Expert teachers saw their students' work as a reflection of their own teaching rather than a reflection of the students' characteristics. They also gave high-quality informative feedback to their students, and more of it than less expert teachers.

Research on exceptionally good teachers confirms much quantitative and qualitative research, and informs this book throughout.

There is a more detailed account of Hattie (2003) and Ayres (2004) in Petty (2009).

Sources of information on quantitative research

All the following make use of quantitative but also qualitative research.

Professor John Hattie

Professor John Hattie has a very deserved global reputation for identifying the factors that most affect student achievement. He does this by collecting all the rigourously sifted summary evidence on effect sizes available, and synthesising this. His books on visible learning are seminal and highly recommended. With Gregory Donoghue he has now synthesised this vast body of summary research into a conceptual model that describes how best to teach a topic (not a lesson), which can be seen in Figure 14.5.

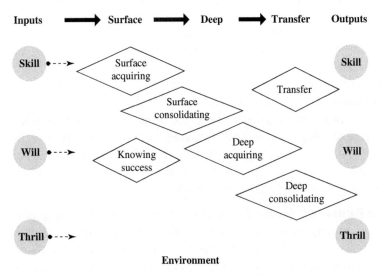

Figure 14.5: The Hattie–Donoghue model of learning

The Hattie–Donoghue model proposes that various learning strategies are powerful at certain stages during the learning of a topic. The teaching methods that work best for introducing surface knowledge are not the same methods that best develop deep understanding and transfer. I have made extensive use of this model in this book, for example with my RAR structure, and particularly with my ladder of tasks.

Notice that within both surface and deep phases there is an acquiring and a consolidation phase in their model. Hattie used his gigantic database of summary evidence containing the work of thousands of academics on millions of students to identify the most effective teaching methods or 'learning strategies'. However, Hattie and Donoghue discovered that the effectiveness of teaching methods depended on where the students were in their learning of the topic. For example, the methods that best helped students acquire surface learning did not help students acquire deep learning, and vice versa. The table below outlines just some of the methods/strategies most effective for each phase in the teaching of a topic. Do read their paper for more detail, which is freely available online. Remember, an effect size of 0.4 is medium and 0.6 is high; all effect sizes are average for many studies.

Which strategies work best at different stages in the model?

Across the whole model and so throughout the teaching of a topic, success criteria has an effect size of 1.1 (see Chapters 6 and 7) and the jigsaw teaching method an effect size of 1.2 (see Chapter 8).

Some powerful learning strategies or teaching methods for different phases in teaching of a topic are shown below. They are a selection from Hattie and Donoghue (2016) and use the terminology in their model. There are more in their paper.

Acquiring surface learning	Effect size	Explanations, and where to find this strategy in this book
Strategy to integrate with prior knowledge	0.93	See Chapter 6 on 'orientation' especially the 'relevant recall questions' method. See also 'peer explaining' in Chapter 7.
Mnemonics	0.76	These are tricks for remembering basic facts, see Chapter 8.
Summarisation	0.66	Students summarising key points, if text is used then underlining (next in the table) might help this summarisation (but it's cheating to add their effect sizes!).
Underlining and highlighting	0.50	See Chapter 13 on skills, also many methods in Chapter 8.
Note-taking (I call this note-making)	0.50	This is students writing their *own* notes, not copying them. See Chapters 7 and 12 for various approaches. This could be in graphic organiser form (Chapter 3) when the effect size might be higher.

Consolidating surface learning	Effect size	Explanations, and where to find this strategy in this book
Deliberate practice	0.77	A process of practising the use of the knowledge and skill, especially to fix a weakness. See Chapter 9 on applying learning and Chapter 11 on check and correct, for example learning loops.
Giving and receiving feedback	0.71	See Chapter 11 on check and correct.
Spaced versus massed practice	0.60	Chapter 12 on the reuse of learning.
Practice testing	0.44	See the end of Chapter 12 on the reuse of learning.
Teaching test-taking, and coaching for tests	0.27	Note, this is not as effective as other approaches in these tables.

Acquiring deep learning involves identifying the reasons why the knowledge is as it is, examining arguments and evidence for and against any claims made in the knowledge, and examining qualifiers. Linking the knowledge with other knowledge is especially important, as explained in Chapter 1.

Acquiring deep learning	Effect size	Explanations, and where to find this strategy in this book
Elaboration and organisation	0.75	Explaining the knowledge in your own words and structuring it.
Strategy monitoring	0.71	The student thinking about their own thinking and learning and monitoring their own strategies to learn.
Elaborative interrogation	0.42	Extending the detail, but asking 'why', justifying and critically appraising the knowledge.

Consolidating deep learning	Effect size	Explanations, and where to find this strategy in this book
Seeking help from peers	0.83	See Chapter 11, also group work methods in Chapter 5.
Class discussion	0.82	See Chapter 5.
Evaluation and reflection	0.75	See Chapter 9, especially evaluative tasks towards the top of the ladder. See also reflective journals and personal targets in Chapter 11.
Problem-solving teaching	0.68	See challenging tasks in Chapters 9 and 10 if the writing is about problem-solving. Problem-solving can be taught as a skill, see Chapter 13.
Self-verbalisation and self-questioning	0.64	See peer explaining, Chapter 7.
Becoming a teacher (peer tutoring)	0.54	See peer explaining, Chapter 7. Also search online for 'learning teams Geoff Petty' for a download.

Transfer	Effect size	Explanation, and where to find this strategy in this book
Similarities and differences	1.32	Comparing two concepts. See Chapter 3 for the method, and for card games based on this.
Seeing patterns to new situations	1.14	Examining *'Where have we seen this before?'* See the ends of Chapters 1 and 9.
Far transfer	0.80	Seeing the relevance of what is being taught in a very wide context. See the end of Chapter 9 for methods for far transfer. Also bridging and meta-cognition in Chapter 13.

The Hattie-Donoghue model describes three 'inputs'. These are attributes a given student should have, at least to some degree, when you begin to teach your topic.

- **The skill:** prior achievement and other attributes the student brings to the task

- **The will:** the habits of mind and basic capacity and confidence of the student to do what is necessary to learn

- **The thrill:** the extent to which learning is seen by students as enjoyable for its own sake, rather than done for approval, marks/grades, or some other externally imposed factor – that is, the degree to which students are intrinsically, rather than extrinsically, motivated to make sense of the learning, linking it to what they already know.

The model states that these same attributes are affected by your teaching of the topic, so the attributes are also 'outputs'. Students will, of course, have more prior achievement if you have taught them the topic. But their 'will' and 'thrill' will be affected too. Hopefully, you will teach in such a way that will increase your students' capacity to learn, and their confidence as a learner (will). Hopefully, your teaching will also increase your students' intrinsic interest in your subject, and in learning for its own sake (thrill).

I worry that some teachers, driven by an overbearing accountability culture and seeking to avoid blame or for other reasons, overuse test preparation methods that their students soon find dull and repetitive, and which fail to excite interest in the subject or in learning itself. Methods that continually compare students with each other, for example grades or percentages, have a negative effect on many students' self-belief, interest in the subject and interest in learning, as described in Chapter 11. Over-emphasis on testing can even sacrifice students' mental health.

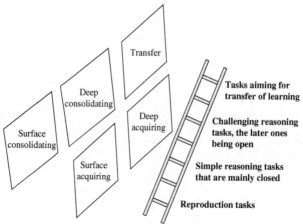

Figure 14.6: The Hattie–Donoghue model can be seen as a ladder of tasks

Interestingly, test-preparation methods are not as effective as other methods according to the model. The best way to prepare students for a test is to teach for deep learning using interesting active teaching methods and allowing for check and correct, though I give some test-preparation methods on pages 236, 227, 151, and 214.

> 'When students take a deep approach they aim to develop understanding and make sense of what they are learning, and create meaning and make ideas their own. This means they [...] relate ideas together and make connections with previous experiences, ask themselves questions about what they are learning, discuss their ideas with others and compare different perspectives. When students are taking a surface approach they aim to reproduce information and learn the facts and ideas – with little recourse to seeing relations or connections between ideas.'
>
> *John Hattie, 'The role of learning strategies in today's classrooms',*
> *The 34th Vernon-Wall Lecture, 2014*

Robert Marzano

Professor Robert Marzano works mainly in the USA, and has long used systematic reviews of research to inform how to improve teaching. His books are highly recommended. There is a free download available online at http://www.marzanoresearch.com/ that lists 'nine essential instructional strategies'.

Marzano's nine essential instructional strategies	Explanation and where to find these in this book
1. Identifying similarities and differences	See Chapter 3.
2. Summarising and note-taking	This is students making their own notes, not copying from the board, see Chapters 7, 8, 10.
3. Reinforcing effort and providing recognition	See Chapter 11, especially medal and mission and goals.
4. Homework and practice	Use any of the methods in Chapters 7, 8, 9, and 11.
5. Non-linguistic representations	See Chapter 3 on graphic organisers.
6. Co-operative learning	See 'jigsaw' Chapter 8.
7. Setting objectives and providing feedback	Setting objectives Chapters 6 and 7, providing feedback Chapter 11.
8. Generating and testing hypotheses	See the end of Chapter 9.
9. Cues, questions, and advance organisers	Chapters 5 and 6.

There is a good deal more to Marzano than this, for example he advocates using a complete six-step process to teach vocabulary that includes teacher explanation, student explanation, student graphic or pictographic representation, review using comparison activities, student discussion of vocabulary terms, and the use of games; this could include card-sorting games in Chapter 3.

His book, *The Art and Science of Teaching,* is highly influential and available as a free download.

The Education Endowment Foundation (EEF): Teaching and Learning Toolkit

The EEF was set up by the Sutton Trust in 2011. Its website can be found here: https://educationendowmentfoundation.org.uk

There is advice on 'big picture' themes such as developing independent learning, mathematics, student engagement and behaviour and many more. They also produce 'evidence summaries', which give rise to a 'Teaching and Learning Toolkit'. This is a very accessible summary of educational research on teaching 5–16-year-olds, though the ideas can often be adapted for older learners. For each factor that might affect achievement, the EEF provides an evaluation of the following:

Cost: This is given in general terms, for example 'low', 'moderate' or 'very high'.

Evidence strength: Evidence is described using general terms such as 'extensive evidence' or 'limited evidence'.

Impact: Rather than using effect sizes, the EEF gives the impact of the factors in its toolkit in terms of 'months of additional progress' made by a typical student. For example, 'feedback' provides eight months of additional progress, if it is done well of course.

Sadly there is not always procedural detail to help you implement some of the strategies, though reports such as their 'Marking Review' are much more helpful in this respect. Here are the factors they identify as providing the greatest 'additional progress'. There are others; please visit the website.

EEF Toolkit strand	Cost	Evidence strength	Impact in months of additional progress	Explanation and where to find this in this book
Feedback (I would call this check and correct)	1/5	3/5	8	Chapter 5 on questioning and Chapter 11 on check and correct.
Meta-cognition and self-regulation	1/5	4/5	8	Students thinking about their own thinking and work, Chapters 7 and 11.
Homework (secondary)	1/5	3/5	5	Chapter 9.
Mastery learning	1/5	3/5	5	Chapter 11.
Peer tutoring	1/5	4/5	5	See peer explaining, Chapter 7.
Reading comprehension strategies	1/5	4/5	5	Chapter 13.
Collaborative learning	1/5	4/5	5	See 'jigsaw', Chapter 8.

BES: Iterative best evidence syntheses

The New Zealand Government is a generous source of free reliable advice for teachers in the form of 'iterative best evidence syntheses'. This is the form of summary evidence advocated by Wiliam (2016). See the references on page 286 under the heading 'Best evidence syntheses (free online)'. These include the excellent:

- 'Effective pedagogy in mathematics' by G. Anthony and M. Walshaw

- 'Teacher professional learning and development best evidence synthesis' by H. Timperley et al.

There is useful detail in the 'Exemplars for quality teaching' on the www.educationcounts.govt.nz website, which are case studies that provide good operational detail. As with most of the following organisations, full reports are provided, but helpful summaries are available too.

EPPI-Centre

The Institute of Education (IoE) University College of London runs the Evidence for Policy and Practice Information and Co-ordinating Centre (EPPI-Centre), which specialises in systematic reviews and the use of research in decision-making. It can be found at: https://eppi.ioe.ac.uk

The reports are succinct and short. However, despite having sections in their reports on 'implications for practice' the advice is often very generalised. For example, a paper on self- and peer assessment found it increased attainment, but the 'implications for practice' runs to three bullet points.

Helpful, but one could not implement self- or peer assessment well from this. However, to be fair the research used to produce this summary very rarely gives the precise methodology used by the teachers, a weakness in most published research on teaching.

IES Institute of Education Sciences

This is focused on education in the USA, and includes the National Centre for Education Research and the What Works Clearing House mentioned below. The website https://ies.ed.gov/ has a search facility. Look out particularly for their 'practice guides', practical summaries of systematic reviews that can be downloaded free of charge. Some of the material is specific to the US curriculum; however, you can adapt it for useful ideas.

What Works Clearing (WWC) House

This can be found at https://ies.ed.gov/ncee/wwc/. It is an organisation in the USA and largely focuses on assessing programmes or products that a school or college might buy, such as schemes to teach reading.

Institute for Effective Education

The IEE, part of the University of York, publishes a fortnightly e-newsletter called 'Best Evidence in Brief' in conjunction with the Center for Research and Reform in Education at Johns Hopkins University in the USA. This excellent publication is very readable and reports on high-quality research. It also focuses on the practical implications for teachers. You can sign up for 'Best Evidence in Brief' for free on the IEE website: https://the-iee.org.uk/.

Best evidence encyclopaedias

The University of York provides us with their best evidence encyclopaedia at www.bestevidence.org.uk This has advice on teaching reading, primary science, technology and mathematics, early childhood education, and mathematics, at both primary and secondary level and much more. There is advice for teachers, headteachers, policy makers and researchers, and for children. However, the main focus is on programmes that a school can purchase, which often involve special training.

There is a best evidence encyclopaedia for the USA at http://www.bestevidence. org/ covering education from Kindergarten to Grade 12, the latter being for 17- to 18-year-olds (K–12). You can search for best evidence summaries, some of which might be in your subject for your age group. Although focused on the USA, there is much advice here for teachers in any country.

Using evidence to improve your teaching

Earlier in this chapter we saw how we could use triangulation and systematic syntheses of advice to inform us about strategies that are likely to work well for us and our students. However, there is no certainty that a method/strategy/technique that has worked for other teachers will work for you and your students. Neither is there any certainty that you can achieve the same effect size. Where should we go from here? Let's use an evidence-based approach to answer this question: how do research reviews on improving teaching suggest you should go about becoming even better?

Figure 14.7 summarises the findings of two such summaries from Timperley (2007) and Joyce and Showers (2002). It shows how high-quality evidence can be used to *suggest* methods that may work for you, and solve your teaching and learning problems or meet the aspirations of you or your students. You then learn to use such methods by repeated trial and error, that is, reflective practice. Note that the evidence is not your dictator, only your advisor. It need not limit your teaching or creativity in any way. You choose a useful-looking method and experiment with it repeatedly, learning how to use it well (this is sometimes called 'action research'). You discuss your experiments with a group of teachers who are also experimenting with their methods. This is called a 'community of practice': research reviews on how to improve teaching show communities of practice are vitally necessary for your own improvement, and that it seems the vast majority of teachers will not improve without them.

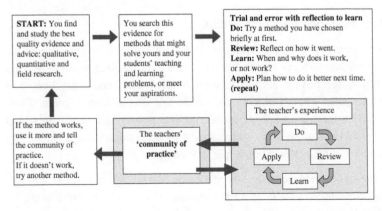

Figure 14.7: How teachers can use evidence to sift for methods that might improve their teaching

If the method you are experimenting with works, great, you use it more and tell others about it. If it doesn't work after at least five trials or so, you abandon it and try another method suggested by the evidence.

Using the evidence as a source of ideas is very helpful, but shouldn't stop you thinking of your own approaches and experimenting with these. However, trialling evidence-based methods will help you understand better what works and what doesn't and why, so you can devise your own methods more successfully. Indeed, that's the whole purpose of using evidence: it improves your understanding of the teaching and learning process, see Timperley et al. (2008) and (2011).

I call these experiments with your teaching 'supported experiments'. They are done for your students, as well as for your team, and they are supported by the team. Once you have found a way of making a strategy work, you tell your team about it and they adopt it on their active scheme of work (a scheme of work with teaching methods on it), or in a course specific best methods manual. That way other teachers benefit from your experiment. You may also coach them in the use of this new method. There is more on this improvement process on my website: http://geoffpetty.com/for-team-leaders/supported-experiments/.

 Consider

Creating a teaching method/strategy/technique manual in your team

One way of using this book is to:

1 experiment with the methods that will improve your teaching, and/or your students' learning in a direction that is important to you

2 trial the methods repeatedly, in short activities at first

3 tell your team about the teaching strategies you have found work best

4 produce an active scheme of work that suggests a selection of activities for each topic or subtopic in your scheme. Or develop a teaching strategy manual for your courses. Share out the work among your team to develop the strategies and their resources in detail, as it is a lot of work. This will take at least a year, and ideally is a permanent improvement project.

Looking closely at Timperley and at Joyce and Showers, they did not find evidence that inspection regimes, league tables or similar accountability systems that judge teachers' work create improvements anywhere near as well as supported experiments within communities of practice. The countries that do best in international comparisons of education systems stress continued professional development (CPD) and teamwork, not accountability.

Further reading

See also the principal references in Chapter 15 Further reading and references.

Free online resources

Search for 'evidence-based teaching', 'meta-study', 'systematic reviews', 'confirmation bias' and 'effect sizes'.

'A new guide on evidence-based practice: identifying and implementing educational practices supported by rigorous evidence'. This is an easy-to-read government guide from the USA.

M. Baker, 'Over half of psychology studies fail reproducibility test' (2015). A *Nature* paper, I would conclude that summaries of research are more reliable than individual studies.

R. Marzano, 'A theory-based meta-analysis of research on instruction' (Aurora, Co: Mid-Continent Research for Education and Learning, 1998). The paper is large and complex but is an example of a meta-analysis on teaching methods.

H. Timperley et al., 'Best evidence synthesis on professional learning and development' (Report to the Ministry of Education, Wellington, New Zealand, 2008). A review of the evidence on how to improve teaching.

D. Wiliam, 'Randomised control trials in education research' (*University of Brighton Research in Education*, Vol. 6, No. 1, 2014).

Books and papers

P. Ayres et al., 'Effective teaching in the context of a Grade 12 high-stakes external examination in New South Wales, Australia' (*British Educational Research Journal*, Vol. 30, No. 1 February 2004).

J.B. Biggs, 'What do inventories of students' learning processes really measure? A theoretical review and clarification' (*British Journal of Educational Psychology*, 63(1), 3–19, 1993).

J.D. Bransford et al., *How People Learn: Brain, Mind, Experience and School* (Washington: National Research Council, 2000).

D. Gough, S. Oliver and J. Thomas, *An Introduction to Systematic Reviews* (London: Sage, 2012).

D. Gough and J. Thomas, 'Systematic reviews of research in education: Aims, myths and multiple methods' (*Review of Education,* Vol. 4, No. 1, pages 84–102, February 2016).

J.A.C. Hattie, 'The role of learning strategies in today's classrooms' (The 34th Vernon-Wall Lecture, the Education Section of The British Psychological Society, 2015). Available online for a small payment.

B.R. Joyce and B. Showers, *Student Achievement Through Staff Development* (3rd Edition) (Alexandria: ASCD, 2002). Very readable review of research with similar findings to Timperley (2008).

T.S. Kuhn, *The Structure of Scientific Revolutions* (Chicago: University of Chicago Press, 1962).

R. Marzano, D. Pickering and J. Pollock, *Classroom Instruction that Works* (Alexandria: ASCD, 2001).

J.C. Nesbit and O. Adesope, 'Learning with concept and knowledge maps: A meta-analysis (*Review of Educational Research* 76, page 413, 2006).

G. Petty, *Evidence-Based Teaching* (Oxford: Oxford University Press, 2009).

K.R. Popper, *The Logic of Scientific Discovery* (3rd Edition) (London: Hutchinson, 1968).

H. Timperley, *Realising the Power of Professional Learning* (Maidenhead: McGraw-Hill: 2011).

D. Wiliam, *Assessment for Learning: Why, What and How?* (London: IoE, 2009). Shows that it takes about two years for teachers in a community of practice to get about the average effect size researchers find.

D. Wiliam, 'Leadership for teacher learning: Creating a culture where all teachers improve so that all students succeed' (LearningSciencesInternational. com, 2016). Useful critique of effect size research but much more.

D. Willingham, *Why Don't Students Like School? A Cognitive Scientist Answers Questions About How the Mind Works and What It Means for the Classroom* (San Francisco: Jossey-Bass, 2010). Very readable summary of cognitive science.

Chapter 15

Further reading and references

Principal references for the Evidence boxes

The references under the three headings below are referred to in the Evidence boxes at the end of each chapter, in order to use the 'triangulation' approach mentioned in the last chapter. The references can mostly be downloaded for free online (search for title and author). Other summaries of research are available, especially in book form, and many will have more detail than most of the free resources below.

Summaries of qualitative research

The following do not include quantitative data, but quantitative research may have been referred to in writing the paper or book The first two are books, the others are free online, search for title and author.

J.D. Bransford et al., *How People Learn: Brain, Mind, Experience and School* (Washington: National Research Council, 2000). This book is the result of more than 20 academics working for two years on a large national project to summarise what is known about learning. Being a book it is much more detailed than the other references below.

D. Willingham, *Why Don't Students Like School? A Cognitive Scientist Answers Questions About How the Mind Works and What it Means for the Classroom* (San Francisco: Jossey-Bass, 2010).

American Psychological Association, 'Coalition for psychology in schools and education' (2015). Top 20 principles from psychology for pre-K–12 teaching and learning.

Deans for Impact, 'The science of learning'. (Austin, TX: Deans for Impact, 2015).

H. Pashler, P. Bain, B. Bottge, A. Graesser, K. Koedinger, M. McDaniel and J. Metcalfe, 'Organising instruction and study to improve student learning (NCER 2007–2004)' (Washington, DC: National Center for Education Research, Institute of Education Sciences, U.S. Department of Education, 2007. Retrieved from http://ncer.ed.gov).

B. Rosenshine, 'Principles of instruction' (International Academy of Education and International Bureau of Education, 2010). This summary makes use of evidence on the classroom practices of teachers who get the highest gains in student learning.

And where relevant: *'Cognitive Load Theory: Research that teachers really need to understand'* (Centre for Education Statistics and Evaluation, 2017).

Summaries of quantitative research

These are all free to download, search for title and author. These references include quantitative data, but qualitative research was referred to in their preparation.

J.A.C. Hattie and G.M. Donoghue, 'Learning strategies: a synthesis and conceptual model' (*NPJ Science of Learning*, 2016). The supplementary appendix at the very end of this paper lists effect sizes, along with the reviews from which they came. See https://www.nature.com/articles/npjscilearn201613.

R. Marzano, *The Art and Science of Teaching: A Comprehensive Framework for Effective Instruction.* (Alexandria, VA: ASCD, 2007). A free pdf 'learning map' of the Teacher Evaluation Model based on this book is also available.

R. Marzano et al., *'Nine Essential Instructional Strategies'* (adapted from *Classroom Instruction that Works,* Alexandria: ASCD, 2001).

Note: Hattie (2009) and Hattie (2013), referenced below, are useful references if you want a quantitative view on a particular factor that affects achievement.

Field research on teachers whose students show the highest gains

P. Ayres et al., 'Effective teaching in the context of a Grade 12 high-stakes external examination in New South Wales, Australia' (*British Educational Research Journal,* Vol. 30, No. 1 February 2004).

J.A.C. Hattie, 'Teachers make a difference: What is the research evidence?' (Paper presented at the Building Teacher Quality: What does the research tell us? ACER Research Conference, Melbourne, Australia, 2003. Retrieved from http://research.acer.edu.au/research_conference_2003/4/).

D. Lemov, *Teach Like a Champion 2.0* (San Francisco: Jossey-Bass, 2015). This is an important book as it gives detail about strategies used by exceptionally good teachers.

B. Rosenshine, 'Principles of instruction' (International Academy of Education and International Bureau of Education, 2010). Makes use of field research on teachers who get the highest gains in student learning.

Best evidence syntheses (free online)

Best evidence syntheses are regarded by Dylan Wiliam as the most reliable source of summarised evidence. The International Bureau of Education publishes a series of short booklets all summarising research in a given field: search for 'International Bureau of Education educational practices' for a full catalogue. Search for title and author for a free download. Here are just a few from a series of more than 20. The last two listed below summarise research on teacher improvement.

G. Aitken and C. Sinnema, 'Effective pedagogy in the social sciences/tikanga ā iwi: Best evidence synthesis iteration' (Ministry of Education, 2008).

G. Anthony and M. Walshaw, 'Effective pedagogy in mathematics/ pāngarau: Best evidence synthesis iteration' (Ministry of Education, 2009).

E. Bernhardt, 'Teaching other languages' (International Academy of Education, 2010).

V. Robinson, M. Hohepa and C. Lloyd, 'School leadership and student outcomes: what works and why: Best evidence synthesis interation' (Ministry of Education, 2009).

H. Timperley et al., 'Teacher professional learning and development: Best evidence synthesis (Ministry of Education, 2007).

More free downloads that summarise research

The following summarise research in a rigorous/reasonably rigorous way. Please search online for the title and author.

O. Caviglioli, summarising J. Sweller's 'Cognitive load theory' (for How2, 2011).

R. Coe et al., 'What makes great teaching?' (Centre for Evaluation and Monitoring University of Durham, 2014).

J. Dunlosky, 'Strengthening the Student Toolbox' (*American Educator,* Fall 2013). This is focused on revision rather than learning for the first time, a point sometimes missed by those who quote it.

R. Marzano, *The Art and Science of Teaching: A Comprehensive Framework for Effective Instruction* (Alexandria, Virginia: ASCD, 2007). This is a whole book and it is very generous of ASCD and Robert Marzano to give it away for free.

R. Marzano, 'Art and Science of Teaching Teacher Evaluation Model Learning Map' (2011). This is a concept map that summarises the excellent book mentioned above.

R. Marzano et al., *The Highly Engaged Classroom* (Bloomington: Marzano Research Laboratory, 2010).

D. Wiliam, 'The nine things every teacher should know' (TES, 2016).

Other references and further reading

P.C. Abrami et al., 'Instructional interventions affecting critical thinking skills and dispositions: A stage 1 meta-analysis' (*Review of Educational Research,* 78 (4), 1102–1134, 2008). Research that shows that critical thinking can be taught – if you do it the right way.

P.C. Abrami et al., 'Strategies for teaching students to think critically: A meta-analysis' (*Review of Educational Research,* 85, 275–314, 2015). Critical thinking needs to be integrated into content teaching.

P. Adey and M. Shayer, *Really Raising Standards* (London: Routledge, 1994). Report on the idea and successes of cognitive acceleration creating highly efficient far transfer – still ahead of its time.

P. Adey and J. Dillon (Eds), *Bad Education: Debunking Myths in Education* (Buckingham: Open University Press, 2012). Very readable with contributions from major figures on issues such as IQ and learning styles.

S. Allison and A. Tharby, *Making Every Lesson Count* (Carmarthen: Crown House Publishing, 2015). Brilliant and highly readable book with lots of detail on strategy.

P. Ayres et al., 'Effective teaching in the context of a Grade 12 high-stakes external examination in New South Wales, Australia' (*British Educational Research Journal,* Vol. 30, No. 1, February 2004). Teachers in the top one per cent nationally for six years running – how do they teach? Fascinating!

J.B. Biggs and K.F. Collis, *Evaluating the Quality of Learning: The SOLO Taxonomy (Structure of the Observed Learning Outcome)* (New York: Academic Press, 1982). One of the greatest contributions to our understanding of what understanding means – highly influential. I summarised it in Petty (2009).

J. Biggs and C. Tang, *Teaching for Quality Learning at University* (4th Edition) (Maidenhead: McGraw-Hill, 2011).

P.J. Black and D. Wiliam, 'Assessment and classroom learning' (*Assessment in Education: Principles, Policy and Practice,* 5 (1), 7–74, 1998). A real classic on what I call 'check and correct' – a very readable review of research on a vital topic.

P. Black et al., *Assessment for Learning: Putting it into Practice* (Buckingham: Open University Press, 2003). Highly practical and readable, lots of ideas on checking and correcting learning.

J.D. Bransford et al., *How People Learn: Brain, Mind, Experience and School* (Washington: National Research Council, 2000). This is still the most accessible and authoritative summary of the psychology of teaching and learning. Dozens of academics laboured for more than two years to come up with this highly readable summary for teachers. There are spin-off *'How People Learn'* books on history, science, and so on.

W.M. Carroll, 'Using worked examples as an instructional support in the algebra classroom' (*Journal of Educational Psychology,* 83, pages 360–367, 1994). A wonderful study showing that peer-explaining a model helps students learn mathematics.

S. Clarke, *Formative Assessment in the Secondary Classroom* (London: Hodder Murray, 2005).

F. Coffield, D. Moseley, E. Hall and K. Ecclestone, 'Learning styles and pedagogy in post-16 learning: A systematic and critical review' (Learning and Skills Research Centre, 2004). Learning styles debunked.

L. Cohen et al., *Research Methods in Education* (7th Edition) (London: Routledge-Falmer, 2011). Looks at most approaches to educational research and finds them all helpful in their way. More importantly, it shows how to do them.

M.S. Donovan and J.D. Bransford (eds), *How Students Learn: History in the Classroom* (Washington: National Academies Press, 2005). One of the spin-offs from Bransford (2000).

J. Dunlosky et al., 'Improving students' learning with effective learning techniques promising directions from cognitive and educational psychology' (*Psychological Science in the Public Interest* 14, 4–58, 2013). This paper mixes teaching methods and student revision techniques, but a method that works for one might not work well for the other. Well worth reading, despite this slight muddle.

C. Dweck, *Mindset: How You Can Fulfil Your Potential* (New York: Hachette, 2012). Learners need to see learning as due to effort, practice, seeking help, checking and correcting and other factors within the student's control, not inherited characteristics that the student cannot control. A readable account by a key researcher in the area.

K. Ericsson et al., 'The role of deliberate practice in the acquisition of expert performance' (*Psychological Review*, Vol. 100, No. 3. 363–406, 1993). We learn from practising in a particular way, then checking and correcting that practice. The antidote to the 'intelligence is inherited' view. There is a summary of this most important paper on my website and you can download the original paper for free.

P. Ginnis, *The Teacher's Toolkit* (Carmarthen: Crown House Publishing, 2002). Lots of teaching methods to try, lots of detail on these, well worth a look.

D. Gough, S. Oliver and J. Thomas, *An Introduction to Systematic Reviews* (London: Sage, 2012).

D. Gough and J. Thomas, 'Systematic reviews of research in education: Aims, myths and multiple methods' (*Review of Education*, Vol. 4, No. 1, pages 84–102, February 2016).

J.A.C. Hattie, *Visible Learning: A Synthesis of Over 800 Meta-Analyses Relating to Achievement* (London: Routledge, 2008). This is the largest synthesis of quantitative research, though informed by qualitative research too. A great reference work if you want to find out about a particular factor that affects learning.

J.A.C. Hattie, *Visible Learning for Teachers* (London: Routledge, 2012).

J.A.C. Hattie, 'The 34th Vernon-Wall Lecture' (British Psychological Society, 2014). This goes into more detail on the Hattie-Donoghue model; you can download it for a small fee.

J.A.C. Hattie and E.M. Anderman (Eds), *International Guide to Student Achievement* (New York: Routledge, 2013). More than 150 short reviews of research by leaders in their field on most of the factors that affect student achievement, including quantitative approaches.

J.A.C. Hattie, J. Biggs and N. Purdie, 'Effects of learning skills interventions on student learning: A meta-analysis' (*Review of Educational Research*, Vol. 66, No. 2 99–136, 1996). A seminal paper showing that academic skills, study skills, thinking skills and the like are teachable – if you do it the right way. There is a summary of this paper on my website.

J.A.C. Hattie and H. Timperley, 'The power of feedback' (*Review of Educational Research,* Vol. 77, No. 1 pages 81–112, 2007). I believe this is still the most read paper on an educational issue.

S. Johnson and H. Siegel, *Teaching Thinking Skills* (London: Continuum, 2010). This gives both sides of the argument about whether thinking skills can be taught, but largely ignores quantitative research.

B.R. Joyce and B. Showers, *Student Achievement Through Staff Development* (3rd Edition) (Alexandria: ASCD, 2002). Very readable review of research with similar findings to Timperley (2008).

T.S. Kuhn, *The Structure of Scientific Revolutions* (Chicago: University of Chicago Press, 1962). How we get to know what we know; one of the great books of the 20th century.

D. Lemov, *Teach Like a Champion 2.0* (San Francisco: Jossey-Bass, 2015). This is an important book as it gives detail about strategies used by excellent teachers.

R.J. Marzano, 'A theory-based meta-analysis of research on instruction' (Aurora, CO: Mid-continent Research for Education and Learning, 1998). This can be downloaded for free. A technical paper, but a wealth of detail, although a little dated now.

R. Marzano, *The Art and Science of Teaching: A Comprehensive Framework for Effective Instruction* (Alexandria, VA: ASCD, 2007). This is a classic, and the whole book can be downloaded as a pdf, which is a very generous gift to teachers and their students.

R. Marzano, 'The Marzano Compendium of Instructional Strategies' (2016). This is a subscription service available from www.marzanoresearch.com with hundreds of strategies.

R. Marzano, D. Pickering and J. Pollock, *Classroom Instruction that Works* (Alexandria, Virginia: ASCD, 2001). I still prefer the first edition of this classic book, well described by its title and quantitative in nature.

R. Marzano et al., *The Highly Engaged Classroom* (Bloomington: Marzano Research Laboratory, 2010). This book can be downloaded for free as a pdf.

E. Mazur, *Peer Instruction: A User's Manual* (London: Pearson, 1996). An astonishingly effective teaching method which I call 'diagnostic questions' explained in detail. If you teach HE this is vital reading.

D. Moseley et al., *Thinking Skill Frameworks for Post-16 Learners: An Evaluation* (Cambridge: Cambridge University Press, 2004). Methods to help you improve your teaching of skills, including a positive review of my own 'icedip' model for creative thinking and working.

D. Mujis and D. Reynolds, *Effective Teaching: Evidence and Practice* (London: Paul Chapman Publishing, 2017). Great book with another slant on evidence-based teaching, good on direct instruction.

J.C. Nesbit and O. Adesope, 'Learning with Concept and Knowledge Maps: A Meta-Analysis' (*Review of Educational Research* 76, pages 413, 2006). More readable than many meta-analyses.

G.A. Nuthall, *The Hidden Lives of Learners* (Wellington: NZCER Press, 2007). Highly influential – shows that learners need to reuse, review, and re-experience learning, and if they do, even-low performing students can learn well.

G. Petty, *Evidence-Based Teaching* (Oxford: Oxford University Press, 2009). See also www.geoffpetty.com.

G. Petty, *Teaching Today: A Practical Guide* (5th Edition) (Oxford: Oxford University Press, 2014).

G. Petty, *How to be Better at Creativity* (2nd Edition) (Raleigh: Lulu, 2017).

S. Pinker, *How the Mind Works* (London: Penguin, 1997). Still a classic and very readable.

K.R. Popper, *The Logic of Scientific Discovery* (3rd Edition) (London: Hutchinson, 1968). How we can ensure that our knowledge is as true as we can hope for. One of the greatest achievements of intellectual work in any field, and highly influential, though still not influential enough.

R. Sadler, 'Formative assessment and the design of instructional systems' (*Instructional Science*, 18, 119–44, 1989). A short paper on what students need to know in order to learn well. A work of genius, born out by all research reviews on feedback and modelling.

R.K. Sawyer (Ed), *The Cambridge Handbook of The Learning Sciences* (Cambridge: Cambridge University Press, 2006). This is a highly authoritative collection of more than 30 essays by leaders in their field on topics such as project-based learning and assessing deep understanding.

M. Shayer and P. Adey, *Learning Intelligence: Cognitive Acceleration Across the Curriculum from 5 to 15 Years* (Buckingham: Open University Press, 2002). A report on arguably the most outstanding contribution to experimentation in education in the UK, it shows astonishing transfer is possible. Not read enough by cognitive scientists.

H. Timperley, *Realising the Power of Professional Learning* (Maidenhead: McGraw-Hill, 2011).

H. Timperley et al., 'Best evidence synthesis on professional learning and development' (Report to the Ministry of Education, Wellington, New Zealand, 2008). Highly authoritative review of research on how to improve teaching, communities of practice, not accountability.

P. Westwood, *Commonsense Methods for Children with Special Educational Needs* (4th Edition) (London: Routledge-Falmer, 2003). Packed with practical ideas and advice.

D. Wiliam, *Assessment for Learning: Why, What and How?* (London: IoE, 2009).

D. Wiliam, 'Randomised control trials in education research' (*University of Brighton Research in Education,* Vol. 6, No.1, 2014). Available online.

D. Wiliam, 'Leadership for teacher learning: Creating a culture where all teachers improve so that all students succeed' (LearningSciencesInternational. com, 2016). Includes a useful critique of effect size research but much more.

D. Wiliam and S. Leahy, *Embedding Formative Assessment* (West Palm Beach: The Learning Sciences, 2015). Very practical ideas on check and correct, and a strong argument for using ladders of tasks in order to differentiate.

D. Willingham, *Why Don't Students Like School? A Cognitive Scientist Answers Questions About How the Mind Works and What it Means for the Classroom* (San Francisco: Jossey-Bass, 2010). A very readable summary of cognitive science.

Index

Acknowledgements

British Psychological Society for excerpts from Hattie, J. A. C., The Role of Learning Strategies in Today's Classrooms (The 34th Vernon-Wall Lecture, 2014). Pages 4 and 7. Reproduced with permission of British Psychological Society through PLSclear.

Cengage for excerpts from Ausubel, D. P., Education Psychology: A Cognitive View (Holt, Rinehart and Winston, 1968).

Center for Effective Performance, Incorporated quote from Mager, R., Developing Attitude toward Learning, (1968).

J. A. C. Hattie and G. M. Donoghue for excerpts from Hattie and G.M. Donoghue, Learning strategies: a synthesis and conceptual model (NPJ Science of Learning, 2016). Reproduced under the terms of the Creative Commons Attribution 4.0 International License, CC-BY 4.0.

Marzano Research for excerpts from Meta-Analysis Database of Instructional Strategies, (2018) https://www.marzanoresearch.com/research/database © 2018 Marzano Research. Reproduced with permission.

McKinsey & Company for excerpt from How to improve student educational outcomes: New insights from data analytics, (2017). https://www.mckinsey. com/industries/social-sector/our-insights/how-to-improve-student-educational-outcomes-new-insights-from-data-analytics Copyright © 2018 McKinsey & Company, www.mckinsey.com. All rights reserved. Reprinted by permission.

McREL International adapted excerpt from Dean, C., Ross Hubbell, E., Pitler, H., and Stone, B., Classroom Instruction that Works: Research-Based Strategies for Increasing Student Achievement, 2nd edition, (2012). Copyright 2012, McREL International. Used by permission.

T. Sherrington for concept from Sherrington, T., Sweet Algebra. A model (2017). https://teacherhead.com/2017/04/05/sweet-algebra-a-model/.

The Sutton Trust for data from Education Endowment Foundation, The Sutton Trust, Teaching and Learning Toolkit, (2018). Reproduced with permission from Stephen Tall, on behalf of the Education Endowment Foundation (EEF).

John Wiley & Sons for excerpts from Lemov, D., Teach Like a Champion (Jossey-Bass, 2010). Pages xi, 40. Reproduced with permission from John Wiley & Sons. Also for extracts from D. Willingham, Why don't students like school? (Jossey-Bass, 2009). Pages 22, 163, 210.

Although we have made every effort to trace and contact all copyright holders before publication this has not been possible in all cases. If notified, the publisher will rectify any errors or omissions at the earliest opportunity.